ASSESSMENT RESOURCES

PHYSICAL SCIENCE

Prentice Hall
Needham, Massachusetts
Upper Saddle River, New Jersey
Glenview, Illinois

PRENTICE HALL
SCIENCE EXPLORER

ASSESSMENT RESOURCES
Physical Science

PRENTICE HALL
Needham, Massachusetts
Upper Saddle River, New Jersey
Glenview, Illinois

Contents

Book M *Motion, Forces, and Energy* (continued)

Book N *Electricity and Magnetism*

Book O *Sound and Light*

About the Assessment Resources

The *Assessment Resources* for *SCIENCE EXPLORER* gives you unparalleled flexibility in creating tests. You can design tests to reflect your particular teaching emphasis. You can use the *Assessment Resources* to create tests for different classes or to create alternative forms of the same test. You can also create tests for one chapter or for any combination of chapters, as well as for unit, midterm, and final examinations.

QUESTION FORMATS

The *Assessment Resources* provides 72 printed Chapter Tests with more than 5,000 questions for the *SCIENCE EXPLORER* program.

Questions are provided in the following formats:
- multiple choice
- modified true/false
- fill-ins
- questions with graphics
- essay questions

AVAILABLE IN WINDOWS AND MACINTOSH FORMATS

The Assessment Resources CD-ROM contains easy-to-use software for the *SCIENCE EXPLORER Assessment Resources*. The software operates in both the Windows and Macintosh environments. For more information, please contact your Prentice Hall Sales Representative or call 1-800-848-9500.

FLEXIBLE TEST-MAKING

The *Assessment Resources* for *SCIENCE EXPLORER* allows you to create tests easily and conveniently. You can select or add exactly the questions you want for each test. You can design tests for students of different ability levels, and create different tests for different classes or alternate versions of the same test. The *Assessment Resources* also allows you to tailor tests to meet your state and local curriculum requirements and to build the appropriate content, skills, and critical thinking into your testing program. And there is no need to cut and paste the maps, graphs, or charts that students need to answer a test item. When you select a test item linked to an illustration, the *Assessment Resources* software will automatically print the illustration along with the question.

HELP IS JUST A PHONE CALL AWAY

Stuck at any point? Simply call our toll-free HELP hotline (1-800-237-7136) for continuous and reliable support.

About the Prentice Hall Dial-A-Test® Service

If you do not have access to a computer or would like the convenience of designing your own tests without typing a word, you may want to take advantage of our free Dial-A-Test® Service. Available to all users of *SCIENCE EXPLORER,* Dial-A-Test® is simple to use.

Dial-A-Test® OFFERS YOU THE ABILITY TO:

• Customize tests for different ability levels.

• Focus your testing on mastery of specific content, skills, or critical thinking.

• Scramble your questions for each class you teach.

• Choose from a variety of formats on the ready-made Chapter Tests.

HERE'S HOW IT WORKS

1. **Choose the questions you want** from the ready-made Chapter Tests.

2. **Enter the numbers of the questions** in the order you want on a Dial-A-Test® Order Form (see page vii). Be sure to include a prefix with the **book letter** and **chapter number** for each question. For example, in the case of test question 17, taken from the Chapter 1 test in Book M, mark the order form with the designation **M01–17.**

3. **Use a separate Dial-A-Test® order form** for each original test you request. You may use one form, however, to order multiple versions of the same original test.

4. **If you would like another version** of your original test with the questions scrambled, or put in another sequence, simply check the blank labeled *Scramble Questions* on the order form. If you would like more than one scrambled version of your original test, note this on your order form or inform the Dial-A-Test® operator. Please note that Prentice Hall reserves the right to limit the number of tests and versions you can request at any one time, especially during the busier times of the year when midterms and finals are given.

5. **Choose the method** by which you would like to order your original test and/or multiple versions of your original test. To order by telephone, call toll free 1-800-468-8378 between 9:00 a.m. and 4:30 p.m. Eastern Standard Time and read the test question numbers to our Dial-A-Test® operator. To order by mail, send your completed Dial-A-Test® order form to the address listed below. Now you may also FAX your order to 1-614-771-7365.

6. **You may order** up to 100 questions per test by telephone on our toll-free 800 number or up to 200 questions per test by mail.

7. **Please allow a minimum of two weeks** for shipping, especially if you are ordering by mail. Although we process your order within 48 hours of your call or the receipt of your form by mail, mailing may take up to two weeks. Thus we ask you to plan accordingly and expect to receive your original test, any alternate test versions that you requested, and complete answer keys, within a reasonable amount of time.

8. **Tests are available all year.** You can order tests before the school year begins, during vacation, or as you need them.

9. **For additional order forms** or to ask questions regarding this service, please write to the following address:

Dial-A-Test®
Prentice Hall School Division
4350 Equity Drive
Columbus, OH 43228

- ORDER FORM -
CTS

DIAL-A-TEST®
PRENTICE HALL SCHOOL DIVISION
CUSTOMIZED TESTING SERVICE
TOLL-FREE NUMBER 800-468-8378 (H O-T-T-E-S-T)

- ORDER FORM -
CTS

You may **call** the PH Dial-A-Test® toll-free number during our business hours (9:00 a.m.-4:30 p.m. EST).
Now you may also FAX your order to 1-614-771-7365 any time.

DIAL-A-TEST®
PRENTICE HALL SCHOOL DIVISION
4350 EQUITY DRIVE
COLUMBUS, OH 43228

FOR PH USE		DATE REC.	DATE SENT
__ PHONE __ MAIL __ FAX		_____	_____

EXACT TEXT TITLE/VOL. _Science Explorer (Physical Science books)_ **© DATE** _2000_
CODE _0-13-436363-9_

CUSTOMER INFORMATION
NAME _____
SCHOOL _____
ADDRESS _____
CITY _____ STATE ____ ZIP _____
PHONE _____ EXT. _____

DATE BY WHICH TEST IS NEEDED _____

TEST USAGE (CHECK ONE)
__ SAMPLE   __ QUIZ   __ CHAPTER TEST
__ UNIT TEST __ SEMESTER TEST __ FINAL EXAM

VERSIONS (SEE Instruction #4)
(CHECK ONE)
__ 1. ORIGINAL   __ 2. SCRAMBLE QUESTIONS

TEST IDENTIFICATION (This information will appear at the top of your test.)

_____
_____
_____
_____

EXAMPLE: Mr. Rodriguez
Comprehensive Science 1
Period 5 Test

1 ____	26 ____	51 ____	76 ____	101 ____	126 ____	151 ____	176 ____
2 ____	27 ____	52 ____	77 ____	102 ____	127 ____	152 ____	177 ____
3 ____	28 ____	53 ____	78 ____	103 ____	128 ____	153 ____	178 ____
4 ____	29 ____	54 ____	79 ____	104 ____	129 ____	154 ____	179 ____
5 ____	30 ____	55 ____	80 ____	105 ____	130 ____	155 ____	180 ____
6 ____	31 ____	56 ____	81 ____	106 ____	131 ____	156 ____	181 ____
7 ____	32 ____	57 ____	82 ____	107 ____	132 ____	157 ____	182 ____
8 ____	33 ____	58 ____	83 ____	108 ____	133 ____	158 ____	183 ____
9 ____	34 ____	59 ____	84 ____	109 ____	134 ____	159 ____	184 ____
10 ____	35 ____	60 ____	85 ____	110 ____	135 ____	160 ____	185 ____
11 ____	36 ____	61 ____	86 ____	111 ____	136 ____	161 ____	186 ____
12 ____	37 ____	62 ____	87 ____	112 ____	137 ____	162 ____	187 ____
13 ____	38 ____	63 ____	88 ____	113 ____	138 ____	163 ____	188 ____
14 ____	39 ____	64 ____	89 ____	114 ____	139 ____	164 ____	189 ____
15 ____	40 ____	65 ____	90 ____	115 ____	140 ____	165 ____	190 ____
16 ____	41 ____	66 ____	91 ____	116 ____	141 ____	166 ____	191 ____
17 ____	42 ____	67 ____	92 ____	117 ____	142 ____	167 ____	192 ____
18 ____	43 ____	68 ____	93 ____	118 ____	143 ____	168 ____	193 ____
19 ____	44 ____	69 ____	94 ____	119 ____	144 ____	169 ____	194 ____
20 ____	45 ____	70 ____	95 ____	120 ____	145 ____	170 ____	195 ____
21 ____	46 ____	71 ____	96 ____	121 ____	146 ____	171 ____	196 ____
22 ____	47 ____	72 ____	97 ____	122 ____	147 ____	172 ____	197 ____
23 ____	48 ____	73 ____	98 ____	123 ____	148 ____	173 ____	198 ____
24 ____	49 ____	74 ____	99 ____	124 ____	149 ____	174 ____	199 ____
25 ____	50 ____	75 ____	100 ____	125 ____	150 ____	175 ____	200 ____

Name _____ Date _____

A. Multiple Choice
Choose the letter of the correct answer.

_____ 1. One example of changing a substance physically is

    a. burning paper.
    b. baking cookies.
    c. heating table sugar.
    d. blending a milkshake.

_____ 2. One example of changing a substance chemically is

    a. filtering.
    b. burning wood.
    c. boiling water.
    d. crushing a can.

_____ 3. A characteristic property that can help tell similar liquids apart is

    a. hardness.
    b. melting point.
    c. boiling point.
    d. smell.

_____ 4. Why might you need to study at least two or three characteristics before you can accurately identify a substance?

    a. All substances have the same melting point.
    b. Many substances share melting points, boiling points, or other characteristic properties.
    c. All substances have different boiling points.
    d. All solids melt at 0°C.

_____ 5. Sugar and salt are examples of

    a. atoms.
    b. elements.
    c. mixtures.
    d. pure substances.

_____ 6. Substances that CANNOT be broken down chemically into other substances are

    a. elements.
    b. compounds.
    c. mixtures.
    d. solutions.

_____ 7. The measurement of the force of gravity on an object is the object's

    a. mass.
    b. volume.
    c. weight.
    d. density.

_____ **8.** The measurement of how much matter an object contains is its

    a. volume.
    b. weight.
    c. mass.
    d. melting point.

_____ **9.** The measurement of how much mass is contained in a given volume is called

    a. weight.
    b. melting point.
    c. boiling point.
    d. density.

_____ **10.** The density of a block of wood with a volume of 50 cubic centimeters and a mass of 100 grams is

    a. 2 g/cm^3
    b. 0.5 g/cm^3
    c. 500 g/cm^3
    d. $5,000 \text{ g/cm}^3$

_____ **11.** All elements are composed of extremely small particles called

    a. compounds.
    b. mixtures.
    c. atoms.
    d. molecules.

_____ **12.** The first person who came up with the idea of atoms was

    a. Dalton.
    b. Fahrenheit.
    c. Asimov.
    d. Democritus.

_____ **13.** According to Dalton's theory of atoms, all atoms in any element

    a. are exactly alike.
    b. can be broken into smaller pieces.
    c. are different.
    d. have a different mass.

_____ **14.** What did Dalton's theory of atoms say about compounds?

    a. Atoms of two or more elements can combine to form compounds.
    b. All compounds are exactly alike.
    c. Only elements of the same mass can combine to form compounds.
    d. Only atoms of the same elements can combine to form compounds.

_____ **15.** A group of atoms that are joined together and act as a single unit is called a(n)

    a. element.
    b. compound.
    c. molecule.
    d. solution.

_____ **16.** What holds atoms together in a molecule?

    a. density

    b. gravity

    c. physical bonds

    d. chemical bonds

_____ **17.** Why can gold be separated easily from surrounding material?

    a. It has a high mass.

    b. It is shiny.

    c. It has a high density.

    d. It has a high volume.

_____ **18.** What technique did miners use to separate gold from sand and dirt?

    a. boiling

    b. panning

    c. heating in charcoal

    d. melting

_____ **19.** Copper can be separated from surrounding material because of its

    a. mass.

    b. volume.

    c. density.

    d. chemical activity.

_____ **20.** In nature, copper usually exists as a

    a. pure element.

    b. compound mixed with other materials.

    c. solution mixed with many elements.

    d. grouping of copper atoms.

_____ **21.** How would you calculate the density of an object?

    a. Divide its weight by its volume.

    b. Divide its mass by its volume.

    c. Multiply its volume times its mass.

    d. Multiply its weight times its mass.

_____ **22.** The SI unit for mass is the

    a. ounce.

    b. pound.

    c. kilogram.

    d. liter.

_____ **23.** Pure substances formed from chemical combinations of two or more different elements are called

    a. elements.

    b. compounds.

    c. mixtures.

    d. solutions.

_____ **24.** Which type of matter consists of two or more substances that are NOT chemically combined?

    a. elements

    b. compounds

    c. mixtures

    d. pure substances

_____ **25.** How do liquid water, ice, and water vapor differ from each other?

    a. They are different states of matter.

    b. They are different compounds.

    c. They are made of different kinds of molecules.

    d. They are made of different kinds of atoms.

_____ **26.** Which statement was NOT part of Dalton's theory of atoms?

    a. Atoms can't be broken into smaller pieces.

    b. All atoms are alike.

    c. Atoms of each element have a unique mass.

    d. The masses of the elements in a compound are always in a constant ratio.

_____ **27.** Dalton's theory of atoms said that the masses of elements in a compound are always

    a. the same.

    b. in a 2 to 1 ratio.

    c. in a 4 to 1 ratio.

    d. in a constant ratio.

_____ **28.** An electric current breaks the chemical bond that joins a metal and other elements in an ore in a process called

    a. electrolysis.

    b. melting.

    c. boiling.

    d. panning.

_____ **29.** Iron can be separated from the oxygen in its ore by

    a. panning.

    b. electrolysis.

    c. by heating the ore in a hot charcoal fire.

    d. breaking the ore into small pieces.

_____ **30.** Which statement was part of Dalton's theory of atoms?

    a. All atoms have the same density.

    b. Every atom has its own unique size and shape.

    c. Atoms of each element have a unique mass.

    d. Atoms of each element form only one compound.

B. True or False
If the statement is true, write true. If it is false, change the underlined word or words to make the statement true.

31. A change that produces one or more new substances is called a <u>physical</u> change.

_____

_____

32. The <u>freezing</u> point of water is 100°C.

_____

_____

33. A <u>pure</u> substance is made of only one kind of matter and has definite properties.

_____

_____

34. An object's <u>mass</u> is a measure of the force of gravity acting on the object.

_____

_____

35. The density of a material is expressed as <u>volume divided by mass</u>.

_____

_____

36. The smallest particle of an element is called an <u>atom</u>.

_____

_____

37. In the early 1800s, John Dalton proposed a theory including the idea that atoms <u>cannot</u> be broken apart.

_____

_____

38. A <u>molecule</u> can contain just a few atoms or as many as a billion atoms.

_____

_____

39. <u>Weight</u> is a physical property that enables miners to distinguish between real gold and "fool's gold," or pyrite.

_____

_____

40. In blast furnaces, iron metal separates from its ore because oxygen in the ore reacts with <u>carbon</u>.

_____

_____

C. Completion

Fill in the word or phrase that best completes each statement.

41. The burning of wood is an example of a(n) _____ change.

_____

_____

42. The characteristic temperature at which a pure solid changes to a liquid is its _____ point.

_____

_____

43. A _____ is formed when two or more substances mix together so well that they appear to be a single substance.

_____

_____

44. Mass is the measure of the total amount of _____ in any object.

_____

_____

45. The units liter, milliliter, and cubic centimeters are all used to measure the _____ of an object or substance.

_____

_____

46. One of the first persons known to have developed the idea of atoms was the ancient Greek philosopher _____.

_____

_____

47. John Dalton said that the masses of the _____ in a compound are always in a constant ratio.

_____

_____

48. A _____ is a group of atoms that are bonded together and act as a single unit.

_____

_____

49. If you slowly pour out a mixture of metallic gold, dirt, and water, the gold will sink and remain behind because of its high _____.

_____

_____

50. Usually a _____ change is needed to release iron from the ore in which it is found.

_____

_____

51. Dissolving a spoonful of sugar in tea or coffee is an example of a _____ change.

_____

_____

52. Boiling point and melting point are two _____ properties, which remain the same for any sample of a substance.

_____

_____

53. A _____ is a pure substance formed from two or more elements.

_____

_____

54. Two objects that have the same _____ will have the same weight when they experience the gravitational force of the same planet.

_____

_____

55. The unit used to measure density is a unit of mass divided by a unit of _____.

_____

_____

56. According to Dalton's theory about matter, the _____ of each element are exactly alike.

_____

_____

57. A _____ is a force that holds the atoms in a molecule together.

_____

_____

58. The metallic element _____ has a high density that causes it to separate from other materials during the panning process.

_____

_____

59. Metallic copper can be separated from its compounds by an electric current during the process called _____.

_____

_____

60. The smallest possible molecule is made of two _____ held together by a chemical bond.

_____

_____

D. Interpreting Diagrams

Use the diagram to answer each question.

Densities of Some Common Substances	
Substance	**Density (g/mL)**
Air	0.0013
Gasoline	0.7
Wood (oak)	0.85
Water (ice)	0.9
Water (liquid)	1.0
Aluminum	2.7
Steel	7.8
Silver	10.5
Lead	11.3
Mercury	13.5
Gold	19.3

61. How does the density of liquid water compare with the density of ice?

_____

_____

_____

_____

62. If samples of silver and lead each had volumes equal to 1 mL, which would have the greater mass, and how much would the difference in the masses be?

_____

_____

_____

_____

63. If gasoline is poured carefully into liquid water, will it sink or float? Explain why.

_____

_____

_____

_____

64. A 54-gram sample of an unknown material has a volume equal to 20 mL. Based on its density, could the sample be aluminum?

_____

_____

_____

_____

_____

65. What is the mass of 150 mL of liquid water? Explain.

_____

_____

_____

_____

66. If a sample of a material has a mass of 21 grams and a volume equal to 2 mL, could it be one of the substances listed in the table? Explain.

_____

_____

_____

_____

Use the diagram to answer each question

Sample Melting Points and Boiling Points

Substance	Melting Point (°C)	Boiling Point (°C)
Butane	−138	0
Methanol	−98	65
Heptane	−91	98
Iodine	114	184

67. Which substance(s) in the table are gas(es) at room temperature (approximately 20°C)?

_____

_____

_____

_____

68. What is the physical state of iodine at 150°C?

_____

_____

_____

_____

69. If the temperature of heptane was changed from 90°C to 100°C, would a physical or chemical change take place? Explain.

_____

_____

_____

_____

70. Which substance in the table changes state when heated from 10°C to 80°C? What change of state occurs?

_____
_____
_____
_____

71. On the basis of its boiling point, which substance in the table would be most difficult to distinguish from water? Explain.

_____
_____
_____
_____

72. Name the substance(s) in the table that are solid(s) at room temperature (approximately 20°C).

_____
_____
_____
_____

E. Essay
Write an answer to each of the following questions.

73. Suppose that a spacecraft from Earth lands on the moon and then returns to Earth. Describe how the mass and weight of a person in the spacecraft would be affected while on Earth and on the moon. Remember that the moon has the weaker force of gravity.

_____
_____
_____
_____
_____

74. Explain the difference between a mixture and a compound.

_____

_____

_____

_____

_____

_____

75. Explain how you could find out whether or not an unknown liquid was water.

_____

_____

_____

_____

_____

_____

_____

76. Describe Dalton's theory of atoms.

_____

_____

_____

_____

_____

_____

77. Explain the difference between atoms and molecules.

_____

_____

_____

_____

_____

_____

_____

78. When an electric current is passed through water during the process of electrolysis, two gases are formed. One gas has a boiling point of -183°C, and the other a boiling point of -253°C. Was this event a physical change or a chemical change? Explain.

_____

_____

_____

_____

_____

_____

79. Explain why panning, which can be used to obtain the element gold, cannot be used to obtain the element iron.

_____

_____

_____

_____

_____

_____

80. The density of gold is 19.3 g/cm^3. What does it mean to say that density is a characteristic property of gold?

_____

_____

_____

_____

_____

_____

Name _____ Date _____

Test 51 Book K, Chapter 1: Introduction to Matter
Answer Key (Short)

    __d__   **1.**
    __b__   **2.**
    __c__   **3.**
    __b__   **4.**
    __d__   **5.**
    __a__   **6.**
    __c__   **7.**
    __c__   **8.**
    __d__   **9.**
    __a__   **10.**
    __c__   **11.**
    __d__   **12.**
    __a__   **13.**
    __a__   **14.**
    __c__   **15.**
    __d__   **16.**
    __c__   **17.**
    __b__   **18.**
    __d__   **19.**
    __b__   **20.**
    __b__   **21.**
    __c__   **22.**
    __b__   **23.**
    __c__   **24.**
    __a__   **25.**
    __b__   **26.**
    __d__   **27.**
    __a__   **28.**
    __c__   **29.**
    __c__   **30.**

31. false, chemical
32. false, boiling
33. TRUE
34. false, weight
35. false, mass divided by volume
36. TRUE
37. TRUE
38. TRUE
39. false, density
40. TRUE
41. chemical

42.	melting
43.	solution
44.	matter
45.	volume
46.	Democritus
47.	elements
48.	molecule
49.	density
50.	chemical
51.	physical
52.	characteristic
53.	compound
54.	mass
55.	volume
56.	atoms
57.	chemical bond
58.	gold
59.	electrolysis
60.	atoms
61.	The density of water, 1.0 g/mL, is slightly greater than the density of ice, 0.9 g/mL.
62.	The mass of lead would be 0.8 g greater than the mass of silver.
63.	Gasoline will float on water because it is less dense.
64.	Yes, because its density is 54 g/20 mL, or 2.7 g/mL, which is the density of aluminum.
65.	150 g; if 1 mL of water has a mass of 1 gram, 150 mL will have a mass of 150 grams; 150 mL • 1 g/1 mL = 150 g
66.	It could be silver, since 21 g/ 2 mL equals 10.5 g/ mL
67.	butane
68.	liquid
69.	A physical change; at 90°C, heptane would be a liquid; at 98°C, it would become a gas.
70.	Methanol changes from a liquid to a gas at 65°C.
71.	The boiling point of heptane (98°C) is only two degrees lower than the boiling point of water (100°C), so heptane would be most difficult to distinguish from water on the basis of its boiling point.
72.	iodine
73.	Mass depends only on the amount of matter in an object, and so the person's mass remains the same throughout the trip. The weight of an object depends on the force of gravity acting on it, and so the person's weight would be greater on Earth than on the moon.
74.	A mixture consists of two or more substances that are mixed together but not chemically combined. The individual substances in a mixture keep their separate properties. A compound is a pure substance formed when two or more elements combine chemically. The properties of a compound are very different from the elements that formed it.
75.	You could investigate some of the characteristic properties of the unknown substance. If the unknown is water, the substance will have the same freezing point, the same boiling point, the same density, and the same chemical reactivity as water.
76.	According to Dalton, all elements are made up of atoms, which cannot be broken into smaller pieces. Atoms of the same element are exactly alike, and they have a unique mass. Atoms of two or more elements can combine to make compounds, and the masses of elements in a compound are always in a constant ratio.

77.   Atoms are the smallest particles of an element. Atoms can combine with other atoms to form molecules. A molecule is a group of atoms that are joined together and act as a single unit. Molecules can vary in size, from just two atoms to billions of atoms. Atoms within a molecule are held together by chemical bonds.

78.   A chemical change has occurred. The boiling point of a substance is a characteristic property. Water's boiling point is 100°C. The two new boiling points are evidence that new substances with different characteristic properties have been formed.

79.   Gold can be separated from dirt by panning because it is present in its elemental form and it has a high density. Iron is not usually present in ores as an element. Instead, it is found chemically bonded to other atoms, often in compounds of iron and oxygen. The iron compounds are usually heated with a source of carbon to cause a chemical change that releases the element iron.

80.   A characteristic property of a substance is the same no matter what amount of the substance is studied. That means that any sample of pure gold should have a density of 19.3 g.cm^3. If a particular sample did not have that density, the sample could not be pure gold.

Test 52 Book K, Chapter 2: Changes in Matter

A. Multiple Choice
Choose the letter of the correct answer.

_____ 1. A solid is a state of matter that has a(n)

    a. indefinite volume and an indefinite shape.

    b. definite volume and a definite shape.

    c. definite volume and an indefinite shape.

    d. indefinite volume and a definite shape.

_____ 2. The resistance of a liquid to flowing is its

    a. pressure.

    b. temperature.

    c. viscosity.

    d. volume.

_____ 3. Particles of a liquid

    a. are tightly packed together and stay in a fixed position.

    b. have no viscosity.

    c. increase in volume with increasing temperature.

    d. are free to move throughout a container but remain in close contact with one another.

_____ 4. In which state of matter do the particles spread apart and fill all the space available to them?

    a. crystal

    b. liquid

    c. gas

    d. solid

_____ 5. The force of a gas's outward push divided by the area of the walls of the container is the gas's

    a. volume.

    b. temperature.

    c. pressure.

    d. density.

_____ 6. According to Boyle's law, when the pressure of a gas increases, its volume

    a. increases.

    b. stays constant.

    c. decreases.

    d. increases, then decreases.

_____ 7. The greater the speed of gas particles, the

    a. fewer collisions there will be.

    b. lower the temperature.

    c. greater the pressure.

    d. lower the pressure.

_____ **8.** When the temperature of a gas decreases, its

    a. pressure increases.

    b. volume increases.

    c. pressure decreases.

    d. particles move faster.

_____ **9.** According to Charles's law when the temperature of a gas increases, its

    a. volume increases.

    b. pressure decreases.

    c. volume decreases.

    d. particles move more slowly.

_____ **10.** When an inflated balloon is exposed to cold air,

    a. the temperature inside the balloon rises.

    b. the pressure inside the balloon rises.

    c. the volume of the balloon decreases.

    d. the volume of the balloon increases.

_____ **11.** A graph of Charles's law shows the relationship between

    a. volume and density of a gas.

    b. volume and pressure of a gas.

    c. temperature and volume of a gas.

    d. temperature and pressure of a gas.

_____ **12.** A graph that shows the pressure of a gas varies inversely with its volume under constant temperature demonstrates

    a. the Pressure law.

    b. the Density law.

    c. Charles's law.

    d. Boyle's law.

_____ **13.** A change that alters the form of a substance without changing it into another substance is called a(n)

    a. physical change.

    b. chemical change.

    c. thermal change.

    d. energy change.

_____ **14.** A chemical change results in

    a. changes in state.

    b. different substances with different properties.

    c. no new substances.

    d. changes in pressure.

_____ **15.** The energy a substance has from the movement of its particles is called

    a. light energy.

    b. chemical energy.

    c. thermal energy.

    d. potential energy.

_____ **16.** In chemical reactions, the law of conservation of energy means that

    a.   energy is always lost.

    b.   energy is always gained.

    c.   the total amount of energy stays the same.

    d.   the total amount of energy before the reaction is less than the total amount of energy at the end of the reaction.

_____ **17.** What is vaporization?

    a.   a gas becoming a liquid

    b.   a liquid becoming a solid

    c.   a gas becoming a solid

    d.   a liquid becoming a gas

_____ **18.** Which process involves a gas changing into a liquid?

    a.   melting

    b.   freezing

    c.   vaporization

    d.   condensation

_____ **19.** What always happens as a result of a chemical reaction?

    a.   New substances are produced.

    b.   Two or more substances are combined.

    c.   The same substance appears in a different form.

    d.   One substance breaks into two or more different substances.

_____ **20.** During chemical reactions, energy is

    a.   either absorbed or released.

    b.   gained or lost.

    c.   condensed.

    d.   not involved.

_____ **21.** A graph that shows the volume of a gas is directly proportional to its temperature under constant pressure demonstrates

    a.   the Pressure law.

    b.   Charles's law.

    c.   the Density law.

    d.   Boyle's law.

_____ **22.** A graph of Boyle's law shows the relationship between

    a.   volume and density of a gas.

    b.   volume and pressure of a gas.

    c.   temperature and volume of a gas.

    d.   temperature and pressure of a gas.

_____ **23.** Data plotted on a graph results in a line that slopes upward from left to right. This graph tells you that

    a.   when one variable increases, the other variable increases.

    b.   when one variable increases, the other variable decreases.

    c.   when one variable increases, the other variable remains the same.

    d.   both variables are decreasing.

_____ **24.** On a long trip, a truck's tires can get very hot and cause

    a.   their volume to decrease.

    b.   their pressure to increase.

    c.   their pressure to decrease.

    d.   the truck to go faster.

_____ **25.** The greater the speed of gas particles, the

    a.   fewer collisions there will be.

    b.   lower the temperature.

    c.   greater the pressure.

    d.   lower the pressure.

_____ **26.** According to Boyle's law, when the pressure of a gas increases, its volume

    a.   increases.

    b.   stays constant.

    c.   decreases.

    d.   increases, then decreases.

_____ **27.** The amount of space that a gas takes up is its

    a.   volume.

    b.   mass.

    c.   pressure.

    d.   density.

_____ **28.** In which state of matter are particles packed tightly together and stay in fixed positions?

    a.   gas

    b.   solid

    c.   liquid

    d.   compound

_____ **29.** Which state of matter can change volume easily?

    a.   solid

    b.   liquid

    c.   gas

    d.   molecule

_____ **30.** The energy a substance has from the movement of its particles is called

    a.   light energy.

    b.   chemical energy.

    c.   thermal energy.

    d.   potential energy.

B. True or False

If the statement is true, write true. If it is false, change the underlined word or words to make the statement true.

31. A <u>liquid</u> does not have a definite shape, but it does have a definite volume.

_____

_____

32. Particles in a liquid move around <u>just as freely as</u> particles in a solid.

_____

_____

33. When the temperature is constant, the volume of a gas will <u>decrease</u> as the pressure decreases.

_____

_____

34. In a rigid container, as the temperature of a gas decreases, the pressure of the gas will <u>decrease</u>.

_____

_____

35. In a flexible container, when the temperature of a gas increases, the volume of the gas will <u>increase</u>.

_____

_____

36. The type of graph that results when the volume of a gas is measured as its pressure is changed is a <u>straight line.</u>

_____

_____

37. Baking a cake is an example of a <u>chemical</u> change.

_____

_____

38. Energy that comes from the chemical bonds within matter is called <u>thermal</u> energy.

_____

_____

39. <u>Condensation</u>, the change of state from a liquid to a solid, is the reverse of melting.

_____

_____

40. In every chemical reaction, the total amount of energy <u>stays the same</u>.

_____

_____

C. Completion
Fill in the word or phrase that best completes each statement.

41. The common state of matter that does not have a definite shape or a definite volume is a(n) _____.

_____

_____

42. The resistance of a liquid to flowing is called _____ .

_____

_____

43. To test Boyle's law, you could change the volume of a gas and measure its _____.

_____

_____

44. When the temperature of a gas in a rigid container increases, the pressure will _____.

_____

_____

45. According to Charles's law, whenever the temperature of a gas decreases, the volume _____.

_____

_____

46. When a graph of two variables shows a straight line passing through the point (0, 0), the two variables are _____ proportional to each other.

_____

_____

47. A_____ change alters the form of a substance, but does not change the material into another substance.

_____

_____

48. When a substance cools, it loses _____ energy to its surroundings.

_____

_____

49. _____ is the process in which a gas becomes a liquid.

_____

_____

50. When a burning match gives off light, energy is being changed from one _____ into another.

_____

_____

51. Solids that have particles arranged in a regular, repeating pattern are known as _____ solids.

_____

_____

52. In a _____, the particles are packed closely together, but they can move past each other freely.

_____

_____

53. Weather balloons are filled with only a small amount of helium because the _____ of the balloon will increase as the air pressure decreases at higher altitudes.

_____

_____

54. In a rigid container, when the speed of the gas molecules increases, the _____ of the gas also increases.

_____

_____

55. When the temperature of a gas in a balloon increases, the volume of the balloon will _____.

_____

_____

56. The graph of Boyle's law shows that as the volume of a gas at constant temperature is changed, its pressure varies _____ with the volume.

_____

_____

57. A substance undergoes a _____ change when it is changed into one or more new substances with different properties.

_____

_____

58. The temperature of a substance increases when the _____ energy of the substance increases.

_____

_____

59. Sublimation is the change of a solid directly into a _____.

_____

_____

60. In a chemical reaction that requires heating, some _____ is being changed from one form to another.

_____

_____

D. Interpreting Diagrams

Use the diagram to answer each question.

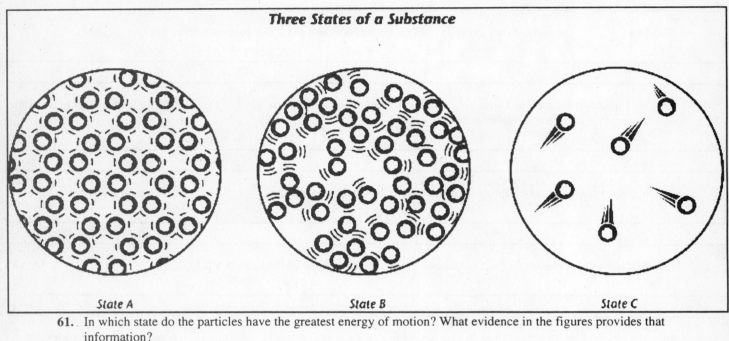

Three States of a Substance

State A   State B   State C

61. In which state do the particles have the greatest energy of motion? What evidence in the figures provides that information?

_____

_____

_____

_____

_____

62. In which state are the particles least able to move? What evidence in the figures provides that information?

_____

_____

_____

63. Which of the three states represents a liquid? What evidence in the figures provides that information?

_____

_____

_____

_____

_____

64. Which of the three states does not have a definite volume and a definite shape?

_____
_____
_____
_____

65. For the same mass of a particular substance, which of the three states would you expect to have the largest volume? Explain.

_____
_____
_____
_____

66. Classify each of the three states as gas, liquid, or solid.

_____
_____
_____
_____

Use the diagram to answer each question.

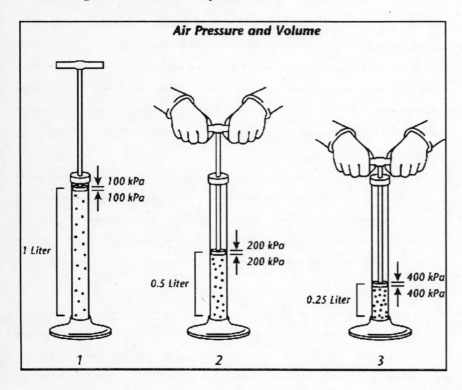

Air Pressure and Volume

1   2   3

67. What pattern in the behavior of gases is shown from Step 1 through Step 3 of the figure?

_____

_____

_____

_____

_____

68. What is the name of the scientific law illustrated in this diagram? Summarize that law.

_____

_____

_____

_____

_____

69. Predict what would happen if the volume of the gas in Step 3 was decreased to 0.125 liter. Compare the new situation with Step 1 or Step 3.

_____

_____

_____

_____

_____

70. What would happen to the pressure in Step 3 if a hole was made that allowed gas particles to move freely in and out of the container?

_____

_____

_____

_____

71. Explain what has happened to the volume and pressure of the gas in the container between Step 1 and Step 2.

_____

_____

_____

_____

72. Predict what would happen if the original volume of the gas in Step 1 was increased to 2 liters.

_____

_____

_____

_____

E. Essay

Write an answer to each of the following questions.

73. Compare solids, liquids, and gases in terms of their shapes and volumes.

_____

_____

_____

_____

_____

_____

74. Suppose you buy some inflated party balloons that are at room temperature (about 20°C). What will happen to those balloons if you take them outside on a cold day? Explain.

_____

_____

_____

_____

_____

_____

75. Explain why a truck tire that has the correct air pressure inside a building at room temperature (about 20°C) is more likely to explode when driven in hot weather than in cold weather.

_____

_____

_____

_____

_____

_____

76. Explain what happens as a puddle dries after a rainstorm.

_____

_____

_____

_____

_____

_____

77. Explain how bakers use energy to control chemical reactions when baking muffins.

_____

_____

_____

_____

_____

_____

78. Explain how the motion of particles differs in gases, liquids, and solids.

_____

_____

_____

_____

_____

_____

_____

79. Compare two graphs. The first graph results when the temperature of a gas is changed and the volume is measured. The second graph results when the volume is changed and the pressure is measured. Explain why the shapes of the graphs are the same or different.

_____

_____

_____

_____

_____

_____

_____

80. Explain why sweating on a hot day can make a person feel cooler.

_____

_____

_____

_____

_____

_____

_____

Test 52 Book K, Chapter 2: Changes in Matter
Answer Key (Short)

__b__	1.
__c__	2.
__d__	3.
__c__	4.
__c__	5.
__c__	6.
__c__	7.
__c__	8.
__a__	9.
__c__	10.
__c__	11.
__d__	12.
__a__	13.
__b__	14.
__c__	15.
__c__	16.
__d__	17.
__d__	18.
__a__	19.
__a__	20.
__b__	21.
__b__	22.
__a__	23.
__b__	24.
__c__	25.
__c__	26.
__a__	27.
__b__	28.
__c__	29.
__c__	30.

31.	TRUE
32.	false, more freely than
33.	false, increase
34.	TRUE
35.	TRUE
36.	false, curve
37.	TRUE
38.	false, chemical
39.	false, freezing
40.	TRUE
41.	gas

42.	viscosity
43.	pressure
44.	increase
45.	decreases
46.	directly
47.	physical
48.	thermal
49.	Condensation
50.	form
51.	crystalline
52.	liquid
53.	volume
54.	pressure
55.	increase
56.	inversely
57.	chemical
58.	thermal
59.	gas
60.	energy
61.	State C; the "tails" on the particles show they have the greatest energy and are moving the fastest; also, the distances between the particles are much greater than in the other two states.
62.	State A; the figure shows that the particles are arranged in a pattern in definite, fixed positions, and so they can vibrate but not move around each other.
63.	State B; the particles are not in a fixed pattern as particles in a solid are; the particles can move around each other, but they remain quite close together; the particles do not have the energy of motion that gas particles have.
64.	State C
65.	State C, because the particles are spread farthest apart and would take up the most space
66.	State A: solid; State B: liquid; State C: gas
67.	The figure shows that the volume and pressure of a gas are related, and that as the volume of a gas decreases, its pressure increases.
68.	Boyle's law; Boyle's law states that when the pressure of a gas increases, its volume decreases; when the pressure of a gas decreases, its volume increases.
69.	The pressure would increase to 800 kPa. That is eight times the pressure of the gas in Step 1, or two times the pressure of the gas in Step 3.
70.	At first, many more particles of the gas would leave the container than would enter, and the pressure in the container would be decreasing. Eventually, the pressure inside the container would be equal to the pressure of the air outside the container.
71.	The volume was decreased by one half, from 1 liter to 0.5 liter. As a result, the pressure of the gas doubled, from 100 kPa to 200 kPa.
72.	The pressure would be reduced to one half the original pressure, or 50 kPa.
73.	A solid has a definite shape and a definite volume. A liquid has a definite volume but not a definite shape; it takes the shape of its container. A gas does not have either a definite volume or a definite shape, and so a gas takes the shape of its container and fills the available volume.

74.   The balloons will decrease in volume. When the temperature of a gas decreases, its volume also decreases. The decrease in temperature means the gas particles have less energy of motion than before.

75.   The volume of the tire is not greatly changed by the changing temperatures, but the gas pressure inside the tire is. In hot weather, the rising air temperature in the tire causes the pressure in the tire to increase also; if the pressure becomes greater than the tire can stand, the tire bursts. However, in cold weather, the air temperature decreases, causing the pressure on the tire walls to be reduced.

76.   As they collide with each other, some water particles gain enough energy of motion to escape at the surface of the puddle. This process gradually reduces the size of the puddle until it dries up. When the change of state occurs at the surface of the liquid, the change from a liquid to a gas is called evaporation. In warm weather, evaporation may occur more quickly because the water is heated by the air, the sun, or the ground.

77.   After bakers mix the ingredients for muffins, they put the muffin batter in a hot oven. The hot oven is a source of thermal energy for chemical reactions in the batter. When the reactions have progressed to the right stage, the baker removes the muffins from the oven. If the muffins were not removed from the source of thermal energy, the chemical reactions would continue, eventually burning the muffins.

78.   Gas particles are spread far apart, and they move in all directions at high speeds, filling all the space available to them. Liquid particles are packed closely together, but they can move freely around each other, and so a liquid can take on the shape of its container. Solid particles are packed tightly together; they can vibrate but not move from their fixed positions.

79.   A graph of the changes in volume resulting from changes in temperature is a straight line with an upward trend. A graph of the changes in pressure resulting from changes in volume is a curved line with a downward trend. The first graph shows that the volume of a gas increases as its temperature increases. The second graph shows that the pressure of a gas decreases as the volume increases.

80.   A person's body produces heat. When sweat, a liquid, forms on body, it gains energy and evaporates, or turns to a gas. Because the person's skin is losing energy to the evaporating sweat particles, the person feels cooler.

Test 53 Book K, Chapter 3: Elements and the Periodic Table

A. Multiple Choice
Choose the letter of the correct answer.

_____ 1. Mendeleev created the first periodic table by arranging elements in order of

   a. decreasing atomic mass.
   b. increasing atomic mass.
   c. increasing atomic number.
   d. increasing melting points and densities.

_____ 2. How did chemists change Mendeleev's periodic table in the early 1900s?

   a. They included chemical properties such as bonding power.
   b. They included physical properties such as melting point and density.
   c. They used atomic mass instead of atomic number to organize the elements.
   d. They used atomic number instead of atomic mass to organize the elements.

_____ 3. From an element's location in the periodic table, you can predict

   a. its properties.
   b. its chemical name.
   c. its chemical symbol.
   d. when it was discovered.

_____ 4. Which of these statements about a column of the periodic table is true?

   a. The elements have similar properties.
   b. The elements have a wide range of properties.
   c. The elements have the same atomic number.
   d. The elements have the same atomic mass.

_____ 5. The factor that determines how an atom interacts with other atoms is its

   a. number of protons.
   b. number of neutrons.
   c. atomic mass.
   d. number of valence electrons.

_____ 6. Which of the following have the same number and arrangement of valence electrons?

   a. the elements in a period
   b. the elements in a group
   c. the elements having similar atomic masses
   d. the elements having similar atomic numbers

_____ 7. Which of the following is NOT a physical property of most metals?

   a. being ductile
   b. being good energy conductors
   c. being a liquid at room temperature
   d. being malleable

_____ 8. Which of the following statements about metals is true?

    a. Metals need to be stored in sealed containers for safety.

    b. Metals show a wide range of chemical properties.

    c. Metals are highly reactive substances.

    d. Metals do not react with oxygen.

_____ 9. In the periodic table, the most reactive metals are found

    a. in Group 1, the first column on the left.

    b. in Period 1, the first row across the top.

    c. in Groups 13 through 16 in the center.

    d. in Periods 6 and 7 at the bottom.

_____ 10. Which group of elements have two valence electrons in their atoms?

    a. transition metals

    b. metal alloys

    c. alkaline earth metals

    d. alkali metals

_____ 11. Where are nonmetals located on the periodic table?

    a. to the left of the zigzag line

    b. to the right of the zigzag line

    c. in the two bottom rows

    d. in Groups 1 through 4

_____ 12. Which group contains the most elements?

    a. metalloids

    b. nonmetals

    c. metals

    d. transition elements

_____ 13. At room temperature, more than half of the nonmetal elements are

    a. alloys.

    b. gases.

    c. liquids.

    d. solids.

_____ 14. Which member of the carbon family is a nonmetal?

    a. carbon

    b. silicon

    c. tin

    d. lead

_____ 15. How does nuclear fusion create new elements inside stars?

    a. All the nuclei repel each other because of their positive charges.

    b. Small nuclei cause large nuclei to break apart.

    c. Large nuclei combine, then form smaller nuclei.

    d. Small nuclei combine to form larger nuclei.

_____ **16.** The sun is made up mostly of

    a. hydrogen.

    b. iron.

    c. carbon.

    d. beryllium.

_____ **17.** Where are metals located in the periodic table?

    a. to the left of the zigzag line

    b. to the right of the zigzag line

    c. in the top rows

    d. in the middle rows

_____ **18.** In which part of an atom are the valence electrons located?

    a. inside the nucleus

    b. closest to the nucleus

    c. farthest from the nucleus

    d. throughout the entire atom

_____ **19.** The elements in a row of the periodic table

    a. are in the same family.

    b. have the same or nearly the same properties.

    c. have the same average atomic mass.

    d. are in the same period.

_____ **20.** The elements in a column of the periodic table

    a. are in the same family.

    b. are in the same period.

    c. have the same atomic mass.

    d. have very similar chemical symbols.

_____ **21.** What information in the periodic table indicates the number of protons in an atom?

    a. the position of the element in its column

    b. the element's chemical symbol

    c. the element's atomic number

    d. the element's atomic mass

_____ **22.** Which part(s) of the atom move around the nucleus?

    a. atomic mass units

    b. electrons

    c. protons

    d. neutrons

_____ **23.** The atomic number of an element is based on the

    a. mass of its nucleus.

    b. number of electrons around its core.

    c. number of protons in its nucleus.

    d. number of neutrons in its nucleus.

_____ **24.** What prediction did Mendeleev make that came true less than 20 years later?

    a. He predicted the atomic numbers of unknown elements.

    b. He predicted that a total of 112 elements would be discovered.

    c. He said that three new elements would be discovered, and he described their properties.

    d. He said that the periodic table would be developed into 18 families.

_____ **25.** The two most common alkaline earth metals are

    a. copper and zinc.

    b. iron and silver.

    c. sodium and potassium.

    d. calcium and magnesium.

_____ **26.** Which of the following statements about transition metals is true?

    a. They are never found uncombined in nature.

    b. They are so similar that it's often difficult to find differences between them.

    c. They are so soft that they can be cut with an ordinary knife.

    d. They are the most reactive of all the types of metals.

_____ **27.** Which group of elements share characteristics with both metals and nonmetals

    a. salts

    b. metalloids

    c. halogens

    d. alloys

_____ **28.** The elements that do not ordinarily form compounds are

    a. the carbon family.

    b. metals.

    c. halogens.

    d. noble gases.

_____ **29.** Which member of the carbon family is a metalloid?

    a. silicon

    b. carbon

    c. tin

    d. lead

_____ **30.** Fluorine, chlorine, bromine, and iodine are part of a group called

    a. noble gases.

    b. metalloids.

    c. halogens.

    d. alkali metals.

B. True or False

If the statement is true, write true. If it is false, change the underlined word or words to make the statement true.

31. The modern periodic table is organized according to <u>atomic mass</u>.

_____

_____

32. The horizontal rows in the periodic table are known as <u>groups</u>.

_____

_____

33. The elements in a group from the periodic table have <u>similar</u> characteristics.

_____

_____

34. The elements in each <u>period</u> of the periodic table generally have the same number of valence electrons.

_____

_____

35. Describing a metal as <u>malleable</u> means that it can be pounded into a new shape.

_____

_____

36. The most chemically active metals are in <u>Group 1</u> of the periodic table.

_____

_____

37. Nonmetals can be found on the <u>left</u> side of the periodic table.

_____

_____

38. In general, the physical properties of nonmetals are <u>similar to</u> the properties of metals.

_____

_____

39. Fusion is the process in which existing nuclei <u>combine</u> and make new nuclei.

_____

_____

40. Atoms of the halogen family elements typically gain <u>two electrons</u> when they react.

_____

_____

C. Completion

Fill in the word or phrase that best completes each statement.

41. Mendeleev discovered that periodic patterns appeared when he arranged the elements in order of increasing _____.

_____

_____

42. The property of an element that indicates the number of protons in its atoms is the _____.

_____

_____

43. A column of elements in the periodic table is called a group, or _____.

_____

_____

44. The electrons in an atom that are involved in forming chemical bonds are called _____.

_____

_____

45. Elements that transmit electricity and heat easily are called good _____.

_____

_____

46. The chemical reactivity of metals tends to _____ from left to right across the periodic table.

_____

_____

47. Some elements on the right side of the periodic table form molecules of two atoms each, which are called _____ molecules.

_____

_____

48. Nonmetals are _____ conductors of heat and electricity.

_____

_____

49. Astronomers generally agree that the matter in the sun and its planets came from a(n) _____ , an explosion that broke apart a massive star billions of years ago.

_____

_____

50. In the 1800s, Dmitri Mendeleev organized the first truly useful _____.

_____

_____

51. An element's _____ can be predicted from its location in the periodic table.

_____

_____

52. Each chemical element is given a specific _____ that usually consists of one or two letters.

_____

_____

53. Elements in Group 1 have _____ valence electron(s).

_____

_____

54. Most metals are in the _____ state at room temperature.

_____

_____

55. Brass is a(n) _____ formed by mixing copper and zinc.

_____

_____

56. Elements known as _____ are located to the right of the metalloids on the periodic table.

_____

_____

57. At room temperature, all the metalloids are solids, while most nonmetals are _____.

_____

_____

58. A substance that will conduct electricity only under certain conditions is called a _____.

_____

_____

59. In stars, matter exists in the _____ state in which electrons have been stripped away from the nuclei of atoms.

_____

_____

60. When two nuclei combine in a _____ reaction, a huge amount of energy is released.

_____

_____

D. Interpreting Diagrams

Use the diagram to answer each question.

Atoms of Some Common Elements

Substance	Atomic Number	Atomic Mass	Protons	Neutrons	Electrons
Sodium	11	?	11	12	?
Magnesium	12	24	12	?	12
Aluminum	?	27	13	14	13
Phosphorus	15	31	?	16	15

61. What is the atomic mass of sodium?

_____

_____

_____

_____

62. What is the total number of electrons in an atom of sodium?

_____

_____

_____

_____

63. How many neutrons are in an atom of magnesium?

_____

_____

_____

_____

64. The element silicon has been omitted from this table. It appears in the periodic table between aluminum and phosphorus, and in the same row. Given that information, which of the five columns could you fill in for silicon?

_____
_____
_____
_____
_____

65. What is the atomic number of aluminum?

_____
_____
_____
_____

66. How many protons are in an atom of phosphorus?

_____
_____
_____
_____

Use the diagram to answer each question.

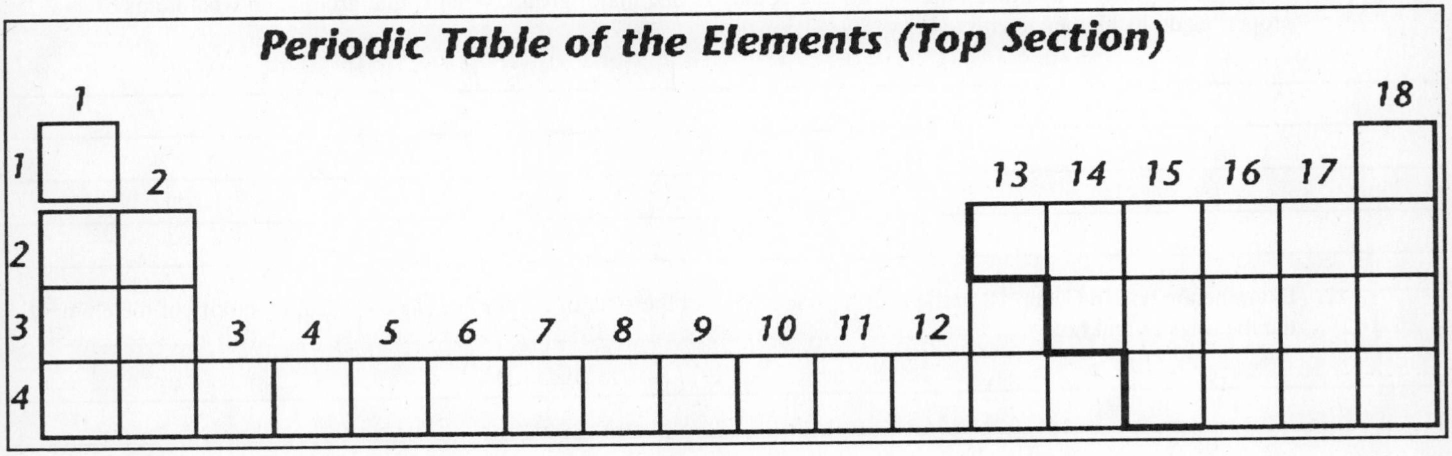

Periodic Table of the Elements (Top Section)

67. Which group of elements has atoms with two valence electrons?

_____
_____
_____
_____

68. If a metal reacts violently with water, in which group is it likely to be found?

_____

_____

_____

_____

69. What name is given to the elements in Groups 3 through 12? How do their properties tend to compare with the elements to the left and right of these groups?

_____

_____

_____

_____

70. What element is located in the first row of Group 1? Why is the box for this element separated from the rest of Group 1 by a slight space?

_____

_____

_____

_____

71. Most of the elements that touch the zigzag line belong to one major group. What is that group, and what kinds of properites do its elements tend to have?

_____

_____

_____

_____

72. Examine the box in Group 18 in the fourth period. Predict the state of matter and the chemical reactivity of the element that belongs in that box.

_____

_____

_____

_____

E. Essay

   Write an answer to each of the following questions.

   73. Explain why the atomic mass of an element is usually not given as a whole number even though each individual atom of the element has a whole number of protons and neutrons.

   _____

   _____

   _____

   _____

   _____

   _____

   _____

   _____

   74. Lithium (atomic number 3), sodium (atomic number 11), and potassium (atomic number 19) all show similar chemical properties. Explain how this is possible.

   _____

   _____

   _____

   _____

   _____

   _____

   _____

   _____

   75. What contribution did the Russian chemist Dmitri Mendeleev make to chemistry? What was he able to do to show the value of his contribution?

   _____

   _____

   _____

   _____

   _____

   _____

   _____

76. Metals show a wide range of chemical behavior. Give examples of that variation by describing some common properties of calcium, gold, iron, and sodium.

_____

_____

_____

_____

_____

_____

77. Compare the properties of metals and nonmetals.

_____

_____

_____

_____

_____

_____

78. Explain why iron and certain other transition metals are used in construction instead of the alkali metals.

_____

_____

_____

_____

_____

_____

79. How do elements with smaller nuclei form heavier elements in the stars? Why does this process occur naturally in stars but not on Earth?

_____

_____

_____

_____

_____

_____

80. Group 17 is called the halogen family, and the group to its right is called the noble gases. How are these elements alike and how are they different?

_____

_____

_____

_____

_____

_____

_____

Test 53 Book K, Chapter 3: Elements and the Periodic Table
Answer Key (Short)

b	**1.**	
d	**2.**	
a	**3.**	
a	**4.**	
d	**5.**	
b	**6.**	
c	**7.**	
b	**8.**	
a	**9.**	
c	**10.**	
b	**11.**	
c	**12.**	
b	**13.**	
a	**14.**	
d	**15.**	
a	**16.**	
a	**17.**	
c	**18.**	
d	**19.**	
a	**20.**	
c	**21.**	
b	**22.**	
c	**23.**	
c	**24.**	
d	**25.**	
b	**26.**	
a	**27.**	
d	**28.**	
a	**29.**	
c	**30.**	

31.   false, atomic number

32.   false, periods

33.   TRUE

34.   false, group, or family

35.   TRUE

36.   TRUE

37.   false, right

38.   false, different from

39.   TRUE

40.   false, one electron

41.   atomic mass

42.	atomic number
43.	family
44.	valence electrons
45.	conductors
46.	decrease
47.	diatomic
48.	poor
49.	supernova
50.	periodic table
51.	properties
52.	symbol
53.	one
54.	solid
55.	alloy
56.	nonmetals
57.	gases
58.	semiconductor
59.	plasma
60.	fusion
61.	23
62.	11
63.	12
64.	Its atomic number is 14, and a silicon atom has 14 protons and 14 electrons. You cannot figure out the number of neutrons and the atomic mass.
65.	13
66.	15
67.	Group 2
68.	Group 1
69.	Transition metals; they are less reactive than the metals in Groups 1 and 2 to their left; they tend to be more reactive than the metals to their right.
70.	Hydrogen; hydrogen is not considered a part of any group, or family, because its chemical properties differ so much from those of other elements.
71.	Metalloids; metalloids have some properties of metals and some properties of nonmetals.
72.	The element is a gas - one of the noble gases. It does not ordinarily react with other elements to form compounds.
73.	All atoms of a given element have the same number of protons, but those atoms may have different numbers of neutrons. That means that the masses of individual atoms are not the same. The atomic mass for the element is the average mass of all the different atoms. That average is not a whole number.
74.	The three elements are members of the same group, the alkali metals. Their chemical behavior results from the fact that their atoms have one valence electron, which tends to be lost during chemical reactions. As a result, these elements are part of the most active group of metals.
75.	Mendeleev organized the first useful periodic table. He arranged the elements in order of increasing atomic mass and grouped them according to properties that repeated in patterns. By using this periodic arrangement, Mendeleev was able to predict the properties of several elements that had not yet been discovered.

76.   Sodium is one of the most chemically active metals; it can react explosively with air or water if not stored properly. Calcium is less reactive than sodium, but it is more reactive than most metals. In nature, sodium and calcium are always found in compounds, and never as elements. Iron also reacts with oxygen, but it does so over a period of time; unprotected iron will gradually turn to rust, a compound of iron and oxygen. Gold is extremely unreactive with air and water; in nature, metallic gold can remain in its elemental form indefinitely.

77.   Metals are generally solid at room temperature, are shiny, malleable, and ductile, are good conductors, and have high melting and boiling points. Nonmetals are generally gases at room temperature and have low melting and boiling points. Solid nonmetals are usually dull and brittle, and are poor conductors. The properties of metals are generally the opposite of the nonmetals.

78.   When people build a structure, they want it to be stable, to be strong enough to hold up under weight, and to last for a long time. Iron and certain other transition metals have these characteristics. Alkali metals, on the other hand, are soft and highly reactive, and so they are not useful for construction.

79.   In stars, atoms exist as plasma. In this state, the atoms are stripped of their electrons; the nuclei move at high speed and collide with one another. Sometimes pairs of nuclei join together, or fuse, making a new, more massive nucleus. In this way, new elements are created through fusion. These reactions require high temperatures and pressures that are found in stars but not on Earth, and so this process does not occur naturally on Earth.

80.   Both groups are nonmetals that appear on the right side of the periodic table. All of Group 18 and all but one element in Group 17 are gases under ordinary conditions. However, their chemical behavior is very different. The halogen atoms have seven valence electrons. They easily gain one electron, making them extremely reactive. The noble gases do not ordinarily gain, lose, or share electrons, making them chemically unreactive.

Test 54 Book K, Chapter 4: Carbon Chemistry

A. Multiple Choice
Choose the letter of the correct answer.

_____ 1. Carbon is able to bond with other elements in many different ways because it has

    a. six protons.

    b. four electrons.

    c. six valence electrons.

    d. four valence electrons.

_____ 2. The element whose atoms can make straight chains, branched chains, and rings is

    a. carbon.

    b. hydrogen.

    c. nitrogen.

    d. oxygen.

_____ 3. Which form of pure carbon is so hard that it can be used in cutting tools?

    a. diamond

    b. graphite

    c. hydrocarbon

    d. fullerene

_____ 4. Which form of pure carbon is formed of layers that slide past one another?

    a. diamond

    b. graphite

    c. fullerene

    d. isomer

_____ 5. What is another name for carbon compounds?

    a. carbohydrates

    b. fullerenes

    c. hydrocarbons

    d. organic compounds

_____ 6. Many organic compounds have similar properties, including

    a. low melting points.

    b. ability to conduct electricity.

    c. ability to dissolve in water.

    d. high boiling points.

_____ 7. What can you tell about methane (CH_4) from its molecular formula?

    a. It contains four carbon atoms.

    b. It contains one hydrogen atom.

    c. It contains four hydrogen atoms.

    d. It forms groups of four molecules.

_____ 8. Which compounds have the same molecular formula but different structures?

    a. hydrocarbons

    b. isomers

    c. organic compounds

    d. polymers

_____ 9. How is a substituted hydrocarbon created from a hydrocarbon chain?

    a. by adding an extra hydrogen atom to the chain of carbon atoms

    b. by forming a double or triple bond between some carbon atoms

    c. by replacing at least one carbon atom with a hydrogen atom

    d. by replacing at least one hydrogen atom with an atom of another element

_____ 10. Which substituted hydrocarbon is formed by replacing atoms with one or more hydroxyl groups?

    a. alcohol

    b. ester

    c. halogen compound

    d. organic acid

_____ 11. Substances that provide the energy and raw materials the human body needs are

    a. nutrients.

    b. substituted hydrocarbons.

    c. esters.

    d. unsaturated hydrocarbons.

_____ 12. Which term describes the breaking down of polymers into monomers in the human body?

    a. reproduction

    b. repair

    c. growth

    d. digestion

_____ 13. Proteins are nutrients used in the body mostly for

    a. energy.

    b. building and repairing body parts.

    c. passing information from one generation to the next.

    d. sending chemical messages.

_____ 14. What factor determines the primary differences among living things?

    a. whether or not their bodies contain nucleic acids

    b. the order of nucleotides in their DNA

    c. the type of complex carbohydrates in their diet

    d. the variety of proteins in their diet

_____ 15. What nutrients needed by the human body are NOT organic compounds?

    a. vitamins

    b. nucleic acids

    c. minerals

    d. simple carbohydrates

_____ **16.** The organic compounds that serve as helper molecules in many of the body's chemical reactions are called

    a. amino acids.

    b. minerals.

    c. nucleotides.

    d. vitamins.

_____ **17.** Which of these compounds has the maximum possible number of hydrogen atoms on its carbon chain?

    a. hydrocarbon with double bonds

    b. hydrocarbon with triple bonds

    c. saturated hydrocarbon

    d. unsaturated hydrocarbon

_____ **18.** Compounds that contain only the elements carbon and hydrogen are called

    a. carbon chains.

    b. hydrocarbons.

    c. isomers.

    d. organic compounds.

_____ **19.** What property do all hydrocarbons have?

    a. They burn easily.

    b. They dissolve in water.

    c. They make good conductors of electricity.

    d. They have high melting points.

_____ **20.** What shapes do hydrocarbons NOT form?

    a. straight chains

    b. branched chains

    c. ring-shaped chains

    d. geodesic domes

_____ **21.** Which of the following is a property of many organic liquids?

    a. They dissolve well in water.

    b. They are good conductors of electricity.

    c. They have strong odors.

    d. They have high boiling points.

_____ **22.** What is the shape of pure carbon fullerenes?

    a. branched chain

    b. hollow ball with a pattern like a geodesic dome

    c. flat layers

    d. hard, solid crystal shaped like a ball

_____ **23.** How many chemical bonds can each carbon atom form?

    a. one

    b. two

    c. four

    d. three

_____ **24.** In which type of substituted hydrocarbon might chlorine be the substituted atom(s)?

    a.   alcohol

    b.   ester

    c.   halogen compound

    d.   organic acid

_____ **25.** A very large organic molecule made up of chains of smaller molecules is called a

    a.   monomer.

    b.   polymer.

    c.   saturated hydrocarbon.

    d.   substituted hydrocarbon.

_____ **26.** The classes of polymers found in all living things are

    a.   vitamins and minerals.

    b.   halogen compounds, alcohols, organic acids, and esters.

    c.   simple carbohydrates and complex carbohydrates.

    d.   carbohydrates, lipids, proteins, and nucleic acids.

_____ **27.** Which class of polymers present in living things consists of chains of amino acids?

    a.   lipids

    b.   proteins

    c.   nucleic acids

    d.   complex carbohydrates

_____ **28.** A carbohydrate is made up of the elements carbon and hydrogen, plus

    a.   oxygen.

    b.   oxygen and nitrogen.

    c.   oxygen and sulfur.

    d.   oxygen and phosphorus.

_____ **29.** Which class of polymers stores the most energy, gram for gram?

    a.   proteins

    b.   nucleic acids

    c.   lipids

    d.   carbohydrates

_____ **30.** Starch is an example of a

    a.   nucleic acid.

    b.   protein.

    c.   simple carbohydrate.

    d.   complex carbohydrate.

B. True or False

If the statement is true, write true. If it is false, change the underlined word or words to make the statement true.

31. One reason carbon can form so many different compounds is that each of its atoms can form <u>eight</u> bonds.

_____

_____

32. The "lead" in a lead pencil is actually graphite, a form of <u>carbon</u>.

_____

_____

33. Most organic compounds <u>do conduct</u> an electric current.

_____

_____

34. A hydrocarbon is made of only carbon and <u>oxygen</u> atoms.

_____

_____

35. In a hydrocarbon, if just one hydrogen atom is replaced by an atom of another element, <u>a different</u> compound is produced.

_____

_____

36. The three elements in a carbohydrate compound are carbon, hydrogen, and <u>nitrogen</u>.

_____

_____

37. One gram of a <u>lipid</u> has more than twice as much energy as one gram of a carbohydrate.

_____

_____

38. Iron and iodine are examples of <u>minerals</u> needed by the body in small amounts.

_____

_____

39. Some carbon compounds can have the same <u>molecular formula</u> but different arrangements of atoms.

_____

_____

40. <u>A halogen compound</u> is a substituted hydrocarbon that contains a carboxyl group.

_____

_____

C. Completion
Fill in the word or phrase that best completes each statement.

41. One reason _____ can form so many compounds is that the same number of atoms can be bonded in different arrangements.

_____

_____

42. The arrangement of carbon atoms in a _____ resembles the pattern on a soccer ball.

_____

_____

43. Like most organic compounds, hydrocarbons do not dissolve well in _____.

_____

_____

44. Two compounds with the same molecular formula but different structures are called _____.

_____

_____

45. In a _____, atoms of other elements replace one or more hydrogen atoms in a hydrocarbon.

_____

_____

46. The simplest kind of carbohydrate is a _____.

_____

_____

47. Your body can digest starch, but another common complex carbohydrate, _____, passes through your body undigested.

_____

_____

48. Vitamins are organic compounds that serve as _____ in a variety of chemical reactions in the body.

_____

_____

49. When one carbon atom is bonded with several other carbon atoms in a single line, the structure is described as a _____.

_____

_____

50. Graphite, fullerenes, and _____ are three forms of the element carbon.

_____

_____

51. Organic compounds that are produced in factories instead of by living things are called _____ compounds.

52. In a molecular formula, the _____ indicates how many atoms of a particular element are present in each molecule of a compound.

53. An alcohol is a substituded hydrocarbon that contains a _____ in place of a hydrogen atom.

54. Amino acids are the building blocks that make up _____.

55. The simple carbohydrate that is present in the blood and that circulates throughout the body is _____.

56. Elements needed by the human body in small amounts are called _____.

57. An organic compound that contains one or more double or triple bonds is described as being _____.

58. The compound formed by the chemical combination of an organic acid and an alcohol is a(n) _____.

59. Cellulose and _____ are two common complex carbohydrates made from simple carbohydrates.

60. The monomers that make up DNA molecules are called _____.

D. Interpreting Diagrams

Use the diagram to answer each question.

Four Organic Molecules

61. Which of the structures is an unsaturated hydrocarbon?

_____

_____

_____

_____

_____

62. Which of the structures is a substituted hydrocarbon?

_____

_____

_____

_____

63. Which two structures have the same molecular formula? What is the formula?

_____

_____

_____

_____

_____

64. Explain how structural formulas like the ones in this diagram provide more information than just a molecular formula alone.

_____

_____

_____

_____

65. Which of the four molecules are hydrocarbons?

_____

_____

_____

_____

66. Identify which molecule has a branched structure and which has a ring structure.

_____

_____

_____

_____

Use the diagram to answer each question.

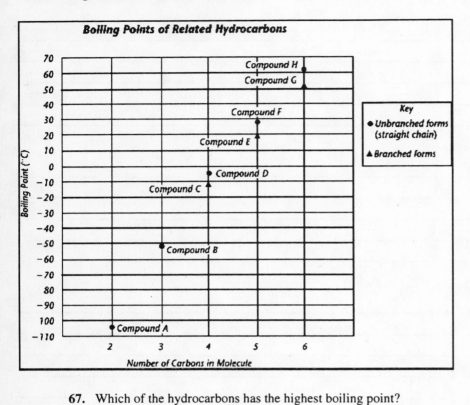

Boiling Points of Related Hydrocarbons

67. Which of the hydrocarbons has the highest boiling point?

_____

_____

_____

_____

68. Which of the hydrocarbons has the lowest boiling point?

_____

_____

_____

_____

69. Which of the hydrocarbons have (has) five carbons?

_____

_____

_____

_____

70. What is the basic difference in structure between Compounds D and C?

_____

_____

_____

_____

71. Compare the boiling points of the hydrocarbons having the same number of carbon atoms. What pattern does this graph show for each pair of compounds?

_____

_____

_____

_____

72. Based on the evidence in this graph, how does the number of carbon atoms in a hydrocarbon affect its boiling point?

_____

_____

_____

_____

E. Essay
  Write an answer to each of the following questions.

73. Explain the difference between a saturated and an unsaturated hydrocarbon, and explain how the name of a hydrocarbon tells you whether or not it is saturated.

_____

_____

_____

_____

_____

_____

74. Why are proteins classified as polymers?

_____

_____

_____

_____

_____

_____

75. Explain what generally happens to the proteins that a person eats.

_____

_____

_____

_____

_____

_____

_____

76. Describe graphite and diamond. Explain why these substances are so different even though both of them are pure forms of carbon.

_____

_____

_____

_____

_____

_____

77. Explain why more compounds can be made from carbon than from any other element.

_____

_____

_____

_____

_____

_____

78. Why can hydrocarbon compounds be used as fuels?

_____

_____

_____

_____

_____

_____

79. Explain what makes an alcohol a substituted hydrocarbon.

_____

_____

_____

_____

_____

_____

_____

80. Explain why vitamins are an important part of a person's diet even though they do not directly provide energy or raw materials for the body.

_____

_____

_____

_____

_____

_____

Test 54 Book K, Chapter 4: Carbon Chemistry
Answer Key (Short)

__d__	**1.**	
__a__	**2.**	
__a__	**3.**	
__b__	**4.**	
__d__	**5.**	
__a__	**6.**	
__c__	**7.**	
__b__	**8.**	
__d__	**9.**	
__a__	**10.**	
__a__	**11.**	
__d__	**12.**	
__b__	**13.**	
__b__	**14.**	
__c__	**15.**	
__d__	**16.**	
__c__	**17.**	
__b__	**18.**	
__a__	**19.**	
__d__	**20.**	
__c__	**21.**	
__b__	**22.**	
__c__	**23.**	
__c__	**24.**	
__b__	**25.**	
__d__	**26.**	
__b__	**27.**	
__a__	**28.**	
__c__	**29.**	
__d__	**30.**	

31. false, four

32. TRUE

33. false, do not conduct

34. false, hydrogen

35. TRUE

36. false, oxygen

37. TRUE

38. TRUE

39. TRUE

40. false, An organic acid

41. carbon

42.	fullerene
43.	water
44.	isomers
45.	substituted hydrocarbon
46.	sugar
47.	cellulose
48.	helper molecules
49.	straight chain
50.	diamond
51.	synthetic
52.	subscript
53.	hydroxyl group
54.	proteins
55.	glucose
56.	minerals
57.	unsaturated
58.	ester
59.	starch
60.	nucleotides
61.	C
62.	D
63.	A and C; C_5H_{10}
64.	A molecular formula indicates the number and type of atoms in the compound. The structural formula gives that information but also indicates the arrangement of the atoms.
65.	A, B, and C
66.	Branched: B; ring: A
67.	Compound H
68.	Compound A
69.	Compounds E and F
70.	Compound D is a straight-chain structure, and Compound C is a branched-chain structure.
71.	For each pair of hydrocarbons with the same number of carbons, the unbranched form has a higher boiling point than the branched form.
72.	The more carbon atoms a hydrocarbon has, the higher its boiling point is.
73.	A saturated hydrocarbon has only single bonds between the carbon atoms, while an unsaturated hydrocarbon has at least one double or triple bond. A hydrocarbon with a name ending in -*ane* is a saturated compound; a hydrocarbon with a name ending in -*ene* or -*yne* is an unsaturated compound.
74.	Polymers are large molecules made up of smaller molecules called monomers. Proteins are large, complex molecules made from amino acids. The amino acids are the monomers that make up the larger protein polymers.
75.	After a person eats proteins, the body digests these large molecules. That means that the proteins are broken down into the amino acids from which they were made. The body then uses those amino acids as building blocks to make new proteins that are part of the human body, such as muscles, hair, skin, and fingernails.

76. Graphite is a solid that is very slippery. It's made from carbon atoms bonded in flat layers that can slide over each other. That arrangement of atoms makes graphite a very effective lubricant. Diamond is a solid that is the hardest known mineral. Its exceptional hardness results from the fact that each carbon atom is bonded to four other carbon atoms.

77. Each carbon atom can form four bonds. In addition, carbon atoms can be arranged in straight chains, branched structures, and rings. Because so many physical structures can be built from these arrangements, more compounds can be formed from carbon than from any other element.

78. Hydrocarbons are made of carbon and hydrogen atoms. These molecules burn easily and release a large amount of heat. The energy in hydrocarbons can be used to heat buildings, generate electricity, and move vehicles such as cars, buses, and airplanes.

79. A substituted hydrocarbon contains another atom or group of atoms in place of a hydrogen atom in the hydrocarbon molecule. If the substituted atoms make up a hydroxyl group, the substance is an alcohol.

80. Unlike the major nutrients, which are needed in large amounts, vitamins are needed in only small amounts. Vitamins serve as helper molecules for many chemical reactions that must take place in order for the body to be healthy. For example, vitamin C is needed to keep skin and gums healthy. Vitamin D is needed for strong bones and teeth.

Test 55 Book L, Chapter 1: Chemical Reactions

A. Multiple Choice
  Choose the letter of the correct answer.

_____ 1.   What is the smallest part of an element?

  a.   atom

  b.   molecule

  c.   compound

  d.   mixture

_____ 2.   Most matter you find in your environment is in the form of

  a.   elements.

  b.   compounds.

  c.   mixtures.

  d.   precipitates.

_____ 3.   Which process changes matter into one or more new substances?

  a.   physical change

  b.   chemical change

  c.   conservation

  d.   freezing

_____ 4.   Water vapor in the air turns to liquid water in the form of rain. This is an example of a

  a.   physical change.

  b.   chemical change.

  c.   chemical equation.

  d.   chemical formula.

_____ 5.   The force that holds atoms together is called

  a.   a chemical bond.

  b.   conservation of matter.

  c.   heat.

  d.   a chemical change.

_____ 6.   What is the result when chemical bonds break and new bonds form?

  a.   a physical change

  b.   a chemical reaction

  c.   matter is destroyed

  d.   surface area increases

_____ 7.   A solid that forms from solution during a chemical reaction is called a(n)

  a.   element.

  b.   bond.

  c.   mixture.

  d.   precipitate.

_____ **8.** The only sure evidence for a chemical reaction is

    a.   the formation of a gas.

    b.   a color change.

    c.   the production of new materials.

    d.   changes in properties.

_____ **9.** A shorter, easier way to show chemical reactions, using symbols instead of words, is called a

    a.   chemical equation.

    b.   chemical formula.

    c.   symbol.

    d.   subscript.

_____ **10.** The substances listed on the left side of a chemical equation are the

    a.   products.

    b.   coefficients.

    c.   precipitates.

    d.   reactants.

_____ **11.** In chemical reactions, what does the principle of conservation of mass mean?

    a.   Matter is not created or destroyed.

    b.   The total mass of the reactants is greater than the total mass of the products.

    c.   The total mass of the reactants is less than the total mass of the products.

    d.   Matter is not changed.

_____ **12.** Which of the following is a balanced chemical equation?

    a. $H_2O_2 \rightarrow H_2O + O_2$

    b. $2\ Fe_2O_3 + 3\ C \rightarrow 4\ Fe + 3\ CO_2$

    c. $SO_2 + O_2 + 2\ H_2O \rightarrow 4\ H_2SO_4$

    d. $2\ Mg + HCl \rightarrow MgCl_2 + H_2$

_____ **13.** When two or more substances combine to make a more complex compound, the process is called a

    a.   decomposition reaction.

    b.   replacement reaction.

    c.   precipitate reaction.

    d.   synthesis reaction.

_____ **14.** A bottle of hydrogen peroxide that eventually turns into a bottle of water and oxygen gas is an example of a

    a.   synthesis reaction.

    b.   decomposition reaction.

    c.   replacement reaction.

    d.   precipitate reaction.

_____ **15.** A chemical reaction that absorbs energy in the form of heat is described as

    a.   endothermic.

    b.   exothermic.

    c.   combustion.

    d.   unbalanced.

_____ **16.** The minimum amount of energy that has to be added to start a reaction is the

    a.   exothermic energy.

    b.   endothermic energy.

    c.   activation energy.

    d.   chemical energy.

_____ **17.** Which of the following does NOT increase the number of particles of a substance available to react in a chemical reaction?

    a.   increasing the concentration

    b.   increasing the surface area

    c.   adding a catalyst

    d.   increasing the mass

_____ **18.** A material used to decrease the rate of a chemical reaction is a(n)

    a.   inhibitor.

    b.   catalyst.

    c.   enzyme.

    d.   fuel.

_____ **19.** Which of these is NOT one of the three things necessary to start and maintain a fire?

    a.   fuel

    b.   oxygen

    c.   carbon dioxide

    d.   heat

_____ **20.** A rapid reaction between oxygen and a fuel is known as

    a.   combustion.

    b.   heat.

    c.   activation.

    d.   decomposition.

_____ **21.** In what way can a fire be brought under control?

    a.   Add fuel.

    b.   Add oxygen.

    c.   Remove oxygen.

    d.   Remove carbon dioxide.

_____ **22.** Water affects most fires by

    a.   cooling the fire and preventing contact between oxygen and fuel.

    b.   decreasing activation energy.

    c.   producing carbon dioxide and removing fuel.

    d.   increasing the temperature.

_____ **23.** What is the best form of fire safety?

    a.   a water hose

    b.   an extinguisher

    c.   the fire department

    d.   fire prevention

_____ **24.** The best way to put out a small kitchen fire is to

    a.   blow it out.

    b.   use a garden hose.

    c.   turn off the appliances.

    d.   use a home fire extinguisher.

_____ **25.** Carbon dioxide is an example of a(n)

    a.   element.

    b.   compound.

    c.   mixture.

    d.   precipitate.

_____ **26.** Each element is represented by a one-letter or two-letter

    a.   formula.

    b.   equation.

    c.   symbol.

    d.   coefficient.

_____ **27.** In an equation, numbers often appear in front of a chemical formula. These numbers tell you the

    a.   number of atoms in a molecule.

    b.   identity of an element in a reaction.

    c.   number of molecules or atoms of each substance in the reaction.

    d.   number of molecules in an atom.

_____ **28.** Every chemical reaction involves a change in

    a.   mass.

    b.   energy.

    c.   concentration.

    d.   state.

_____ **29.** Chemicals that act as biological catalysts by speeding up reactions in living things are

    a.   inhibitors.

    b.   enzymes.

    c.   fuels.

    d.   reactants.

_____ **30.** The simplest type of substance that cannot be broken down into any other substance is a(n)

    a.   precipitate.

    b.   compound.

    c.   mixture.

    d.   element.

B. True or False
If the statement is true, write true. If it is false, change the underlined word or words to make the statement true.

31. A <u>mixture</u> is a substance made of two or more elements chemically combined in a specific ratio.

_____

_____

32. A change that produces a new substance is a <u>chemical</u> change.

_____

_____

33. In a chemical reaction, chemical <u>bonds</u> are formed or broken.

_____

_____

34. A chemical reaction can be identified by observing changes in the <u>properties</u> of matter.

_____

_____

35. The materials present at the beginning of a chemical reaction are called the <u>products</u>.

_____

_____

36. The amount of matter in a chemical reaction <u>changes</u>.

_____

_____

37. <u>Synthesis</u> is the process of making a more complex compound from simpler substances.

_____

_____

38. Chemical reactions that absorb energy are said to be <u>exothermic</u>.

_____

_____

39. The rate of a chemical reaction is <u>independent of</u> temperature.

_____

_____

40. A gas necessary for combustion to take place is <u>carbon dioxide</u>.

_____

_____

C. Completion

Fill in the word or phrase that best completes each statement.

41. A(n) _____ is a substance that cannot be broken down into any other substance by either chemical or physical means.

_____

_____

42. In a(n)_____ change, elements and/or compounds rearrange to form different materials.

_____

43. Atoms are held together by forces known as _____.

_____

_____

44. A precipitate is a _____ that forms from solution during a chemical reaction.

_____

_____

45. A subscript shows the number of _____ of an element in a molecule.

_____

_____

46. The principle of _____ states that during a chemical reaction, matter is not created or destroyed.

_____

_____

47. A reaction in which one element replaces another in a compound or in which two elements in different compounds trade places is called a _____ reaction.

_____

_____

48. A chemical reaction that releases energy in the form of heat is a(n) _____ reaction.

_____

_____

49. The _____ is the amount of one material present in a given volume of another material.

_____

_____

50. A fuel is a material that will release _____ when it burns.

_____

_____

51. When added to a fire, water _____ and prevents the fuel from coming in contact with oxygen.

_____

_____

52. One of the most effective ways to fight a small fire is to use a _____.

_____

_____

53. Two or more atoms may combine to form a _____.

_____

_____

54. The process of dissolving sugar in water is a _____ change.

_____

_____

55. The gas production when acid is added to a sample of chalk is an indication of a _____ reaction.

_____

_____

56. The _____ of a compound shows the ratio of elements present in the compound.

_____

_____

57. In a _____ reaction, the products are simpler substances than the reactant.

_____

_____

58. The _____ is the minimum amount of energy that must be added to start a chemical reaction.

_____

_____

59. A material used to decrease the rate of a reaction is called a(n) _____.

_____

_____

60. A wet log will not burn easily because a large amount of _____ must be added to the log to evaporate the water.

_____

_____

D. Interpreting Diagrams

Use the diagram to answer each question.

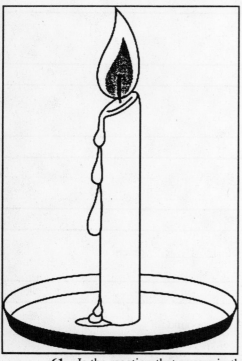

61. Is the reaction that occurs in the diagram endothermic or exothermic? Explain.

_____

_____

_____

_____

_____

62. When the candle was lit, a pool of liquid wax formed in the area around the wick, and then spilled over the side and resolidified. Does this observation refer to a physical change or a chemical change? Explain.

_____

_____

_____

_____

_____

63. If the candle is covered by a large glass beaker, the flame will go out. How does the beaker affect the conditions described by the fire triangle?

_____
_____
_____
_____
_____

64. If the products formed from the burning candle are mostly carbon (C), carbon dioxide (CO_2), and water (H_2O), what elements were in the reactants? How do you know?

_____
_____
_____
_____

65. The flame from the candle gives off black smoke. Does this statement describe evidence for a physical change or a chemical change? Explain.

_____
_____
_____
_____

66. Candles often are made of several different kinds of waxes, and sometimes colorful dyes and pleasing scents. Does this statement describe a compound or a mixture? Explain.

_____
_____
_____
_____

Use the diagram to answer each question.

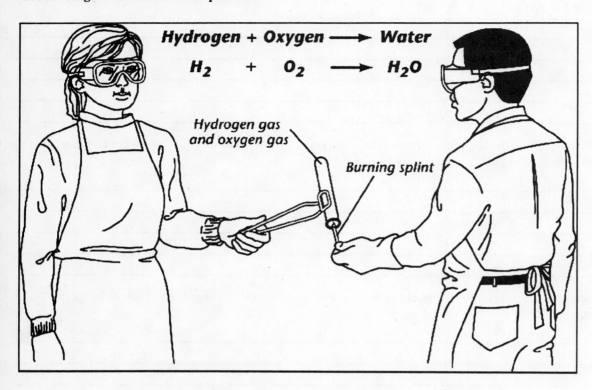

Hydrogen + Oxygen ⟶ Water

$$H_2 \quad + \quad O_2 \quad \longrightarrow \quad H_2O$$

Hydrogen gas
and oxygen gas

Burning splint

67. What type of chemical reaction is represented in the diagram? Explain.

_____

_____

_____

_____

_____

68. How would the mass of water formed in the reaction compare to the mass of oxygen that reacts?

_____

_____

_____

_____

_____

69. Identify the reactant(s) and product(s) of the reaction.

_____

_____

_____

_____

_____

70. Where does the water come from in the reaction?

_____

_____

_____

_____

_____

71. What is the purpose of the burning splint in the reaction?

_____

_____

_____

_____

_____

72. Write a balanced equation for the reaction.

_____

_____

_____

_____

_____

E. Essay
Write an answer to each of the following questions.

73. List some common sources of home fires and describe three items that can be kept in the home to help protect your family and your belongings in case of fire.

_____

_____

_____

_____

_____

_____

74. For each situation described below, tell whether the reaction is endothermic or exothermic, and explain your reasoning in terms of energy, reactants, and products. A) A log burns in a fireplace, giving off gases and leaving behind ash. B) When vinegar and baking soda are mixed, new substances form and the solution becomes cooler.

_____

_____

_____

_____

_____

_____

75. Explain each of the following in terms of factors that affect the rate of a chemical reaction: A) Chemical reactions in living things would not be possible without the enzymes found in cells. B) Wood burns at a steady rate, but sawdust may explode if a spark ignites it.

_____

_____

_____

_____

_____

_____

76. Compare a physical change and a chemical change.

_____

_____

_____

_____

_____

77. Relate the writing and balancing of a chemical equation to the principle of conservation of mass.

_____
_____
_____
_____
_____
_____
_____

78. Explain which bonds are broken and which bonds are formed during the reaction of magnesium and oxygen to form magnesium oxide. Identify which substances are compounds and which are elements. $2\,Mg + O_2 \rightarrow 2\,MgO$

_____
_____
_____
_____
_____
_____
_____

79. In terms of the fire triangle, explain why water is effective in fighting fires.

_____
_____
_____
_____
_____
_____

80. Describe the difference between a synthesis reaction and a decomposition reaction.

_____
_____
_____
_____
_____
_____

Test 55 Book L, Chapter 1: Chemical Reactions
Answer Key (Short)

__a__	1.
__c__	2.
__b__	3.
__a__	4.
__a__	5.
__b__	6.
__d__	7.
__c__	8.
__a__	9.
__d__	10.
__a__	11.
__b__	12.
__d__	13.
__b__	14.
__a__	15.
__c__	16.
__c__	17.
__a__	18.
__c__	19.
__a__	20.
__c__	21.
__a__	22.
__d__	23.
__d__	24.
__b__	25.
__c__	26.
__c__	27.
__b__	28.
__b__	29.
__d__	30.

31.	false, compound
32.	TRUE
33.	TRUE
34.	TRUE
35.	false, reactants
36.	false, remains the same
37.	TRUE
38.	false, endothermic
39.	false, dependent on
40.	false, oxygen
41.	element

42.	chemical
43.	chemical bonds
44.	solid
45.	atoms
46.	conservation of mass
47.	replacement
48.	exothermic
49.	concentration
50.	energy
51.	cools the fire
52.	fire extinguisher
53.	molecule
54.	physical
55.	chemical
56.	chemical formula
57.	decomposition
58.	activation energy
59.	inhibitor
60.	heat
61.	exothermic; heat is released when the candle (wax) burns
62.	A physical change; the substance was still wax, but it changed to a liquid and then back to a solid.
63.	Oxygen is needed for the candle to burn. The beaker prevents oxygen in the air from getting to the candle, so when the oxygen in the beaker is used up, the candle goes out.
64.	Carbon, hydrogen, and oxygen; no matter is created or destroyed in a chemical reaction, and so the elements present in the products must have been present in the reactants.
65.	A chemical change; the black smoke is evidence of the formation of a new substance, which means a chemical change occurs.
66.	A mixture; a compound is one substance made of two or more elements. The statement describes several materials that are not elements but are all mixed together in the candle.
67.	Synthesis; two elements (hydrogen and oxygen) combine to form a compound (water).
68.	According to the principle of conservation of mass, the mass of water formed equals the combined masses of hydrogen and oxygen that react. Therefore, the mass of water formed must be greater than the mass of oxygen that reacts.
69.	Hydrogen and oxygen are the reactants, and water is the product.
70.	Water forms from the reaction between hydrogen and oxygen.
71.	The burning splint supplies the activation energy needed to start the reaction between hydrogen and oxygen.
72.	$2 H_2O + O_2 \rightarrow 2 H_2O$
73.	Common sources of home fires include heaters, faulty electrical wiring, carelessness with cigarettes, and kitchen fires that start during cooking. Smoke detectors can give an early warning in case of a fire. A fire extinguisher can be used to put out a small fire. Baking soda can be used to extinguish a small fire on the stove.
74.	A) The reaction is exothermic because heat and light are given off. The energy of the products is less than the energy of the reactants. B) The reaction is endothermic. Energy is absorbed in the reaction, making the solution feel cooler. The energy of the products is greater than the energy of the reactants.

75.   A) Enzymes are catalysts. They speed up chemical reactions by lowering the activation energy of reactions needed for life. Without the presence of enzymes in cells, life functions would occur too slowly or require temperatures that are too high for cells to survive. B) Sawdust has a greater surface area than wood. Increased surface area of a reactant will increase the rate of a chemical reaction because more of the reactant will come in contact with oxygen.

76.   A physical change is a change only in form or appearance of a substance, but the substance does not change into any other substance(s). A chemical change occurs when elements and compounds combine in different ways, producing one or more substances that were not present before.

77.   The principle of conservation of mass states that matter cannot be created or destroyed during a chemical reaction. Therefore, the number and kind of atoms going into a chemical reaction must exactly equal the number and kind of atoms coming out of the reaction. A balanced chemical equation should show that all the elements present in the reactants are present in equal amounts in the products.

78.   The bonds between oxygen atoms in O_2 are broken. Bonds form between magnesium and oxygen in MgO. Mg and O_2 are elements, and MgO is a compound.

79.   The three parts of the fire triangle are fuel, oxygen, and heat. When one or more of the factors are removed, a fire will go out. When water is added to a fire, it covers the fuel so that oxygen cannot react with it. Water also cools the fire so that there is not enough heat for fuel to continue to ignite.

80.   A synthesis reaction produces a more complex substance from simpler substances. A decomposition reaction produces simpler substances from a more complex substance. These two reactions are opposite processes.

Name _____   Date _____

A. Multiple Choice
Choose the letter of the correct answer.

_____ **1.** How are the noble gases different from other groups of elements?

      a. Their atoms do not react easily with other atoms.

      b. They are nonmetals.

      c. They have no valence electrons.

      d. Their atoms react only with each other.

_____ **2.** Each family in the periodic table has its own characteristic properties based on the number of

      a. neutrons.

      b. valence electrons.

      c. protons.

      d. ions.

_____ **3.** When an atom loses an electron, it becomes a

      a. positive ion.

      b. negative ion.

      c. neutral ion.

      d. neutral atom.

_____ **4.** An ionic bond is the attraction between

      a. similarly charged ions.

      b. oppositely charged ions.

      c. neutral ions.

      d. neutral atoms.

_____ **5.** Ions that are made of more than one atom are examples of

      a. polyatomic ions.

      b. negative ions.

      c. positive ions.

      d. neutral ions.

_____ **6.** What is the chemical name for the compound with the formula NaS?

      a. sodium fluoride

      b. magnesium sulfide

      c. lithium oxide

      d. sodium sulfide

_____ **7.** Which of the following is a characteristic property of ionic compounds?

      a. They have low melting points.

      b. They have low boiling points.

      c. They form crystals with characteristic shapes.

      d. They contain no charged particles.

_____ **8.** In what form can an ionic compound conduct electricity?

    a.   as a solid

    b.   when dissolved in water

    c.   as a crystal

    d.   when warmed slightly

_____ **9.** A chemical bond formed when two atoms share electrons is called a(n)

    a.   ionic bond.

    b.   covalent bond.

    c.   polyatomic bond.

    d.   crystal bond.

_____ **10.** What is a double bond?

    a.   a bond between two atoms

    b.   one pair of electrons shared between two atoms

    c.   two pairs of electrons shared between two atoms

    d.   two pairs of electrons shared between four atoms

_____ **11.** Which is a property shared by most molecular compounds?

    a.   high boiling point

    b.   high melting point

    c.   low melting point

    d.   nonpolar bonds

_____ **12.** Molecular compounds do not conduct electricity because they

    a.   break up into ions.

    b.   do not break up into ions.

    c.   do not dissolve in water.

    d.   have high melting points.

_____ **13.** A covalent bond in which electrons are shared unequally is

    a.   polar.

    b.   a double bond.

    c.   ionic.

    d.   polyatomic.

_____ **14.** Molecules that contain two polar bonds are

    a.   ionic.

    b.   always polar.

    c.   always nonpolar.

    d.   sometimes polar.

_____ **15.** The properties of a mineral crystal are determined by the arrangement of its particles and the

    a.   number of particles present.

    b.   color of the mineral.

    c.   shape of the crystal.

    d.   bonds holding the particles together.

_____ **16.** Which of the following is a characteristic of halite?

     a.   It cannot be scratched with a steel knife.

     b.   It does not dissolve in water.

     c.   If you break it, the smaller pieces all have the same shape as the bigger piece.

     d.   It has round-shaped crystals.

_____ **17.** A naturally occurring solid with a crystal structure and a definite chemical composition is a(n)

     a.   ion.

     b.   mineral.

     c.   electron.

     d.   atom.

_____ **18.** Very energetic particles that move rapidly in all directions in the space outside the nucleus of an atom are

     a.   ions.

     b.   neutrons.

     c.   electrons.

     d.   protons.

_____ **19.** Which particles in an atom are in the nucleus?

     a.   protons and neutrons

     b.   protons and electrons

     c.   protons and ions

     d.   electrons and neutrons

_____ **20.** Atoms are electrically neutral because they have

     a.   equal numbers of protons and neutrons.

     b.   equal numbers of electrons and neutrons.

     c.   equal numbers of protons and electrons.

     d.   no charged particles.

_____ **21.** Which of these particles has a positive charge?

     a.   atom

     b.   proton

     c.   neutron

     d.   electron

_____ **22.** Electrons involved in bonding between atoms are

     a.   valence electrons.

     b.   inside the nucleus.

     c.   closest to the nucleus.

     d.   positively charged.

_____ **23.** What is the greatest number of valence electrons a neutral atom can have?

     a.   1

     b.   3

     c.   8

     d.   12

_____ **24.** The atomic number is the number of

    a.   protons in the nucleus of an atom.

    b.   neutrons in the nucleus of an atom.

    c.   valence electrons in an atom.

    d.   electrons in the nucleus of an atom.

_____ **25.** A row across the periodic table is called a

    a.   group.

    b.   family.

    c.   section.

    d.   period

_____ **26.** Water is polar and oil is nonpolar. What happens when the two liquids are poured into the same container?

    a.   Both liquids become nonpolar.

    b.   A gas is produced.

    c.   The liquids mix well.

    d.   The liquids do not mix.

_____ **27.** How many groups are in the periodic table?

    a.   7

    b.   8

    c.   18

    d.   112

_____ **28.** If atoms of a halogen nonmetal gain one electron, the atoms then have

    a.   no valence electrons.

    b.   7 valence electrons.

    c.   8 valence electrons.

    d.   17 valence electrons.

_____ **29.** Ionic compounds are electrically

    a.   charged.

    b.   positive.

    c.   negative.

    d.   neutral.

_____ **30.** Which is a list of mineral crystals?

    a.   halite, water, carbon dioxide, quartz

    b.   halite, sugar, oxygen, mica

    c.   sugar, sulfur, salt, methane

    d.   halite, sulfur, mica, quartz

B. True or False

   If the statement is true, write true. If it is false, change the underlined word or words to make the statement true.

31. The <u>nucleus</u> of an atom is the region where the protons and neutrons can be found.

_____

_____

32. The valence electrons are those electrons found <u>closest to</u> the nucleus.

_____

_____

33. The <u>atomic number</u> is the number of protons in the nucleus of the atom.

_____

_____

34. Each family in the periodic table has its own characteristic properties based upon its number of <u>valence electrons</u>.

_____

_____

35. When an atom gains an electron it becomes a <u>positive</u> ion.

_____

_____

36. The attraction between a positive ion and a negative ion results in a <u>covalent</u> bond.

_____

_____

37. Orderly crystal shapes, high melting points, and electrical conductivity when dissolved in water are properties of <u>ionic</u> compounds.

_____

_____

38. When electrons are <u>transferred</u> between two atoms, a covalent bond is formed.

_____

_____

39. Low melting points and lack of electrical conductivity are properties of <u>molecular</u> compounds.

_____

_____

40. A <u>nonpolar</u> bond is formed when two atoms share electrons unequally.

_____

_____

C. Completion
Fill in the word or phrase that best completes each statement.

41. Neutrons are particles that have _____ charge.

_____

_____

42. Chemical bonds form when valence electrons are _____ between atoms.

_____

_____

43. In the periodic table, atoms are arranged from left to right and from top to bottom in order of increasing _____.

_____

_____

44. Group 18 elements, also known as the noble gases, _____ with other elements.

_____

_____

45. Nitrate (NO_3^-), ammonium (NH_4^+), and carbonate (CO_3^{2-}) are examples of ____ ions.

_____

_____

46. When ions having a charge of 2+ form bonds with ions having a charge of 2-, the charge on the resulting compound is _____.

_____

_____

47. Ionic compounds that dissolve in water conduct electricity because they _____.

_____

_____

48. Bonds that form between two nonmetal ions usually are _____ bonds.

_____

_____

49. Molecular compounds that dissolve in water do not conduct electricity because no _____ are present.

_____

_____

50. Fluorine (F_2) is a _____ molecule because the valence electrons are shared equally between the two fluorine atoms.

_____

_____

51. A naturally occurring solid that has a crystal structure and a definite chemical composition is called a(n) _____.

_____

_____

52. Three properties used to identify mineral crystals are _____.

_____

_____

53. _____ are very energetic particles moving about in the space outside the nucleus.

_____

_____

54. A neutral atom never has more than _____ valence electrons.

_____

_____

55. Elements in the same row of the periodic table are in the same _____.

_____

_____

56. Elements in Group 17 (the halogens) are the _____ reactive nonmetals.

_____

_____

57. Elements in Group 1 lose one electron to form ions with a _____ charge.

_____

_____

58. When an ionic compound forms, the total number of positive charges and the total number of negative charges must be _____.

_____

_____

59. In a double covalent bond, _____ electrons are shared between two atoms.

_____

_____

60. Because the electrons in a molecule of hydrogen fluoride (HF) are more strongly pulled toward the fluorine atom, the molecule is _____.

_____

_____

D. Interpreting Diagrams

Use the diagram to answer each question.

Five Groups of Elements From the Periodic Table

1	2	13	17	18
				2 **He** Helium 4.003
3 **Li** Lithium 6.941	4 **Be** Beryllium 9.012	5 **B** Boron 10.811	9 **F** Fluorine 18.998	10 **Ne** Neon 20.180
11 **Na** Sodium 22.990	12 **Mg** Magnesium 24.305	13 **Al** Aluminum 26.982	17 **Cl** Chlorine 35.453	18 **Ar** Argon 39.948
19 **K** Potassium 39.098	20 **Ca** Calcium 40.078	31 **Ga** Gallium 69.723	35 **Br** Bromine 79.904	36 **Kr** Krypton 83.80
37 **Rb** Rubidium 85.468	38 **Sr** Strontium 87.62	49 **In** Indium 114.818	53 **I** Iodine 126.904	54 **Xe** Xenon 131.29
55 **Cs** Cesium 132.905	56 **Ba** Barium 137.327	81 **Tl** Thallium 204.383	85 **At** Astatine (210)	86 **Rn** Radon (222)
87 **Fr** Francium (223)	88 **Ra** Radium 226.025			

61. Which group contains elements with two valence electrons?

_____

_____

_____

_____

_____

62. List three elements from the group containing the most reactive nonmetals.

_____

_____

_____

63. In each period, how does the number of electrons in each kind of atom change from left to right between Groups 1 and 2? Explain how you know.

_____

_____

_____

_____

64. How many atoms of a Group 17 element would be needed to react with one atom of a Group 2 element? Explain.

_____

_____

_____

_____

65. In an electron dot diagram of aluminum (Al), how many dots should be drawn around the element's symbol? Why?

_____

_____

_____

_____

66. Which group of elements loses electrons most easily?

_____

_____

_____

_____

Use the diagram to answer each question.

Protons, Neutrons, and Electrons

Particle	Relative Mass	Charge	Location
Proton	1	+1	Nucleus
Neutron	1	0	Nucleus
Electron	Approximately $\frac{1}{1836}$	−1	Electron Cloud

67. How do protons, neutrons, and electrons differ in charge?

_____

_____

_____

_____

68. How do electrons differ in mass from protons and neutrons?

_____

_____

_____

_____

69. What are two ways that a proton and a neutron are similar?

_____

_____

_____

_____

70. Where and what is the electron cloud of an atom?

_____

_____

_____

_____

71. The mass of an atom may be determined by adding the masses of the protons and neutrons in the nucleus. Why is it unnecessary to include the electrons when determining the mass of an atom?

_____

_____

_____

_____

72. Explain how it is possible for an atom to have no charge even though it is made up of protons, neutrons, and electrons.

_____

_____

_____

_____

E. Essay

Write an answer to each of the following questions.

73. Explain how a bond forms between potassium and bromine in potassium bromide (KBr).

_____

_____

_____

_____

_____

74. Explain what makes the Group 1 elements the most reactive metals.

_____

_____

_____

_____

_____

_____

75. How do valence electrons relate to the chemical reactions of an element?

_____

_____

_____

_____

_____

_____

76. Compare a covalent bond and an ionic bond.

_____

_____

_____

_____

_____

_____

77. Describe properties that would help you to distinguish an ionic compound from a molecular compound.

_____

_____

_____

_____

_____

_____

78. Explain why elements such as argon (Ar) and krypton (Kr) from Group 18 in the periodic table are not usually found in compounds.

_____

_____

_____

_____

_____

_____

79. Compare the properties of the minerals halite and quartz.

_____

_____

_____

_____

_____

_____

80. Explain what is meant by the term "polar bond."

_____

_____

_____

_____

_____

_____

Test 56 Book L, Chapter 2: Atoms and Bonding

Answer Key (Short)

__a__	1.
__b__	2.
__a__	3.
__b__	4.
__a__	5.
__d__	6.
__c__	7.
__b__	8.
__b__	9.
__c__	10.
__c__	11.
__b__	12.
__a__	13.
__d__	14.
__d__	15.
__c__	16.
__b__	17.
__c__	18.
__a__	19.
__c__	20.
__b__	21.
__a__	22.
__c__	23.
__a__	24.
__d__	25.
__d__	26.
__c__	27.
__c__	28.
__d__	29.
__d__	30.

31.		TRUE
32.		false, farthest from
33.		TRUE
34.		TRUE
35.		false, negative
36.		false, an ionic
37.		TRUE
38.		false, shared
39.		TRUE
40.		false, polar
41.		no

42. transferred or shared

43. atomic number

44. do not usually react

45. polyatomic

46. zero

47. break into ions that move freely

48. covalent

49. charged particles (ions)

50. nonpolar

51. mineral

52. Accept any three: color, shininess, density, crystal shape, hardness, the way the mineral breaks apart or grows, chemical composition.

53. Electrons

54. eight

55. period

56. most

57. 1+

58. equal

59. four (or two pairs of)

60. polar

61. Group 2

62. Accept any three elements from Group 17: Fluorine (F), Chlorine (Cl), Bromine (Br), Iodine (I), Astatine (At)

63. From Group 1 to Group 2, the number of electrons in each kind of atom increases by one in each period. This is the case because the number of protons (atomic number) increases by one from Group 1 to Group 2, and atoms have equal numbers of electrons and protons.

64. Two; atoms of elements in Group 17 form ions with a charge of 1-, and atoms of elements in Group 2 form ions with a charge of 2+. It would take two ions of a Group 17 element to balance the charge of one ion of a Group 2 element.

65. Three; elements in Group 13 have 3 valence electrons.

66. Group 1

67. A proton is positively charged, an electron is negatively charged, and a neutron has no charge (or a charge of zero).

68. Electrons have a much lower mass than protons and neutrons.

69. Protons and neutrons have the same mass. Both are found in the nucleus.

70. The electron cloud is outside the nucleus of the atom. It forms from the electrons, which move rapidly in a spherical space around the nucleus.

71. The mass of an electron is much lower than the mass of either a proton or a neutron. When adding the masses of the particles together, the mass of the electrons will be too small by comparison to matter. Electrons do not add a significant amount to the total mass of an atom.

72. The numbers of protons and electrons in any atom are the equal, and so the positive charges of the protons cancel the negative charges of the electrons. Neutrons have no charge to begin with, and so they do not affect the charge on the atom.

73. Potassium has one valence electron and bromine has seven valence electrons. The lone valence electron from potassium is lost and is transferred to the bromine atom. The result is a potassium ion with a charge of 1+ and a bromide ion with a charge of 1-. The oppositely charged ions attract each other and the charges balance to make a compound that is electrically neutral.

74.   Atoms of Group 1 elements each have a single valence electron. These atoms easily lose their valence electrons, reacting with other elements that can gain electrons, and becoming more chemically stable. The easy loss of the one valence electron makes the Group 1 elements more reactive than metals that must lose two or three electrons in reactions.

75.   Valence electrons are the electrons that are farthest away from the nucleus and the ones that are involved in chemical reactions. Chemical reactions occur whenever valence electrons are shared or transferred between atoms. The number of valence electrons determines how these reactions take place and what kind of bonds atoms can form.

76.   A covalent bond is formed when two atoms share valence electrons. Neither atom loses electrons or takes electrons from the other. No charged particles form. In an ionic bond, one or more electrons are transferred from one atom to another. Atoms that lose electrons become positively charged ions, and atoms that gain electrons become negatively charged ions. These charged particles then attract each other.

77.   Ionic compounds have high melting points and high boiling points compared to molecular compounds. Ionic compounds that are dissolved in water or melted will conduct electricity. Molecular compounds do not conduct electricity in either case.

78.   These elements have eight valence electrons. They do not gain or lose electrons easily. As a result, these elements do not usually react with other elements to form compounds.

79.   Halite is a mineral made of sodium chloride. It is an ionic crystal, and it dissolves in water. If a piece of halite is broken, the smaller pieces have the same shape as the bigger piece. Quartz is a mineral made of silicon and oxygen atoms covalently bonded together. Quartz is harder than halite and it does not dissolve in water. If a quartz crystal is broken, the smaller pieces have irregular shapes.

80.   When two atoms form a covalent bond, electrons are shared between them. If the atoms are different, the electrons may be shared unequally. This means the electrons may be pulled closer to one atom, making the bond slightly negative at one end and slightly positive at the other end. This unequal sharing of electrons is known as a polar bond.

Test 57 Book L, Chapter 3: Acids, Bases, and Solutions

A. Multiple Choice
   Choose the letter of the correct answer.

_____ 1.   A liquid mixture in which particles can be seen and easily separated by settling or filtration is a

   a.   solution.

   b.   suspension.

   c.   solvent.

   d.   solute.

_____ 2.   How is a solute different from a solvent in a solution?

   a.   The solute is present in a smaller amount.

   b.   The solute is present in a greater amount.

   c.   The solute is a solid and the solvent is a liquid.

   d.   The solute is a liquid and the solvent is a gas.

_____ 3.   How can a scientist tell whether a solution is salt in water or sugar in water?

   a.   by tasting the solution

   b.   by smelling the solution

   c.   by testing the conductivity of the solution

   d.   by filtering the solution

_____ 4.   Weak tea is an example of a

   a.   dilute solution.

   b.   concentrated solution.

   c.   suspension.

   d.   solvent.

_____ 5.   When you add so much solute that no more dissolves, you have a

   a.   saturated solution.

   b.   unsaturated solution.

   c.   neutralization.

   d.   suspension.

_____ 6.   A substance that tastes bitter, feels slippery, and turns red litmus paper blue is a(n)

   a.   acid.

   b.   base.

   c.   indicator.

   d.   solvent.

_____ 7.   What is one way to increase the solubility of sugar in water?

   a.   Heat the water.

   b.   Chill the water.

   c.   Increase the amount of sugar.

   d.   Decrease the amount of water.

_____ 8. What happens when you add salt to the water when cooking spaghetti?

    a. It brings the water to a boil faster.

    b. It makes the water hotter when it boils.

    c. It reduces evaporation of the water.

    d. It makes the spaghetti cook more slowly.

_____ 9. When a solute is added to a solvent, the freezing point of the solution is

    a. higher than the freezing point of either substance alone.

    b. lower than the freezing point of either substance alone.

    c. the same as the freezing point of the solute.

    d. the same as the freezing point of the solvent.

_____ 10. Which is a characteristic property of acids?

    a. They turn blue litmus paper red.

    b. They turn red litmus paper blue.

    c. They taste bitter.

    d. They do not react with metals.

_____ 11. Acids are described as corrosive because they

    a. turn litmus blue.

    b. taste bitter.

    c. "eat away" at other materials.

    d. feel slippery.

_____ 12. Which is a likely use for a base?

    a. as a vitamin in your food

    b. etching metals for printing

    c. making foods taste sour

    d. making soaps and detergents

_____ 13. Any substance that forms hydrogen ions (H^+) in water is a(n)

    a. acid.

    b. base.

    c. indicator.

    d. salt.

_____ 14. In water, bases form

    a. hydroxide ions.

    b. hydrogen ions.

    c. hydrogen gas.

    d. oxide ions.

_____ 15. The pH scale measures

    a. the strength of an acid.

    b. the strength of hydrogen ions.

    c. the concentration of hydrogen ions.

    d. the concentration of an acid.

_____ 16. If a solution has a pH of 9, the solution is

    a.   acidic.

    b.   basic.

    c.   neutral.

    d.   saturated.

_____ 17. Neutralization is a reaction between a(n)

    a.   acid and a base.

    b.   acid and a metal.

    c.   base and a salt.

    d.   salt and water.

_____ 18. What does a neutralization reaction produce?

    a.   acids

    b.   bases

    c.   water and a salt

    d.   carbonated water

_____ 19. The process that breaks down complex molecules of food into smaller molecules is called

    a.   neutralization.

    b.   conduction.

    c.   digestion.

    d.   solution.

_____ 20. Which process tears, grinds, and mashes large food particles into smaller ones?

    a.   chemical digestion

    b.   indigestion

    c.   neutralization

    d.   mechanical digestion

_____ 21. How is pH important during digestion?

    a.   Digestion needs a constant pH to take place.

    b.   Different foods have different pH values.

    c.   Enzymes react best with acids.

    d.   Different enzymes work best at different pH values.

_____ 22. Compared to the pH of the mouth and the small intestine, the pH of the stomach is

    a.   the same.

    b.   higher.

    c.   lower.

    d.   changing constantly.

_____ 23. Normal rainfall is slightly acidic, which means its pH must be

    a.   less than 2.

    b.   between 5 and 7.

    c.   between 2 and 4.

    d.   between 7 and 9.

_____ **24.** When a few spoonfuls of sugar are mixed into a cup of water, sugar is the

   a.   acid.
   b.   base.
   c.   solvent.
   d.   solute.

_____ **25.** When a compound dissolves in water,

   a.   it breaks up into individual crystals.
   b.   it always conducts electricity.
   c.   its particles surround individual water molecules.
   d.   each of its particles become surrounded by water molecules.

_____ **26.** A measure of how well a solute can dissolve in a solvent at a given temperature is that substance's

   a.   saturation point.
   b.   acidity.
   c.   solubility.
   d.   concentration.

_____ **27.** What does it mean if a compound has a solubility of 15 g in 100 g of water at 0°C?

   a.   100 g of the compound will dissolve in 15 g of water at 0°C.
   b.   15 g of the compound will dissolve in 100 g of water at 0°C.
   c.   The compound will not dissolve until 15 g of it are present.
   d.   The compound will dissolve only if the water temperature is 0°C.

_____ **28.** What do enzymes in the digestive system do?

   a.   speed up chemical digestion
   b.   speed up mechanical digestion
   c.   make the stomach acidic
   d.   neutralize stomach acid

_____ **29.** Acids present in food are safe to eat because they usually are

   a.   concentrated.
   b.   dilute.
   c.   strong.
   d.   weak.

_____ **30.** You can find the pH of a substance by using

   a.   litmus paper.
   b.   thermometer.
   c.   an indicator.
   d.   a conductivity tester.

B. True or False

If the statement is true, write true. If it is false, change the underlined word or words to make the statement true.

31. A <u>solute</u> is a mixture in which particles can be seen and easily separated.

_____

_____

32. A substance that is present in a solution in a smaller amount and is dissolved by the solvent is called the <u>solute</u>.

_____

_____

33. Among the factors that affect the solubility of a substance are type of solvent and <u>time</u>.

_____

_____

34. Adding a solute to a solvent will <u>raise</u> the freezing point of the solvent.

_____

_____

35. Acids will turn litmus paper <u>red</u>.

_____

_____

36. Bases feel slippery and taste <u>sour</u>.

_____

_____

37. Bases form <u>hydrogen ions (H^+)</u> when dissolved in water.

_____

_____

38. The pH is a scale used to measure the concentration of <u>hydrogen ions</u>.

_____

_____

39. The products of a neutralization reaction are <u>acids and bases</u>.

_____

_____

40. <u>Concentration</u> is the process of breaking down complex molecules of foods into smaller molecules.

_____

_____

C. Completion

Fill in the word or phrase that best completes each statement.

41. A _____ is a mixture that appears uniform throughout and whose particles cannot easily be separated.

_____

_____

42. When a solution forms, particles of a solute _____ and become surrounded by particles of the solvent.

_____

_____

43. If you can continue to add more solute to a solution, the solution is said to be _____.

_____

_____

44. The presence of a solute makes it harder for solvent molecules to escape when heated, and so the boiling point of a solution is _____ than that of the pure solvent.

_____

_____

45. A(n) _____ is a compound that tastes sour and reacts with some metals.

_____

_____

46. A(n) _____ is a compound that turns litmus blue and is often found in soaps and detergents.

_____

_____

47. Substances that form hydrogen ions when released in water are called _____.

_____

_____

48. When the pH is high, the concentration of hydrogen ions is _____.

_____

_____

49. In a reaction of an acid with a base, the pH changes to a value that is closer to _____.

_____

_____

50. _____ digestion tears, grinds, and mashes large food particles into smaller particles.

_____

_____

51. Chemical digestion happens with the help of _____ that are sensitive to pH.

_____

_____

52. Because it will dissolve so many solutes, _____ is sometimes called the universal solvent.

_____

_____

53. _____ solids break up into individual neutral particles when dissolved in a solvent.

_____

_____

54. Ionic and polar compounds _____ in water because water molecules are polar.

_____

_____

55. At the same concentrations, strong acids produce more _____ than weak acids.

_____

_____

56. Foods such as oranges, tomatoes, and apples have a pH that is _____ than 7.

_____

_____

57. A(n) _____ is an ionic compound produced from the neutralization of an acid with a base.

_____

_____

58. Digestion breaks down _____ into simpler substances that your body can use for raw materials and energy.

_____

_____

59. The organ with the most acidic contents in the digestive system is the _____.

_____

_____

60. Acids are _____, which means that they "eat away" at other materials.

_____

_____

D. Interpreting Diagrams

Use the diagram to answer each question.

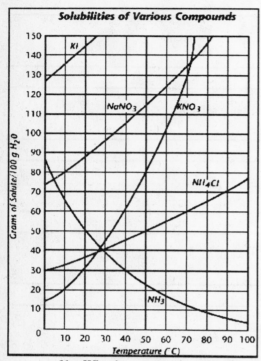

Solubilities of Various Compounds

61. What happens to the solubility of potassium nitrate (KNO_3) as the temperature rises?

_____

_____

_____

_____

_____

62. According to the graph, which of the compounds is most soluble at 0°C? Which is least soluble at 100°C?

_____

_____

_____

_____

63. Compare the solubility of sodium nitrate ($NaNO_3$) to that of ammonia (NH_3).

_____

_____

_____

_____

64. How many grams of potassium nitrate (KNO_3) will settle out when a saturated solution containing 100 grams of water is cooled from 70°C to 50°C?

_____

_____

_____

_____

_____

65. At a high temperature, what other compounds besides ammonia (NH_3) have a lower solubility than that of potassium nitrate (KNO_3)?

_____

_____

_____

_____

66. At 70°C, 60 grams of ammonium chloride (NH_4Cl) are added to 100 grams of water. What will happen if 10 grams more of ammonium chloride are added to the solution? Explain.

_____

_____

_____

_____

_____

Use the diagram to answer each question.

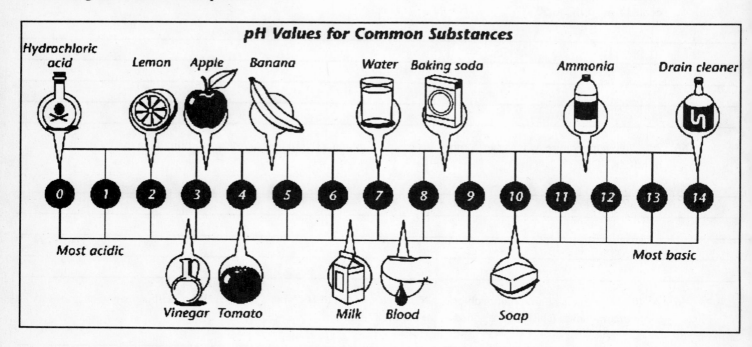

pH Values for Common Substances

Hydrochloric acid   Lemon   Apple   Banana   Water   Baking soda   Ammonia   Drain cleaner

0 1 2 3 4 5 6 7 8 9 10 11 12 13 14

Most acidic

Most basic

Vinegar   Tomato   Milk   Blood   Soap

67. Use the pH scale to predict how the taste of an apple and a lemon would compare. Which has the more sour taste? Explain.

_____

_____

_____

_____

68. In terms of pH, explain what would happen if you mixed vinegar with a solution of ammonia. What type of products would form?

_____

_____

_____

_____

_____

69. What does the pH of drain cleaner tell you about the dangers of such a product?

_____

_____

_____

_____

_____

70. What color would litmus turn in a solution of baking soda? Explain your answer in terms of pH.

_____

_____

_____

_____

_____

71. Why does soap taste bitter?

_____

_____

_____

_____

_____

72. What does the pH of water tell you about how the water differs from the other items shown in the diagram?

_____

_____

_____

_____

_____

E. Essay
   Write an answer to each of the following questions.

73. Explain why the coolant in a car's radiator protects the engine from damage.

_____

_____

_____

_____

_____

_____

_____

74. Describe how solutions of acids and bases differ in terms of particles. How do the differences relate to the properties of acids and bases?

_____

_____

_____

_____

_____

_____

_____

75. Describe how particles of table salt (an ionic compound) and sugar (a molecular compound) differ in the way they dissolve in water.

_____

_____

_____

_____

_____

_____

76. Describe how you would separate the parts of a water-and-sand suspension as compared to how you would separate the parts of a water-and-sugar solution.

_____

_____

_____

_____

_____

_____

_____

77. Describe the changes in pH that occur as food passes through your digestive system. Why are these changes important?

_____

_____

_____

_____

_____

_____

_____

_____

78. Explain the roles of chemical and mechanical digestion in preparing food for use in the body.

_____

_____

_____

_____

_____

_____

_____

_____

79. You are given three clear, colorless, unknown solutions, and red and blue litmus papers. Describe the steps you might take to correctly identify each solution as acidic, basic, or neutral.

_____

_____

_____

_____

_____

_____

_____

_____

80. Describe the neutralization process and give an example of the reaction using hydrochloric acid (HCl) and potassium hydroxide (KOH).

_____

_____

_____

_____

_____

_____

_____

__b__	1.
__a__	2.
__c__	3.
__a__	4.
__a__	5.
__b__	6.
__a__	7.
__b__	8.
__b__	9.
__a__	10.
__c__	11.
__d__	12.
__a__	13.
__a__	14.
__c__	15.
__b__	16.
__a__	17.
__c__	18.
__c__	19.
__d__	20.
__d__	21.
__c__	22.
__b__	23.
__d__	24.
__d__	25.
__c__	26.
__b__	27.
__a__	28.
__d__	29.
__c__	30.

31.	false, suspension
32.	TRUE
33.	false, temperature
34.	false, lower
35.	TRUE
36.	false, bitter
37.	false, hydroxide ions (OH^-)
38.	TRUE
39.	false, water and a salt
40.	false, Digestion
41.	solution

42.	separate
43.	unsaturated
44.	higher
45.	acid
46.	base
47.	acids
48.	low
49.	7 (or neutral)
50.	Mechanical
51.	enzymes
52.	water
53.	Molecular
54.	dissolve
55.	hydrogen ions
56.	less (or lower)
57.	salt
58.	foods
59.	stomach
60.	corrosive
61.	The solubility increases.
62.	KI is most soluble at 0°C, and NH_3 is least soluble at 100°C.
63.	Ammonia (NH_3) is more soluble than sodium nitrate ($NaNO_3$) at low temperatures and less soluble than sodium nitrate ($NaNO_3$) at high temperatures. (Some students may add that the two compounds have the same solubility at approximately 5°C.)
64.	130 g - 80 g = 50 g
65.	sodium nitrate ($NaNO_3$) and ammonium chloride (NH_4Cl)
66.	Most of the additional ammonium chloride will fall to the bottom of the container because the solution will be saturated. At 70°C, the solubility of ammonium chloride in 100 grams of water is just over 60 grams.
67.	Lemons have a pH of about 2 and apples have a pH of about 3. A lemon is more acidic, and so it would taste more sour.
68.	Vinegar is an acid and ammonia is a base, and so a neutralization reaction would occur. The pH would be closer to 7 than either the vinegar or ammonia alone. A salt and water would be produced.
69.	A high pH means that drain cleaner is very basic. The solution can burn and irritate skin.
70.	Baking soda has a pH of about 8.5, which means it is a base. Bases turn litmus blue.
71.	Soap is a base and bases taste bitter.
72.	Water has a pH of 7, which is neutral. It is not an acid or a base.
73.	The antifreeze in the coolant lowers its freezing point and raises its boiling point. As a result, the engine is less likely to overheat. In cold weather, the liquid is less likely to freeze and cause damage.
74.	When acids dissolve in water, they produce hydrogen ions (H^+). Bases produce hydroxide ions (OH^-). Acids have similar properties (turn litmus red, react with some metals) because of the presence of hydrogen ions (H^+). Bases have similar properties (turn litmus blue, do not react with metals) because of the presence of hydroxide ions (OH^-).

75. When table salt dissolves in water, the water molecules surround and separate the ions from each other. The salt crystal breaks up, forming positive and negative ions in the solution. When sugar dissolves in water, the sugar molecules separate from each other and become surrounded by water molecules, but no ions form.

76. The sand particles are large and they could be separated from the water by filtering or letting the particles settle. Sugar will not settle out, but the solution can be separated by letting the water evaporate.

77. The pH of the mouth is near 7, or neutral. The stomach is very acidic, having a pH of about 2. In the small intestine, the pH rises to a slightly basic level of about 8. The changes in pH are important because enzymes in the different parts of the digestive system work best at different pH levels.

78. When you eat, your teeth chew and grind food into smaller pieces. This is mechanical digestion. Then reactions aided by digestive enzymes break down large food molecules into smaller molecules. This is chemical digestion. The two processes change the food into simpler substances that can be used by the body for raw materials and energy.

79. Dip red litmus paper into each solution and watch for color changes. Then do the same with blue litmus paper. Any solution that turns red litmus blue is basic. Any solution that turns blue litmus red is acidic. A solution that does not turn either litmus paper another color is neutral.

80. A neutralization reaction occurs between an acid and a base and produces a salt and water. The final solution is closer to a neutral pH than either the acid or base alone. Hydrochloric acid (HCl) reacts with potassium hydroxide (KOH), producing a solution of potassium chloride (KCl) and water (H_2O). (Some students also may add an equation for the reaction: $HCl + KOH \rightarrow H_2O + KCl$ A few students may show the potassium chloride product as ions: $K^+ + Cl^-$.)

Test 58 Book L, Chapter 4: Exploring Materials

A. Multiple Choice
Choose the letter of the correct answer.

_____ 1. A large, complex molecule built from smaller molecules joined together is a(n)

   a. composite.
   b. polymer.
   c. monomer.
   d. alloy.

_____ 2. A natural polymer that gives shape to plant cells is

   a. silk.
   b. nylon.
   c. cellulose.
   d. wood.

_____ 3. A polymer may be combined with one or more substances to make a new material called a(n)

   a. alloy.
   b. monomer.
   c. ceramic.
   d. composite.

_____ 4. Which material is an example of a natural composite?

   a. fiberglass
   b. wood
   c. Kevlar
   d. nylon

_____ 5. A substance made of two or more elements that has the properties of metal is a(n)

   a. polymer.
   b. monomer.
   c. alloy.
   d. ceramic.

_____ 6. What is an advantage that alloys might have over many pure metals?

   a. Alloys occur naturally.
   b. Alloys resist rust.
   c. Alloys are weaker.
   d. Alloys can bend easily.

_____ 7. Steel is an alloy of one or more elements combined with

   a. copper.
   b. gold.
   c. iron.
   d. lead.

_____ **8.** Which of the following properties is NOT characteristic of steel?

    a. hardness

    b. resistance to corrosion

    c. strength

    d. reacts readily with air

_____ **9.** Hard, crystalline solids made by heating clay and other minerals to high temperatures are

    a. alloys.

    b. glasses.

    c. ceramics.

    d. polymers.

_____ **10.** One useful property of ceramics is their ability to

    a. resist moisture.

    b. conduct electricity.

    c. melt at low temperatures.

    d. resist breaking when struck.

_____ **11.** What materials are being used to replace copper telephone and cable television lines?

    a. composites

    b. optical fibers

    c. alloys

    d. polymer fibers

_____ **12.** Which is NOT a way in which glass may be useful?

    a. bending light in useful ways

    b. resistance to heat

    c. carrying light messages

    d. conducting electricity

_____ **13.** During radioactive decay, atomic nuclei of unstable isotopes

    a. give off nuclear radiation.

    b. are broken down by radioactive bacteria.

    c. form chemical bonds.

    d. are unchanged.

_____ **14.** A piece of paper or a thin piece of metal will provide protection from

    a. alpha radiation.

    b. beta radiation.

    c. gamma radiation.

    d. gamma rays.

_____ **15.** Measurements of half-life make radioactive isotopes useful for

    a. radiation therapy.

    b. tracing oil spills.

    c. building shields to absorb nuclear radiation.

    d. determining the ages of rocks and fossils.

_____ 16. The half-life of an isotope is the length of time needed for half the mass of the sample to

    a. decay.

    b. double in size.

    c. become radioactive.

    d. rust.

_____ 17. The reason radioactive isotopes can be followed through the steps of a chemical reaction or industrial process is that they

    a. have half-lives.

    b. give off radiation.

    c. do not react chemically as nonradioactive isotopes do.

    d. do not decay.

_____ 18. In radiation therapy,

    a. ancient fossils can be dated.

    b. unhealthy human cells are destroyed.

    c. radioactive isotopes are used as fuel.

    d. weak spots in water pipes are found.

_____ 19.
Which pair are isotopes?

    a. $^{12}_{6}C$ and $^{14}_{6}C$

    b. $^{14}_{6}C$ and $^{14}_{7}C$

    c. $^{14}_{6}C$ and $^{14}_{6}C$

    d. $^{14}_{6}C$ and $^{12}_{6}C$

_____ 20. You find the mass number of an isotope by

    a. adding the number of protons and electrons.

    b. subtracting the number of protons from the number of neutrons.

    c. adding the number of protons, electrons, and neutrons.

    d. adding the number of protons and neutrons.

_____ 21. If a polymer is compared to a long train of identical train cars, each car represents a

    a. monomer.

    b. composite.

    c. alloy.

    d. chemical bond.

_____ 22. What is an example of a synthetic polymer?

    a. cellulose

    b. a spider's web

    c. a protein

    d. plastic

_____ **23.** Beta radiation consists of particles that are identical to

    a.   helium nuclei.

    b.   hydrogen atoms.

    c.   X-rays.

    d.   electrons.

_____ **24.** Which of these is an alloy?

    a.   bronze

    b.   tin

    c.   copper

    d.   gold

_____ **25.** What is the advantage in making an alloy by mixing the elements as powders and then heating them?

    a.   The amount of each metal does not have to be carefully measured.

    b.   The metals blend at lower temperatures so they may be quickly molded.

    c.   Less pressure is needed.

    d.   More energy is used.

_____ **26.** Tiles on space shuttles that must withstand extremely high heat are made from

    a.   alloys.

    b.   ceramics.

    c.   glass.

    d.   pure metals.

_____ **27.** The main ingredient used to make glass is

    a.   water.

    b.   lead.

    c.   sand.

    d.   crystal.

_____ **28.** The disposal of radioactive materials must be carefully managed because they

    a.   are expensive.

    b.   take up too much space in landfills.

    c.   sometimes have long half-lives.

    d.   may be traced.

_____ **29.** Reactions involving the particles in the nucleus of an atom are called

    a.   physical reactions.

    b.   chemical reactions.

    c.   nuclear reactions.

    d.   composite reactions.

_____ **30.** The reason radioactive isotopes can be followed through the steps of a chemical reaction or industrial process is that they

    a. have half-lives.

    b. give off radiation.

    c. do not react chemically as nonradioactive isotopes do.

    d. do not decay.

B. True or False

    If the statement is true, write true. If it is false, change the underlined word or words to make the statement true.

31. A polymer is a complex molecule made from smaller units called <u>monomers</u>.

_____

_____

32. Two or more substances may be combined to produce a new material with different properties. This new material is called a <u>plastic</u>.

_____

_____

33. In every alloy, at least one of the components is a <u>metal</u>.

_____

_____

34. <u>Brass</u> is an alloy of iron with other elements.

_____

_____

35. <u>Gold alloys</u> resist moisture, do not conduct electricity, and can withstand very high temperatures.

_____

_____

36. Glass has <u>an orderly</u> crystal structure.

_____

_____

37. Unstable isotopes decompose and release fast-moving particles and energy in a process called <u>radioactive decay</u>.

_____

_____

38. The time needed for half the mass of a radioactive isotope to decay is known as the <u>radiation period</u> of the isotope.

_____

_____

39. A radioactive isotope that can be followed through the steps of a chemical reaction is <u>an indicator</u>.

_____

_____

40. The <u>atomic number</u> is the sum of the numbers of protons and neutrons in the nucleus of an atom.

_____

_____

C. Completion
Fill in the word or phrase that best completes each statement.

41. _____ is a strong and flexible natural polymer that gives shape to plant cells.

_____

_____

42. _____ is a natural composite made of long fibers of cellulose held together by another polymer called lignin.

_____

_____

43. Many _____ are made by melting metals and mixing them together in carefully measured amounts.

_____

_____

44. About 5,000 years ago, an alloy of copper and tin was discovered to be stronger and harder than either metal alone. This alloy is called _____.

_____

_____

45. Hard, crystalline solids made by heating _____ and other minerals to high temperatures are called ceramics.

_____

_____

46. Glass is made by heating _____ to make a thick liquid that is shaped and then cooled.

_____

_____

47. A(n) _____ particle has the same structure as a helium nucleus.

_____

_____

48. If the half-life of a radioactive isotope is 5,730 years, the fraction of the original sample that will be left after 17,190 years is _____.

_____

_____

49. The disposal of radioactive wastes is an environmental concern because radiation is _____.

_____

_____

50. Different isotopes of a single element have different numbers of _____.

_____

_____

51. Plastics, nylon, and PVC piping are examples of _____ polymers.

_____

_____

52. A composite known as _____ is made of strands of glass fiber that are woven together and strengthened with a liquid plastic that sets like glue.

_____

_____

53. Pure gold is not used for jewelry because it is too _____.

_____

_____

54. Aluminum alloys are used for the outer covering of airplanes because the alloys are strong, resistant to corrosion, and _____.

_____

_____

55. Ceramics are used as electrical insulators because they do not _____.

_____

_____

56. A threadlike piece of glass that is used to transmit light messages is called a(n) _____

_____

_____

57. When a neutron breaks apart in the nucleus of an unstable atom, a proton and a(n) _____ are formed.

_____

_____

58. Because radioactive isotopes decay at a predictable rate, the half-life can be used to tell how old a material is by the process of _____.

_____

_____

59. In medicine, radioactive isotopes can be used to kill cancerous cells in a process known as _____.

_____

_____

60. An atom of phosphorus-32 has 15 protons and _____ neutrons.

_____

_____

D. Interpreting Diagrams
Use the diagram to answer each question.

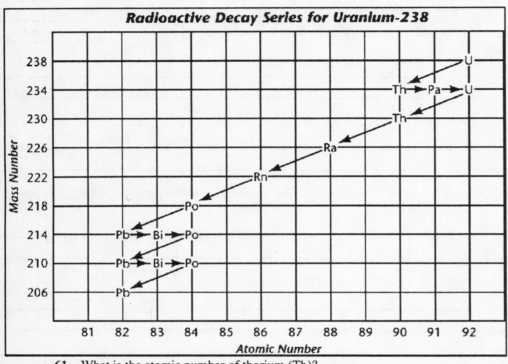

Radioactive Decay Series for Uranium-238

61. What is the atomic number of thorium (Th)?

_____

_____

_____

_____

62. What are the atomic number and mass number of the radon (Rn) isotope shown?

_____

_____

_____

_____

_____

63. What particle is given off during the change from radium (Ra) to radon (Rn)? Explain how you know.

_____

_____

_____

_____

_____

64. What particle is given off during the change from protactinium (Pa) to uranium (U)? Explain how you know.

_____

_____

_____

_____

_____

65. What is the difference in atomic number between the original isotope of uranium (U) that begins the decay series and the final isotope of lead (Pb)?

_____

_____

_____

_____

_____

66. How many isotopes of polonium (Po) are part of the decay process of uranium-238? How do you know?

_____

_____

_____

_____

Use the diagram to answer each question.

Models of Polymers and Monomers

A

B

C

D

E

F

67. Which of the diagrams represent models of polymers?

_____

_____

_____

_____

68. How many different models of monomers are shown in the diagram, and which ones are they?

_____

_____

_____

_____

69. What is the difference between a monomer and a polymer?

_____

_____

_____

_____

70. Describe an example of another polymer model that could be built from monomers shown in the diagram.

_____

_____

_____

_____

71. What kind of atom forms the backbone of monomer and polymer molecules?

_____

_____

_____

_____

72. How does each polymer modeled in the diagram differ from the other polymers shown?

_____

_____

_____

_____

E. Essay

Write an answer to each of the following questions.

73. Describe some useful properties of synthetic polymers, and explain why they are often used in place of natural polymers. Give three examples of how synthetic polymers are used.

_____

_____

_____

_____

_____

_____

74. Why are alloys often more useful than pure metals?

_____

_____

_____

_____

_____

_____

75. Explain why a bicycle made from polymer composites may be better than a bicycle made from steel.

_____

_____

_____

_____

_____

_____

76. Explain how glass can be used for different purposes. Give three examples of how different kinds of glass may be used.

_____

_____

_____

_____

_____

_____

77. Explain why ceramic tiles are used to protect the space shuttle during reentry from space.

_____

_____

_____

_____

_____

_____

78. Compare and contrast types of radioactive decay involving alpha particles, beta particles, and gamma radiation.

_____

_____

_____

_____

_____

_____

_____

_____

79. Explain the structure of a polymer. Include a description of the role of carbon in your answer.

_____

_____

_____

_____

_____

_____

_____

_____

80. Give several examples of how radioactive isotopes are useful. Explain why the same properties that make these isotopes useful also make them hazardous.

_____

_____

_____

_____

_____

_____

_____

_____

Test 58 Book L, Chapter 4: Exploring Materials
Answer Key (Short)

b	1.
c	2.
d	3.
b	4.
c	5.
b	6.
c	7.
d	8.
c	9.
a	10.
b	11.
d	12.
a	13.
a	14.
d	15.
a	16.
b	17.
b	18.
a	19.
d	20.
a	21.
d	22.
a	23.
a	24.
b	25.
b	26.
c	27.
c	28.
c	29.
b	30.

31.   TRUE
32.   false, composite
33.   TRUE
34.   false, Steel
35.   false, Ceramics
36.   false, no
37.   TRUE
38.   false, half-life
39.   false, a tracer
40.   false, mass number
41.   Cellulose

42.	Wood
43.	alloys
44.	bronze
45.	clay
46.	sand
47.	alpha
48.	1/8
49.	dangerous to living things
50.	neutrons
51.	synthetic
52.	fiberglass
53.	soft
54.	lightweight
55.	conduct electricity
56.	optical fiber
57.	beta particle (or electron)
58.	radioactive dating
59.	radiation therapy
60.	17
61.	90
62.	86, 222
63.	An alpha particle; the atomic number decreases by 2 and the mass number decreases by 4. This is the way a nucleus changes when an alpha particle is given off.
64.	A beta particle (or an electron); the atomic number increases by one, but the mass number stays the same. A neutron breaks down, producing a proton in the nucleus, which increases the atomic number but does not change the mass number. A beta particle (or an electron) is released.
65.	10
66.	3; there are three isotopes with an atomic number of 84. They have mass numbers (218, 214, 210).
67.	A, E, and F
68.	three; B, C, and D
69.	A monomer is a small molecule. Monomers are joined together in repeating patterns, forming large molecules that are polymers.
70.	Answers may vary. Possible answers: A polymer could be built from monomers B and C in repeating patterns; A polymer could be built from monomers C and D in repeating patterns; A polymer could be built from monomer B alone.
71.	carbon
72.	Models A and F both are polymers made of single, but different, monomers. Model E is made of two different monomers that alternate in a repeating pattern.
73.	Synthetic polymers tend to be strong, lightweight, heat resistant, flexible, and long lasting. They are often used in place of natural polymers that are too expensive or wear out too quickly. Synthetic polymers are used to make such items as fabrics, food containers, toys, pipes, carpets, drinking cups, packing materials, furniture, and insulation. (Student answers will vary. Accept any three that are correct.)

74.   Alloys usually have increased strength, hardness, and resistance to chemical reactions than pure metals. However, alloys still have metallic properties, such as the ability to conduct heat and electricity. The properties of alloys often make them more useful than the pure metals in tools, machines, and other items.

75.   Polymer composites are lighter than steel but just as strong, and so the bicycle is not as heavy and will be easier to ride. The rider will not tire as easily when pedaling the bicycle made from composites.

76.   When glass is made, different materials can be added to give it different properties. Glass can be made heat resistant for use in cookware. It can be made to bend light in useful ways so that it can be used in eyeglasses, microscopes, and telescopes. Glass also can be beautifully colored for use in artwork.

77.   Ceramic tiles are very resistant to heat, and so the tiles protect the surface of the space shuttle when it comes through the atmosphere for landings. This allows the space shuttle to be reused many times.

78.   During alpha decay, an alpha particle made of two protons and two neutrons is released. The atomic number decreases by two and the mass number decreases by four. In beta decay, a neutron breaks down, giving off a proton and a beta particle, or electron. The proton remains in the nucleus and the beta particle is released. The atomic number increases by one and the mass number stays the same. Alpha and beta decay are almost always accompanied by gamma radiation, a form of high-energy waves. Gamma radiation is the most penetrating, beta particles are less penetrating, and alpha particles are the least penetrating.

79.   A polymer is a large complex molecule built from smaller molecules called monomers. Large numbers of one or more monomers are connected by chemical bonds in a repeating pattern that forms a chain or a web. Carbon atoms form the backbone of these molecules. Carbon atoms are unusual because they can bond to each other in chains and ring-shaped groups.

80.   Student examples may vary. Possible answers: Radioactive isotopes are used as tracers in chemical reactions or in industrial processes. They also are used to generate electricity in nuclear power plants, to find out about and treat medical problems, and to find the ages of fossils. Radioactive isotopes are useful because they give off radiation that can be detected. But radiation makes these isotopes dangerous because it damages living cells. Radiation can cause illness or death. Some isotopes have long half-lives, which means they can last for thousands or millions of years or more. They must be handled and stored in ways that reduce risk.

Test 59 Book M, Chapter 1: Motion

A. Multiple Choice
Choose the letter of the correct answer.

_____ 1. When an object's distance from another object is changing,

    a. it is in motion.

    b. it is speeding.

    c. it has a high velocity.

    d. it is accelerating.

_____ 2. The basic SI unit of length is the

    a. meter.

    b. foot.

    c. inch.

    d. mile.

_____ 3. Speed equals distance divided by

    a. time.

    b. velocity.

    c. size.

    d. motion.

_____ 4. When you know both the speed and direction of an object's motion, you know the

    a. average speed of the object.

    b. acceleration of the object.

    c. distance the object has traveled.

    d. velocity of the object.

_____ 5. You can show the motion of an object on a line graph in which you plot distance against

    a. velocity.

    b. time.

    c. speed.

    d. direction.

_____ 6. In graphing motion, the steepness of the slope depends on

    a. how quickly or slowly the object is moving.

    b. how far the object has moved.

    c. the velocity of the object.

    d. the direction the object is moving.

_____ 7. The upper layer of Earth consists of more than a dozen major pieces called

    a. units.

    b. plates.

    c. continents.

    d. tectonics.

_____ **8.** In 1,000 years, Earth's plates have moved

    a. 5 kilometers.

    b. 50 centimeters.

    c. 50 meters.

    d. 50 kilometers.

_____ **9.** The rate at which velocity changes is called

    a. speed.

    b. direction.

    c. acceleration.

    d. motion.

_____ **10.** Which of these is an example of deceleration?

    a. a bird taking off for flight

    b. a baseball released by a pitcher

    c. a car approaching a red light

    d. an airplane turning to change its course

_____ **11.** To determine the acceleration rate of an object, you must calculate the change in velocity during each unit of

    a. speed.

    b. time.

    c. motion.

    d. deceleration.

_____ **12.** If velocity is measured in kilometers per hour and time is measured in hours, the unit of acceleration is

    a. hours.

    b. kilometers per hour.

    c. kilometers per hour per hour.

    d. kilometers.

_____ **13.** A train that travels 100 kilometers in 4 hours is traveling at what average speed?

    a. 50 km/h

    b. 100 km/h

    c. 2 km/h

    d. 25 km/h

_____ **14.** As Earth orbits the sun, it is moving about

    a. 30 kilometers per hour.

    b. 300 kilometers per second.

    c. 3 kilometers per minute.

    d. 30 kilometers per second.

_____ **15.** A place or object used for comparison to determine if something is in motion is called

    a. a position.

    b. a reference point.

    c. a constant.

    d. velocity.

_____ **16.** Gallons, inches, and pounds are all

    a. distances.

    b. reference points.

    c. units.

    d. velocities.

_____ **17.** On a graph showing distance versus time, a horizontal line represents an object that is

    a. moving at a constant speed.

    b. increasing its speed.

    c. decreasing its speed.

    d. not moving at all.

_____ **18.** The International System of Units is used

    a. only in the United States.

    b. only in France.

    c. in most of Europe.

    d. all over the world.

_____ **19.** According to the theory of plate tectonics,

    a. Earth's crust is made of molten lava.

    b. Earth's plates move ever so slowly.

    c. Earth's surface has not changed over time.

    d. Earth's core is magnetic.

_____ **20.** Scientists believe that all continents were connected as recently as

    a. 250 years ago.

    b. 25,000 years ago.

    c. 250 million years ago.

    d. 25 years ago.

_____ **21.** If you know the distance an object has traveled in a certain amount of time, you can determine

    a. the size of the object.

    b. the speed of the object.

    c. the location of the object.

    d. the velocity of the object.

_____ **22.** In a conversion factor, what is special about the fraction used?

    a. The denominator is always 1.

    b. The numerator is always 1.

    c. The denominator and numerator are equal.

    d. The denominator is always zero.

_____ **23.** It is rare for any motion to

    a. stay the same for very long.

    b. change quickly.

    c. increase in velocity.

    d. decrease in speed.

_____ **24.** If the speed of an object does NOT change, the object is traveling at a

     a.   constant speed.

     b.   average speed.

     c.   increasing speed.

     d.   decreasing speed.

_____ **25.** Changing direction is an example of a kind of

     a.   acceleration.

     b.   speed.

     c.   velocity.

     d.   constant rate.

_____ **26.** If a bicyclist travels 30 kilometers in two hours, her average speed would be

     a.   30 km/h.

     b.   60 km/h.

     c.   15 km/h.

     d.   2 km/h.

_____ **27.** The moon accelerates because it is

     a.   in a vacuum in space.

     b.   continuously changing direction.

     c.   a very large sphere.

     d.   constantly increasing its speed of orbit.

_____ **28.** If an object moves in the same direction and at a constant speed for 4 hours, which of the following is true?

     a.   The object's speed changed during the 4 hours.

     b.   The object's speed and average speed were equal during the entire 4 hours.

     c.   The object accelerated during the 4 hours.

     d.   The object decelerated during the 4 hours.

_____ **29.** If you know a car traveled 300 kilometers in 3 hours, you can find its

     a.   acceleration.

     b.   direction.

     c.   average speed.

     d.   velocity.

_____ **30.** In an acceleration graph showing speed versus time, a straight line shows the acceleration is

     a.   decreasing.

     b.   increasing.

     c.   changing.

     d.   constant.

B. True or False
If the statement is true, write true. If it is false, change the underlined word or words to make the statement true.

31. Motion is measured relative to a <u>reference point</u>.

_____

_____

32. A person standing on a <u>moving</u> escalator is moving relative to another person standing on the escalator.

_____

_____

33. A cyclist travels 20 km in half an hour. Her average speed is <u>10 km/h</u>.

_____

_____

34. If a toy car traveling at 10 cm/s passes a toy car moving at 10 cm/s in the opposite direction, both cars have the same <u>velocity</u>.

_____

_____

35. A straight line on a <u>motion</u> graph indicates constant speed.

_____

_____

36. A <u>slanted</u> line on a motion graph means that the object is at rest.

_____

_____

37. The upper layer of Earth is broken into more than a dozen <u>continents</u> that move very slowly in various directions.

_____

_____

38. A child riding on a merry-go-round is accelerating because his direction is <u>changing</u>.

_____

_____

39. The SI unit of <u>velocity</u> is the meter per second per second.

_____

_____

40. A straight line on a graph of <u>speed versus time</u> means that the object has a constant acceleration.

_____

_____

C. Completion

Fill in the word or phrase that best completes each statement.

41. A reference point is assumed to be _____, or not moving.

_____

_____

42. A change in an object's position relative to a reference point is called _____.

_____

_____

43. When riding a bicycle past a building, you are not moving relative to the _____.

_____

_____

44. Suppose you are standing on a corner when a car moving toward the north passes you. If you use the car as a reference point, the direction in which you appear to be moving is toward the ____.

_____

_____

45. The distance traveled by a moving object per unit of time is called _____.

_____

_____

46. The basic SI unit of length is the ____.

_____

_____

47. Speed that does not change is referred to as _____ speed.

_____

_____

48. The statement that the motion of a hurricane is 20 kilometers per hour in an easterly direction is a description of the hurricane's _____.

_____

_____

49. A speed of 15 kilometers per hour is abbreviated as 15 _____.

_____

_____

50. According to the theory of plate _____, Earth's plates move very slowly in various directions.

_____

_____

51. The boundaries between the plates that make up the upper layer of Earth are cracks in Earth's _____.

_____

_____

52. Acceleration is the rate of change in _____.

_____

_____

53. _____ occurs when an object slows down.

_____

_____

54. A golf ball _____ when either its speed or direction changes.

_____

_____

55. The motion of a car stopping at a traffic light is an example of a _____ acceleration, also called deceleration.

_____

_____

56. The abbreviation of the unit of acceleration (meters per second per second) is _____.

_____

_____

57. If a ship has an acceleration of 3 km/h^2, its speed is expressed in the unit _____.

_____

_____

58. If a car is speeding up, its initial speed is _____ than its final speed.

_____

_____

59. If a train traveling north at 30 m/s brakes to a stop in 1 minute, its acceleration is _____ southward.

_____

_____

60. If two lines appear on the same motion graph, the line with the steeper _____ indicates a greater speed.

_____

_____

D. Interpreting Diagrams
Use the diagram to answer each question.

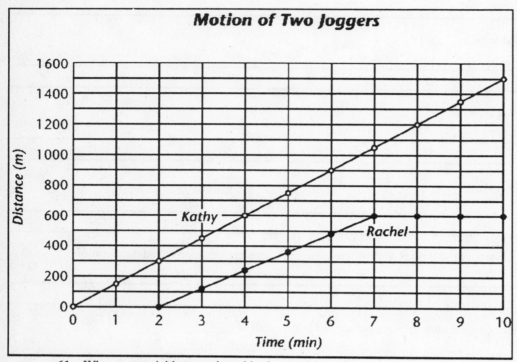

Motion of Two Joggers

61. What two variables are plotted in the graph?

_____

_____

_____

_____

_____

62. How would you describe Kathy's motion? What does such motion mean?

_____

_____

_____

_____

_____

63. How far did Kathy jog in the first 4 minutes?

_____

_____

_____

_____

_____

64. What is Kathy's average speed?

_____
_____
_____
_____

65. How long after Kathy started jogging did Rachel begin jogging?

_____
_____
_____
_____

66. Describe Rachel's motion at 9 minutes.

_____
_____
_____
_____

Use the diagram to answer each question.

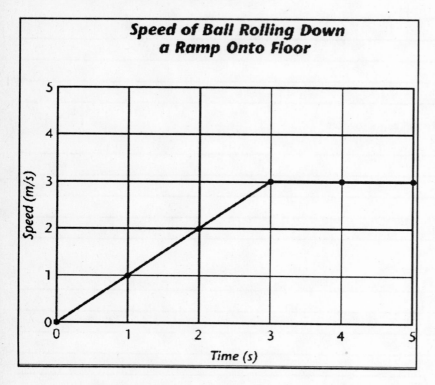

Speed of Ball Rolling Down a Ramp Onto Floor

67. What two variables are plotted in the graph?

_____

_____

_____

_____

_____

68. What does the line segment on the graph from 0 to 3 seconds represent? Explain your answer.

_____

_____

_____

_____

69. What is the acceleration of the ball between 0 and 3 seconds?

_____

_____

_____

_____

_____

70. What happened to the speed of the ball during the final two seconds?

_____
_____
_____
_____
_____

71. Does the graph indicate that the ball decelerated? Explain your answer.

_____
_____
_____
_____
_____

72. How far did the ball move in the final 2 seconds?

_____
_____
_____
_____
_____

E. Essay
Write an answer to each of the following questions.

73. You are riding in a car traveling at 80 km/h. A fly trapped in the car rests on your shoulder. Describe the speed of the fly using two different reference points.

_____
_____
_____
_____
_____
_____

74. You are in a speedboat on a river moving in the same direction as the current. The speedometer on the boat shows that its speed is 20 km/h. However, a person on the shore measures the boat's speed as 23 km/h. How is this possible?

_____

_____

_____

_____

_____

_____

75. Explain how to find the average speed of a car that travels 300 kilometers in 6 hours. Then find the average speed.

_____

_____

_____

_____

_____

76. Two toy wind-up cars are traveling in the same direction. Car A is 5 cm ahead of car B. On a motion graph, the two straight lines that represent their motions cross. Which toy wind-up car is traveling faster? Explain.

_____

_____

_____

_____

_____

_____

77. Two satellite tracking stations are on plates that are moving toward each other. One plate is moving east at a rate of 5 cm/yr. The other plate is moving west at a rate of 5 cm/yr. If the stations are now separated by 200 km, in how many years will the stations be 198 km apart? Explain.

_____

_____

_____

_____

_____

_____

_____

78. People living at Earth's equator are traveling at a speed of about 1670 km/h as Earth spins on its axis. Are these people being accelerated? Explain.

_____

_____

_____

_____

_____

_____

_____

79. Car A is traveling north at 30 m/s and car B is traveling south at 30 m/s. If both cars have a southward acceleration of 1 m/s^2, compare their speeds after 1 second. Explain your comparison.

_____

_____

_____

_____

_____

_____

80. A roller coaster is moving at 10 m/s at the top of a hill and 22 m/s at the bottom of the hill two seconds later. Explain how to find the average acceleration of the roller coaster, and then find the average acceleration.

_____

_____

_____

_____

_____

_____

_____

Test 59 Book M, Chapter 1: Motion
Answer Key (Short)

__a__	1.
__a__	2.
__a__	3.
__d__	4.
__b__	5.
__a__	6.
__b__	7.
__c__	8.
__c__	9.
__c__	10.
__b__	11.
__c__	12.
__d__	13.
__d__	14.
__b__	15.
__c__	16.
__d__	17.
__d__	18.
__b__	19.
__c__	20.
__b__	21.
__c__	22.
__a__	23.
__a__	24.
__a__	25.
__c__	26.
__b__	27.
__b__	28.
__c__	29.
__d__	30.

31.   TRUE
32.   false, stationary
33.   false, 40 km/h
34.   false, speed
35.   TRUE
36.   false, horizontal
37.   false, plates
38.   TRUE
39.   false, acceleration
40.   TRUE
41.   stationary

42.	motion
43.	bicycle
44.	south
45.	speed
46.	meter
47.	constant
48.	velocity
49.	km/h
50.	tectonics
51.	crust
52.	velocity
53.	Deceleration
54.	accelerates
55.	negative
56.	m/s^2
57.	km/h
58.	lower
59.	$0.5 \ m/s^2$
60.	slope
61.	distance and time
62.	Kathy is jogging at a constant speed. Her speed does not change as she moves.
63.	600 m
64.	Average speed = distance/time = 1,500 m/10 min = 150 m/min
65.	2 minutes
66.	Rachel is not moving; she is at rest.
67.	speed and time
68.	The segment represents constant acceleration. The speed increases by the same amount during each second.
69.	$1 \ m/s^2$ (3m/s - 0 m/s)/3 s = (3 m/s)/(3 s) = (1 m/s)/s = $1 \ m/s^2$
70.	The ball's speed was constant; it did not change.
71.	No, deceleration is a negative acceleration, which means an object slows down. According to the graph, the ball's velocity increased in the first three seconds and then remained the same. It did not slow down. Deceleration would be indicated by a line that slopes downward.
72.	6 m (3.0 m/s x 2 s = 6 m)
73.	From the reference point of Earth, the fly is moving at a speed of 80 km/h - the same as the car. From the reference point of the car or your shoulder, the speed of the fly is 0 km/h because it is not moving with respect to the car or your shoulder.
74.	From the reference point of the river, the speed of the boat is 20 km/h. From the reference point of someone standing on the shore, the speed of the boat is the speed on the speedometer plus the downstream speed of the current.
75.	To find average speed, divide the distance traveled, 300 km, by the time to travel the distance, 6 h.

$$\text{Average speed} = \frac{\text{Distance}}{\text{Time}} = \frac{300km}{6h} = 50km/h$$

76.   Car B is traveling faster. At the point where the two lines cross, car B and car A are at the same place after traveling the same amount of time. Since the cars are traveling in the same direction, car B must travel the distance that car A moves plus the 5 cm head start. So, car B must be moving faster because it moves a greater distance in the same amount of time as car A.

77.   Since both plates are moving toward each other, the two plates will be 198 km apart when each plate has moved 1 km. *Time = Distance / Speed* = 1 km / (5 cm/yr) = 1,000 m / (5 cm/yr) = 100,000 cm / (5 cm/yr) = 20,000 yr. The plates will be 198 km apart in 20,000 years.

78.   They are being accelerated because the direction of their motion is constantly changing as they spin in a circle.

79.   After 1 second, Car A's speed is 29 m/s and car B's speed is 31 m/s. For Car A, a southward acceleration is a deceleration, or negative acceleration. For car A to have a negative acceleration, its final velocity must be less than its initial velocity. So car A slows down by 1 m/s in 1 second of travel. Car B speeds up by 1 m/s in 1 second of travel.

80.   To find average acceleration, divide the change in velocity by the time during which the change in velocity took place. *Average acceleration = (Final velocity - Initial velocity) / Time* = (6m/s) / s = 6m/s^2 = (22 m/s - 10 m/s) / 2 s = (12 m/s) / 2 s

A. Multiple Choice
Choose the letter of the correct answer.

_____ 1. Which of the following is an example of exerting a force?

    a. a child running through a field

    b. a train speeding down a track

    c. a carpenter hammering a nail

    d. an airplane soaring through the sky

_____ 2. What happens when two forces act in the same direction?

    a. They cancel each other out.

    b. The stronger one prevails.

    c. They add together.

    d. Their sum divided by two is the total force.

_____ 3. The tendency of an object to resist change in its motion is known as

    a. mass.

    b. inertia.

    c. force.

    d. balance.

_____ 4. The greater the mass of an object,

    a. the more force it can exert.

    b. the greater its inertia.

    c. the more balanced it is.

    d. the more space it takes up.

_____ 5. Force = mass •

    a. speed.

    b. motion.

    c. acceleration.

    d. inertia.

_____ 6. One way to increase acceleration is by

    a. increasing mass.

    b. decreasing mass.

    c. decreasing force.

    d. increasing both force and mass equally.

_____ 7. The force that one surface exerts on another when the two rub against each other is called

    a. friction.

    b. acceleration.

    c. inertia.

    d. gravity.

_____ 8. Which of the following is an example of rolling friction?

    a. your shoes on a sidewalk as you walk

    b. bike tires on the road as you ride

    c. a boat on the water as it sails

    d. two hands rubbing together

_____ 9. When the only force acting on a falling object is gravity, the object is said to be

    a. stationary.

    b. decelerating.

    c. in free fall.

    d. a projectile.

_____ 10. Air resistance is a type of

    a. motion.

    b. acceleration.

    c. velocity.

    d. friction.

_____ 11. The force of gravity on a person or object at the surface of a planet is known as

    a. mass.

    b. inertia.

    c. air resistance.

    d. weight.

_____ 12. Weight = mass •

    a. force due to balanced forces.

    b. acceleration due to gravity.

    c. inertia due to force.

    d. air resistance.

_____ 13. The law of universal gravitation states that any two objects in the universe, without exception,

    a. attract each other.

    b. repel each other.

    c. combine to provide a balanced force.

    d. create friction.

_____ 14. If you were on the moon, your weight would be roughly what fraction of your weight on Earth?

    a. one third

    b. one fourth

    c. one fifth

    d. one sixth

_____ 15. Two figure skaters who push off of each other will move at the same speed if

    a. they push with the same force.

    b. the ice does not cause any friction.

    c. there is no air resistance.

    d. they have the same mass.

_____ **16.** Forces can be added together only if they are

    a. acting on the same object.

    b. balanced forces.

    c. unaffected by gravity.

    d. substantial.

_____ **17.** The product of an object's mass and velocity is called its

    a. inertia.

    b. momentum.

    c. acceleration.

    d. force.

_____ **18.** According to the law of conservation of momentum, when two objects collide in the absence of friction,

    a. velocity decreases.

    b. velocity increases.

    c. momentum is not lost.

    d. only the object with the larger mass continues on.

_____ **19.** The achievement of lifting a rocket off the ground and into space can be explained by

    a. Newton's first law.

    b. Newton's second law.

    c. Newton's third law.

    d. the law of conservation of momentum.

_____ **20.** What is required for a rocket to lift off into space?

    a. thrust that is greater than Earth's gravity

    b. mass that is greater than Earth's

    c. very little air resistance

    d. more velocity than friction

_____ **21.** An object that travels around another object in space is called a

    a. projectile.

    b. inertia.

    c. mass.

    d. satellite.

_____ **22.** Any force that causes an object to move in a circle is called a

    a. balanced force.

    b. unbalanced force.

    c. gravitational force.

    d. centripetal force.

_____ **23.** In physical science, a push or a pull is called a(n)

    a. force.

    b. acceleration.

    c. inertia.

    d. motion.

_____ **24.** The momentum of an object is in the same direction as its

    a. force.

    b. acceleration.

    c. velocity.

    d. inertia.

_____ **25.** How can you increase the momentum of an object?

    a. by decreasing its velocity

    b. by increasing its mass

    c. by increasing its friction

    d. by decreasing its acceleration

_____ **26.** The amount of matter in an object is called its

    a. inertia.

    b. mass.

    c. force.

    d. balance.

_____ **27.** Which of the following is an example of increasing friction intentionally?

    a. waxing skis

    b. adding grease to gears on a bike

    c. throwing sand on an icy driveway

    d. oiling a squeaky door

_____ **28.** The force that pulls falling objects toward Earth is called

    a. gravity.

    b. free fall.

    c. acceleration.

    d. air resistance.

_____ **29.** A leaf flutters instead of dropping straight to the ground when it falls from a tree because it experiences

    a. terminal velocity.

    b. air resistance.

    c. inertia.

    d. rolling friction.

_____ **30.** According to Newton's third law of motion, when a hammer strikes and exerts force on a nail, the nail

    a. creates a friction with the hammer.

    b. disappears into the wood.

    c. exerts an equal force back on the hammer.

    d. moves at a constant speed.

B. True or False

If the statement is true, write true. If it is false, change the underlined word or words to make the statement true.

31. <u>Unbalanced</u> forces maintain motion at constant velocity.

_____

_____

32. The property of matter that resists a change in motion is called <u>inertia</u>.

_____

_____

33. According to Newton's second law of motion, force equals mass times <u>weight</u>.

_____

_____

34. Friction depends on the types of surfaces involved and how <u>hard</u> the surfaces push together.

_____

_____

35. The force of gravity <u>decreases</u> as the masses of objects increase.

_____

_____

36. When the only force acting on a falling object is <u>air resistance</u>, the object is said to be in free fall.

_____

_____

37. Newton's third law of motion explains that forces act <u>alone</u>.

_____

_____

38. A unit of <u>momentum</u> is kg•m/s.

_____

_____

39. A rocket will move upward as long as the <u>thrust</u> is greater than the pull of gravity.

_____

_____

40. The force that keeps a satellite in Earth orbit is always directed <u>away from</u> the center of Earth.

_____

_____

C. Completion
Fill in the word or phrase that best completes each statement.

41. The overall force on an object after all the forces are added together is called the _____ force.

_____

_____

42. Unbalanced forces acting on an object produce _____ motion.

_____

_____

43. A measure of an object's _____ is a measure of the object's inertia.

_____

_____

44. One _____ is the force required to accelerate one kilogram of mass at 1 meter per second per second.

_____

_____

45. A person traveling in a car that stops suddenly keeps moving forward due to _____.

_____

_____

46. Wet pavement is more slippery than dry pavement because the force needed to overcome _____ friction is less than the force needed to overcome sliding friction.

_____

_____

47. The downward force acting on an object in free fall is the force of _____.

_____

_____

48. A(n) _____ is an object that is thrown.

_____

_____

49. When _____ equals the force of gravity on a falling object, the object reaches terminal velocity.

_____

_____

50. The metric unit that is most often used to describe weight is the _____.

_____

_____

51. The force of gravity between you and Earth is greater than the force of gravity between you and a car because Earth has more ___ than the car.

_____

_____

52. As the distance between two objects decreases, the gravitational force between them _____.

_____

_____

53. According to Newton's third law of motion, the strength of a reaction force is _____ the strength of the action force.

_____

_____

54. If the action force of a bat striking a ball accelerates the ball in one direction, the reaction force accelerates the bat in the ____ direction.

_____

_____

55. The momentum of an object is in the same _____ as its velocity.

_____

_____

56. The momentum of a roller skater is not conserved because ____ acts on the skates.

_____

_____

57. During lift-off, the thrust on a rocket is directed _____.

_____

_____

58. The moon is a natural ____ of Earth.

_____

_____

59. The force of gravity is responsible for continuously changing the _____ in which a satellite moves.

_____

_____

60. Friction acts in a direction _____ to an object's direction of motion.

_____

_____

D. Interpreting Diagrams

Use the diagram to answer each question.

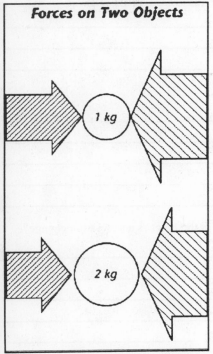

Forces on Two Objects

1 kg

2 kg

61. What does the head of each arrow indicate?

_____

_____

_____

_____

_____

62. What does the width of each arrow represent?

_____

_____

_____

_____

_____

63. In what direction is the net force acting on the 1-kg object?

_____

_____

_____

_____

_____

64. In what direction must a force be applied so that the forces on the 1-kg object are balanced?

_____

_____

_____

_____

65. Compare the acceleration of the 1-kg object with that of the 2-kg object.

_____

_____

_____

_____

66. Suppose a third force is applied to the 1-kg object in an upward direction. How will the object's acceleration change?

_____

_____

_____

_____

Use the diagram to answer each question.

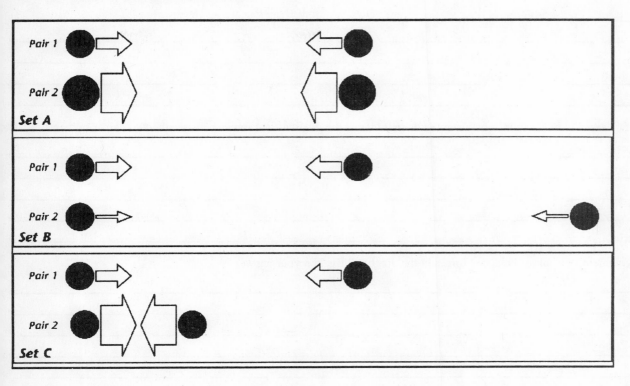

67. Compare the size and direction of the gravitational force exerted by each object in pair 1 of Set A.

_____
_____
_____
_____
_____

68. In Set A, is the gravitational force greater between the objects in pair 1 or pair 2? Explain why.

_____
_____
_____
_____
_____

69. In Set A, what would you have to do to the objects to make the gravitational forces between the objects in pair 2 the same as the forces between the objects in pair 1?

_____
_____
_____
_____
_____

70. In Set B, explain the difference between the magnitudes of the gravitational forces between the two pairs of objects.

_____

_____

_____

_____

71. In Set C, explain the difference between the magnitudes of the gravitational forces between the two pairs of objects.

_____

_____

_____

_____

72. Can you identify a pair of balanced forces in the diagram? Explain your answer.

_____

_____

_____

_____

E. Essay

Write an answer to each of the following questions.

73. In an amusement park ride, a girl stands with her back against the inside wall of a circular room. The room begins to whirl around. After the room reaches a constant speed, the floor drops down, but she doesn't fall. Identify three forces acting on her and give the direction of each. Explain which forces are balanced forces.

_____

_____

_____

_____

_____

_____

_____

74. A book is sitting on the dashboard of a car that is stopped at a traffic light. As the car starts to move forward, the book slides backward off the dashboard. Use the term *inertia* to explain what happened.

_____

_____

_____

_____

_____

_____

_____

75. A skydiver with a mass of 70 kg accelerates to Earth at a rate of 9.8 m/s^2 due to gravity. What is the force on the skydiver? Explain how you determined the answer and its units.

_____

_____

_____

_____

_____

_____

_____

76. A block of wood is at rest on a wooden ramp. When wheels are attached to the block of wood, it moves down the ramp. Explain each situation in terms of friction.

_____

_____

_____

_____

_____

_____

_____

77. Compare the effects of gravity and air resistance on a falling skydiver before and after she opens her parachute.

_____
_____
_____
_____
_____
_____
_____

78. What is the law of conservation of momentum? How can you show that the law is true for two objects that collide?

_____
_____
_____
_____
_____
_____
_____

79. Why don't action-reaction forces cancel out?

_____
_____
_____
_____
_____
_____

80. An object must attain a speed of 8,100 m/s to achieve a low orbit. What happens if the object's speed is less than 8,100 m/s?

_____
_____
_____
_____
_____
_____

Test 60 Book M, Chapter 2: Forces
Answer Key (Short)

__c__	1.
__c__	2.
__b__	3.
__b__	4.
__c__	5.
__b__	6.
__a__	7.
__b__	8.
__c__	9.
__d__	10.
__d__	11.
__b__	12.
__a__	13.
__d__	14.
__d__	15.
__a__	16.
__b__	17.
__c__	18.
__c__	19.
__a__	20.
__d__	21.
__d__	22.
__a__	23.
__c__	24.
__b__	25.
__b__	26.
__c__	27.
__a__	28.
__b__	29.
__c__	30.

31.	false, Balanced
32.	TRUE
33.	false, acceleration
34.	TRUE
35.	false, increases
36.	false, gravity
37.	false, in pairs
38.	TRUE
39.	TRUE
40.	false, toward
41.	net

42.   accelerated

43.   mass

44.   newton

45.   inertia

46.   fluid

47.   gravity

48.   projectile

49.   air resistance

50.   newton

51.   mass

52.   increases

53.   equal to

54.   opposite

55.   direction

56.   friction

57.   upward

58.   satellite

59.   direction

60.   opposite

61.   The head indicates the direction of the force.

62.   The width represents the size, or magnitude, of the force.

63.   to the left

64.   to the right

65.   The acceleration of the 1-kg object is twice the acceleration of the 2-kg object.

66.   The object will accelerate upward and to the left.

67.   The gravitational forces are equal in size but opposite in direction.

68.   The gravitational force between the objects in pair 2 is greater because the objects have a greater mass than those in pair 1.

69.   The forces between the objects in pair 2 could be decreased by moving the objects apart.

70.   The gravitational forces between the objects in pair 1 are greater than the forces between the objects in pair 2 because the objects in pair 2 are farther apart.

71.   The gravitational forces between the objects in pair 2 are greater than the forces between the objects in pair 1 because the objects in pair 2 are closer together.

72.   No pair of forces in the diagram is an example of a pair of balanced forces because each force in the pair acts on a different object. Balanced forces can only act on one object.

73.   The three forces are centripetal force (inward), weight (downward), and friction (upward). Because the girl does not move up or down, the forces that act upward and downward on her must be balanced. These two forces are friction and weight.

74.   When the car was stopped at the traffic light, the book and dashboard were both at rest. As the car accelerated forward, the dashboard moved forward because the car exerted an unbalanced force on it. The dashboard did not exert an unbalanced force on the book, so it remained at rest because of its inertia. As a result, the dashboard moved forward while the book remained at rest. From the reference point of the car, the book appeared to move backward, causing it to fall off the dashboard.

75.   Force = Mass • Acceleration = 70 kg • 9.8 m/s^2 = 686 kg • m/s^2 = 686 N   According to Newton's second law of motion, force equals mass times acceleration. This means that if you know both mass and acceleration, you can find the force. In this case, the mass of the person and the acceleration due to gravity were known. Since 1 N = 1 kg • m/s^2, the final unit is the newton.

76.   Without wheels, the force of sliding friction balances the gravitational force pulling the block down the ramp. There is no net force on the block, so it does not slide down the incline. When wheels are attached, the force of rolling friction is much smaller than the force of sliding friction. Now there is a net force on the block pulling the block down the ramp, so the block begins to move in the direction of this unbalanced force.

77.   There is no difference in the force of gravity on the skydiver before and after she opens her parachute. The downward force on the skydiver equals her weight and the weight of the parachute. The air resistance on the falling skydiver without her parachute open is less than with the parachute open because the larger surface area of the parachute has greater air resistance acting on it.

78.   The law of conservation of momentum states that the total momentum of objects that interact does not change. In other words, the total momentum before and after a collision between two objects is the same. You can show that the law is true by calculating the momentum of each object before the collision and again after the collision. The total momentum of before the collision will equal the total after the collision.

79.   Forces cancel out only of they are acting on the same object. Action and reaction forces act on different objects. For example, when a person kicks a ball, the action force is on the ball but the reaction force is on the person's foot. Therefore, the forces cannot cancel.

80.   The object will not have enough speed to escape Earth's gravity. It will eventually fall back to Earth's surface.

Test 61 Book M, Chapter 3: Forces in Fluids

A. Multiple Choice
Choose the letter of the correct answer.

_____ 1. Snowshoes enable a person to walk on deep snow because the snowshoes

    a. decrease the person's weight on the snow.

    b. increase the area over which the person's weight is distributed.

    c. increase the pressure on the snow.

    d. increase the buoyancy of the person.

_____ 2. A unit of pressure is called a

    a. bernoulli.

    b. pascal.

    c. pound.

    d. meter.

_____ 3. Air pressure exerted equally on an object from different directions is

    a. balanced pressure.

    b. gravitational pressure.

    c. fluid pressure.

    d. constant pressure.

_____ 4. Given that the air pressure outside your body is so great, why aren't you crushed?

    a. Human skin is extremely strong.

    b. Earth's gravity cancels out the air pressure.

    c. Pressure inside your body balances the air pressure outside your body.

    d. Inertia changes the pressure before it comes into contact with you.

_____ 5. Air pressure decreases as

    a. velocity increases.

    b. elevation increases.

    c. acceleration decreases.

    d. gravity increases.

_____ 6. Water pressure increases as

    a. depth increases.

    b. gravity increases.

    c. force decreases.

    d. acceleration decreases.

_____ 7. Which type of substance does Pascal's principle deal with?

    a. solids

    b. fluids

    c. powders

    d. metals

_____ **8.** One application of Pascal's principle is

    a. a hydraulic car lift.

    b. the flight of an airplane.

    c. a speedboat's bottom slapping against the waves.

    d. the buoyancy shown by ducks and other waterfowl.

_____ **9.** What scientific rule do hydraulic systems use?

    a. Bernoulli's principle

    b. Archimedes' principle

    c. Pascal's principle

    d. Newton's first law of motion

_____ **10.** What does a hydraulic system do?

    a. decrease pressure

    b. increase velocity

    c. multiply force

    d. reduce inertia

_____ **11.** Which of the following is true of the buoyant force?

    a. It acts in the downward direction.

    b. It acts with the force of gravity.

    c. It acts in the upward direction.

    d. It makes an object feel heavier.

_____ **12.** What effect does a buoyant force have on a submerged object?

    a. It causes the object to sink in a fluid.

    b. It causes a net force acting upward on the object.

    c. It causes the object to float in a fluid.

    d. It causes a net force acting downward on the object.

_____ **13.** According to Archimedes' principle, if an object floats, the volume of displaced water is equal to the volume of

    a. the entire object.

    b. the portion of the object that is above water.

    c. the portion of the object that is submerged.

    d. exactly half of the object.

_____ **14.** What scientific rule states that the buoyant force on an object is equal to the weight of the fluid displaced by the object?

    a. Archimedes' principle

    b. Pascal's principle

    c. Bernoulli's principle

    d. Newton's third law of motion

_____ **15.** How is the density of a submarine decreased?

    a. It propels faster through the water.

    b. It slows down.

    c. It releases water from its flotation tanks.

    d. It takes in water.

_____ **16.** A ship stays afloat as long as the buoyant force is

    a.   less than the ship's weight.

    b.   greater than the ship's weight.

    c.   less than the ship's speed.

    d.   greater than the ship's speed.

_____ **17.** The pressure exerted by a moving stream of fluid

    a.   is greater than the pressure of the surrounding fluid.

    b.   is less than the pressure of the surrounding fluid.

    c.   depends on the nature of the fluid.

    d.   depends on the volume of the fluid.

_____ **18.** Smoke rises up a chimney partly because of

    a.   Archimedes' principle.

    b.   Pascal's principle.

    c.   Bernoulli's principle.

    d.   Newton's third law of motion.

_____ **19.** Bernoulli's principle explains

    a.   hydraulic brakes.

    b.   buoyancy.

    c.   momentum.

    d.   flight.

_____ **20.** How can an airplane fly?

    a.   The powerful engines force it up into the air.

    b.   The long, sleek design of the body cuts through the air.

    c.   The curvature of the wings causes air to move faster on top of them, creating lift.

    d.   The materials used for the shell cause little friction.

_____ **21.** The mass per unit volume of a substance is its

    a.   density.

    b.   buoyancy.

    c.   weight.

    d.   fluid pressure.

_____ **22.** If the density of an object is equal to the density of the fluid in which it is immersed,

    a.   the object sinks.

    b.   the object rises.

    c.   the object will sink, then rise, then keep repeating this.

    d.   the object neither rises nor sinks but instead floats at a constant level.

_____ **23.** Which of these substances is the LEAST dense?

    a.   wood

    b.   copper

    c.   mercury

    d.   rubber

_____ **24.** Pressure can be measured in units of

    a.   newtons.

    b.   newtons per square centimeter.

    c.   newtons per centimeter.

    d.   newtons per cubic centimeter.

_____ **25.** A substance whose shape can easily change is a

    a.   solid.

    b.   powder.

    c.   fluid.

    d.   metal.

_____ **26.** Fluid pressure is the total force exerted by the fluid divided by

    a.   the area over which the force is exerted.

    b.   the acceleration of the force.

    c.   the gravitational pull within the fluid.

    d.   water pressure or depth.

_____ **27.** What scientific rule states that the pressure exerted by a moving stream of fluid is less than the pressure of the surrounding fluid?

    a.   Archimedes' principle

    b.   Pascal's principle

    c.   Bernoulli's principle

    d.   Newton's third law of motion

_____ **28.** The pressure in the deepest parts of the ocean is roughly how many times the usual air pressure you experience?

    a.   10

    b.   100

    c.   1,000

    d.   1,000,000

_____ **29.** Which of these multiplies a force by transmitting it to a large surface area?

    a.   a hydraulic system

    b.   a buoyant force

    c.   a balanced pressure

    d.   a force pump

_____ **30.** The braking system on a car is an example of

    a.   a hydraulic system.

    b.   buoyancy.

    c.   Bernoulli's principle.

    d.   Newton's third law of motion.

B. True or False

If the statement is true, write true. If it is false, change the underlined word or words to make the statement true.

31. The pressure you exert on the floor <u>decreases</u> when you stand on your toes because the area on which you exert force decreases.

_____

_____

32. The air pressure at an altitude of 3 km is <u>less</u> than the air pressure at 1 km.

_____

_____

33. Air enters your lungs when you inhale because the pressure inside your lungs and the pressure outside are <u>balanced</u>.

_____

_____

34. In the Heimlich maneuver, pressure is quickly applied slightly above the abdomen of someone who is choking, and material is forced out of the person's throat. The Heimlich maneuver is an application of <u>Archimedes'</u> principle.

_____

_____

35. Hydraulic systems use two pistons with different <u>surface areas</u> to lift heavy objects.

_____

_____

36. <u>More</u> force is required to lift an object in water than on land because of the buoyant force of the water.

_____

_____

37. The volume of liquid displaced by a floating cork is <u>less than</u> the volume of the object.

_____

_____

38. As a ship is unloaded, it rises higher in the water because the density of the ship and its cargo <u>increases</u>.

_____

_____

39. Wind blowing across the top of a chimney helps to draw air up the chimney. This is an example of <u>Bernoulli's</u> principle.

_____

_____

40. As an airplane wing moves, air moves <u>faster</u> above the wing than below it.

_____

_____

C. Completion

Fill in the word or phrase that best completes each statement.

41. The pressure resulting from a force of 50 N exerted over an area of 5 m^2 is _____ Pa.

_____

_____

42. Water pressure _____ with depth.

_____

_____

43. A mountain climber might carry oxygen because the air pressure at the top of the mountain is _____ than the air pressure at the bottom.

_____

_____

44. The pressure inside an air mattress _____ the pressure caused by your weight when you lie on it.

_____

_____

45. The _____ of the air inside a bubble submerged in water is equal to the pressure of the surrounding water.

_____

_____

46. When force is applied to a confined fluid, an increase in _____ is transmitted equally to all parts of the fluid.

_____

_____

47. When you squeeze one end of an inflated balloon, the other end bulges out. This behavior is an example of _____ principle.

_____

_____

48. In a hydraulic device, the surface area of the small piston is 20 cm^2 and the surface area of the large piston is 80 cm^2. To lift a 400-N barrel placed on the large piston, you must apply a force of _____ to the small piston.

_____

_____

49. In a hydraulic device, the distance the small piston moves is _____ than the distance the large piston moves.

_____

_____

50. A net force acts on a submerged object because the upward pressure on the bottom of the object is greater than the _____ pressure on the top of the object.

_____

_____

51. You float higher in salt water than in fresh water because the buoyant force on you in the salt water is _____ than the buoyant force in the fresh water.

_____

_____

52. A block of wood is placed in a jar of water. According to Archimedes' principle, the _____ on the block is equal to the weight of the displaced fluid.

_____

_____

53. As a tennis ball is pushed beneath the surface of a liquid, the buoyant force on it _____.

_____

_____

54. Chocolate syrup sinks in milk because chocolate syrup is more ____ than milk.

_____

_____

55. A wooden block floats both in water, which has a density of 1.0 g/cm^3 and in corn oil, which has a density of 1.38 g/cm^3. Less of the wooden block will be submerged in the _____.

_____

_____

56. According to Bernoulli's principle, the pressure in a moving stream of fluid is _____ than the pressure of the surrounding fluid.

_____

_____

57. During high winds, the windows in a building may bulge outward because the air pressure outside the building is _____ than the air pressure inside the building.

_____

_____

58. A shower curtain is pushed toward the running water of the shower because the air pressure near the water is _____ than the air pressure outside the curtain.

_____

_____

59. An eagle can glide through the air on a windy day thanks to _____ principle.

_____

_____

60. A _____ is one newton per square meter.

_____

_____

D. Interpreting Diagrams

Use the diagram to answer each question.

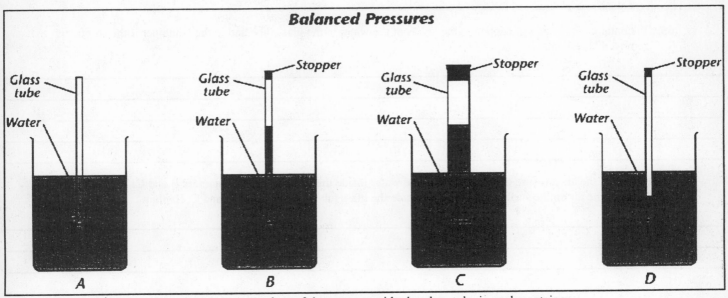

61. Compare the air pressure on the surface of the water outside the glass tube in each container.

_____
_____
_____
_____
_____

62. Compare the air pressure on the surface of the water inside the glass tube in container A and inside the glass tube in container B.

_____
_____
_____
_____
_____

63. In which container is the air pressure inside the glass tube the greatest?

_____
_____
_____
_____
_____

64. Compare the fluid pressure on the bottom of containers A and B.

_____

_____

_____

_____

65. In container B, what will happen to the levels of the water in the glass tube and in the container if the stopper is removed? Explain.

_____

_____

_____

_____

66. Compare the air pressure on the surface of the water inside the glass tubes in containers B and C. Then compare the force of the air on the surface of the water inside the glass tubes in containers B and C. Explain.

_____

_____

_____

_____

Use the diagram to answer each question.

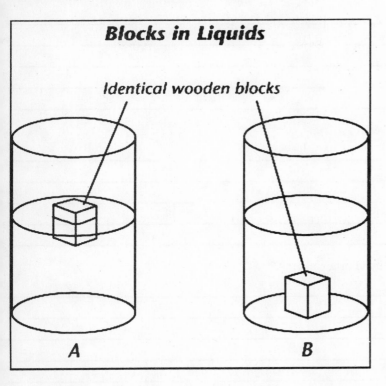

Blocks in Liquids

Identical wooden blocks

A   B

67. When the block was placed in the liquid in container A, the level of the liquid rose. Why?

_____

_____

_____

_____

_____

68. In what direction is the buoyant force acting on the block in container A?

_____

_____

_____

_____

69. Compare the buoyant force on the block in container A with the weight of the block.

_____

_____

_____

_____

70. In which container is the buoyant force of the liquid on the block greater? Explain.

_____

_____

_____

_____

71. In which container is the density of the liquid greater?

_____

_____

_____

_____

72. How is the buoyant force related to the displaced liquid in container A?

_____

_____

_____

_____

E. Essay

Write an answer to each of the following questions.

73. How can a woman wearing high heels exert a greater pressure than an elephant?

_____

_____

_____

_____

_____

_____

74. Why do the small bubbles of air exhaled by a submerged scuba diver get larger as they float to the surface of the water?

_____

_____

_____

_____

_____

_____

75. Suppose you shake a closed can containing a carbonated beverage. Explain what happens when you open the can.

_____

_____

_____

_____

_____

_____

76. Explain how a light push applied to the lever of a hydraulic barber shop chair can lift a person in the chair.

_____

_____

_____

_____

_____

_____

77. If you hold a sheet of notebook paper just under your lips and blow hard across the top of it, the paper will rise. Explain this result.

_____

_____

_____

_____

_____

_____

78. When the flap at the rear of an airplane is in the downward position, the curvature of the wing increases. How will this affect the amount of lift on the wing? Explain.

_____

_____

_____

_____

_____

_____

79. A solid plastic bead floats between a layer of water, which has a density of 1.00 g/cm^3, and glycerin, which has a density of 1.26 g/cm^3. What is the possible range for the density of the plastic used to make the bead? Explain.

_____

_____

_____

_____

_____

_____

80. A block is gently lowered into a large container that is completely filled with water. The block is then released. The water that the partially submerged block displaces is caught in a cup and weighed. If the weight of the water is 2.0 N, what is the weight of the block? Explain.

_____

_____

_____

_____

_____

_____

Test 61 Book M, Chapter 3: Forces in Fluids
Answer Key (Short)

__b__	1.
__b__	2.
__a__	3.
__c__	4.
__b__	5.
__a__	6.
__b__	7.
__a__	8.
__c__	9.
__c__	10.
__c__	11.
__b__	12.
__c__	13.
__a__	14.
__c__	15.
__b__	16.
__b__	17.
__c__	18.
__d__	19.
__c__	20.
__a__	21.
__d__	22.
__a__	23.
__b__	24.
__c__	25.
__a__	26.
__c__	27.
__c__	28.
__a__	29.
__a__	30.

31.	false, increases
32.	TRUE
33.	false, unbalanced
34.	false, Pascal's
35.	TRUE
36.	false, Less
37.	TRUE
38.	false, decreases
39.	TRUE
40.	TRUE
41.	10

42. increases
43. less
44. balances
45. pressure
46. pressure
47. Pascal's
48. 100 N
49. greater
50. downward
51. greater
52. buoyant force
53. increases
54. dense
55. corn oil
56. lower
57. lower
58. lower
59. Bernoulli's
60. pascal
61. The air pressure on the surface of the water outside the glass tube in each container is the same.
62. The air pressure is greater in container A because the height of the water's surface inside the tube is lower.
63. Container D, because the surface of the water is lowest
64. The fluid pressure is the same, because the water has the same depth.
65. When the stopper is removed, air pressure returns to normal in the glass tube. The weight of the water in the tube and air pressure will push the water down, causing the surrounding water to rise until the levels are the same.
66. The pressure on the surface of the water is the same inside the tubes in both containers because the water is at the same height. The force on the surface of the water inside the tube in container C is greater because the pressure is acting over a greater area.
67. The block displaced some of the liquid.
68. The buoyant force is acting upward on the block of wood.
69. The buoyant force and the weight of the block of wood are equal and opposite.
70. The buoyant force of the liquid in container A is greater than in container B because the buoyant force in container A is holding up the block while the buoyant force in container B is not holding up an identical block.
71. Container A
72. The weight of the displaced liquid equals the buoyant force on the block.
73. The elephant has a much greater weight, and therefore stronger force. However, the force is exerted over a large area - the elephant's four feet. The woman exerts a smaller force over a much smaller area - the tips of her two heels.
74. Because water pressure increases with depth, the pressure of water on the bubbles at the depth of the scuba diver is greater than the pressure near the surface. So as the bubbles rise, the pressure on them decreases and they expand.
75. Shaking up the beverage increases its pressure. When the can is opened, gas and liquid escape rapidly, until the pressure inside the can becomes equal to the pressure outside the can.

76. The light push on the lever causes a small piston to exert pressure on the liquid in the hydraulic system. The pressure is exerted equally throughout the system. The fluid exerts this pressure on a larger piston, which is attached to the chair seat. Because the piston has a large surface area, the pressure creates a larger force on it. This force is large enough to lift the piston, the attached chair, and the person in the chair.

77. Blowing across the paper causes the air on top of the paper to travel faster than the air beneath it. The slower moving air beneath the paper exerts greater pressure upward on the paper than the downward pressure caused by the faster moving air on top of the paper. The greater upward pressure causes an unbalanced force on the paper, which lifts it.

78. When the curvature of the wing increases, air moving across the top of the wing moves more rapidly. Also, the air under the wing encounters increased resistance and moves more slowly than when the flap is straight. The increased difference in speeds of the air above and below the wing will cause an increased lift on the wing.

79. The density of the plastic is greater than 1.00 g/cm^3 because the bead sinks in the water, but less than 1.26 g/cm^3 because it floats in the glycerin.

80. The weight of the block is 2.0 N. Because the block was floating (partially submerged), the weight of the block equals the buoyant force on it. According to Archimedes' principle, the buoyant force is the weight of the fluid displaced, which is 2.0 N.

Test 62 Book M, Chapter 4: Work and Machines

A. Multiple Choice
   Choose the letter of the correct answer.

_____ 1. For work to be done on an object, such as pushing a child on a swing,

   a. some force need only be exerted on the object.

   b. the object must move some distance as a result of a force.

   c. the object must move, whether or not a force is exerted on it.

   d. the object must move a distance equal to the amount of force exerted on it.

_____ 2. Which of these is an example of work being done on an object?

   a. holding a heavy piece of wood at a construction site

   b. trying to push a car that doesn't move out of deep snow

   c. pushing a child on a swing

   d. holding a door shut on a windy day so it doesn't blow open

_____ 3. If you exert a force of 20 newtons to push a desk 10 meters, how much work do you do on the desk?

   a. 200 joules

   b. 30 joules

   c. 10 joules

   d. 100 joules

_____ 4. Work is measured in

   a. meters.

   b. pounds.

   c. joules.

   d. newtons.

_____ 5. What do machines do?

   a. change force or distance

   b. increase work

   c. decrease work

   d. eliminate friction

_____ 6. Pulling down on a rope to hoist a sail on a sailboat is an example of a machine

   a. multiplying force.

   b. multiplying distance.

   c. changing direction.

   d. reducing friction.

_____ 7. If you exert a force of 20 newtons on a can opener, and the opener exerts a force of 60 newtons on the can, the ideal mechanical advantage of the can opener is

   a. 6.

   b. 2.

   c. 1,200.

   d. 3.

_____ 8. Without friction there would be

    a. less machine efficiency.

    b. greater output work than input work.

    c. greater input work than output work.

    d. equal input and output work.

_____ 9. An ideal machine would have an efficiency of

    a. 1 percent.

    b. 10 percent.

    c. 50 percent.

    d. 100 percent.

_____ 10. The efficiency of a machine compares

    a. force to mass.

    b. output work to input work.

    c. force to friction.

    d. friction to mass.

_____ 11. A ramp is an example of a simple machine called a(n)

    a. inclined plane.

    b. wedge.

    c. lever.

    d. pulley.

_____ 12. The ideal mechanical advantage for an inclined plane is equal to the length of the incline divided by the

    a. mass of the incline.

    b. slope of the incline.

    c. height of the incline.

    d. angle of the incline.

_____ 13. Which of these is an example of a third-class lever?

    a. scissors

    b. pliers

    c. fishing pole

    d. nutcracker

_____ 14. The ideal mechanical advantage of a wheel and axle is equal to the

    a. radius of the wheel divided by the radius of the axle.

    b. radius of the axle divided by the radius of the wheel.

    c. radius of the wheel divided by the length of the axle.

    d. length of the axle divided by the radius of the wheel.

_____ 15. A machine that utilizes two or more simple machines is called a

    a. combination machine.

    b. compound machine.

    c. mechanical machine.

    d. mixed machine.

_____ **16.** One example of a compound machine is a

    a. door.

    b. pair of scissors.

    c. bicycle.

    d. shovel.

_____ **17.** Which body parts act as the fulcrums of levers?

    a. muscles

    b. bones

    c. joints

    d. tendons

_____ **18.** Which body parts are shaped like wedges?

    a. muscles

    b. tendons

    c. incisors

    d. bones in your legs

_____ **19.** A simple machine that might be thought of as an inclined plane that moves is a

    a. lever.

    b. wheel and axle.

    c. wedge.

    d. pulley.

_____ **20.** Which of these could be considered an inclined plane wrapped around a cylinder?

    a. lever

    b. screw

    c. wheel and axle

    d. pulley

_____ **21.** The fixed point that a lever pivots around is called the

    a. axle.

    b. pulley.

    c. gear.

    d. fulcrum.

_____ **22.** In order to do work on an object, the force you exert must be

    a. the maximum amount of force you are able to exert.

    b. in the same direction as the object's motion.

    c. in a direction opposite to Earth's gravitational force.

    d. quick and deliberate.

_____ **23.** Work = force •

    a. energy.

    b. velocity.

    c. distance.

    d. mass.

_____ 24. When you raise or lower a flag on a flagpole, you are using a

    a. wheel and axle.

    b. pulley.

    c. wedge.

    d. inclined plane.

_____ 25. A term that means the same thing as output force is

    a. input force.

    b. resistance force.

    c. effort force.

    d. multiplying force.

_____ 26. A device with toothed wheels that fit into one another is called a

    a. system of gears.

    b. wheel and axle.

    c. pulley.

    d. fulcrum.

_____ 27. How can a hockey stick be considered a machine?

    a. It multiplies force.

    b. It multiplies distance.

    c. It changes direction.

    d. It reduces friction.

_____ 28. The mechanical advantage of a machine that changes the direction of force only is

    a. 1

    b. less than 1.

    c. greater than 1.

    d. zero.

_____ 29. Most machines in your body, which consist of bones and muscles, are

    a. wedges

    b. levers.

    c. pulleys.

    d. compound machines.

_____ 30. If tight scissors have an efficiency of 50 percent, how much of your work is wasted overcoming friction?

    a. all of it

    b. none of it

    c. one half

    d. 10 percent

B. True or False

If the statement is true, write true. If it is false, change the underlined word or words to make the statement true.

31. Holding a 25-N bag of sugar 1 meter above the floor requires <u>25 joules</u> of work.

_____

_____

32. The work done by a machine is called the <u>output</u> work.

_____

_____

33. The mechanical advantage of a machine that only changes the direction of a force is <u>one</u>.

_____

_____

34. Efficiency compares the output work to the <u>output force</u>.

_____

_____

35. A wheel and axle is a <u>compound</u> machine.

_____

_____

36. A second-class lever always multiplies <u>distance</u>.

_____

_____

37. The ideal mechanical advantage of a wheel and axle is the radius of the wheel <u>times</u> the radius of the axle.

_____

_____

38. Your jaw and teeth act together as a <u>simple</u> machine.

_____

_____

39. When you raise your leg, the <u>knee</u> acts as a fulcrum for the upper leg.

_____

_____

40. You do <u>work</u> on an object when you lift it from the floor to a shelf.

_____

_____

C. Completion
Fill in the word or phrase that best completes each statement.

41. When you drop a rock, the object that does work on the rock as it falls is _____.

_____

_____

42. A gardener pushes on the angled handle of a lawnmower, causing it to move forward across a lawn. The only portion of the gardener's force that does work on the lawnmower is the force in the ____ direction.

_____

_____

43. A newton-meter is a measure of work also known as the _____.

_____

_____

44. The amount of work done in lifting a 25-N bag of sugar 2 meters is the same as lifting two 25-N bags of sugar ___ meter(s).

_____

_____

45. The force applied to a machine is called the _____ force.

_____

_____

46. A simple machine makes work easier by multiplying force or _____, or by changing direction.

_____

_____

47. The ____ mechanical advantage of a machine cannot be predicted in advance because it depends on the efficiency of the machine.

_____

_____

48. The ideal mechanical advantage would equal the actual mechanical advantage if there were no losses due to _____.

_____

_____

49. The efficiency of an actual machine is always less than ____%

_____

_____

50. The output work of a certain machine is 12,600 J. If the input work is 18,000 J, the efficiency is ____.

_____

_____

51. When you use a paint can opener to open a can of paint, you use the paint can opener as a simple machine called a(n) _____.

_____

_____

52. A jar lid is an example of a simple machine called a(n) _____.

_____

_____

53. A screwdriver is a simple machine called a(n) _____.

_____

_____

54. A ramp in a parking garage is an example of a simple machine called a(n) _____.

_____

_____

55. You can increase the ideal mechanical advantage of a first class lever by moving the fulcrum closer to the _____ force.

_____

_____

56. Raising one end of a ramp will _____ its ideal mechanical advantage.

_____

_____

57. The set of gears on a bicycle wheel is classified as a(n) _____ machine.

_____

_____

58. A chef sometimes holds the tip of a knife stationary when chopping food. Held this way, the knife is a compound machine made up of a wedge and a _____.

_____

_____

59. As you wave your hand at the wrist, your hand is acting as a simple machine called a(n) _____.

_____

_____

60. As you bite into a peach, your front teeth act as a simple machine called a(n) _____.

_____

_____

D. Interpreting Diagrams

Use the diagram to answer each question.

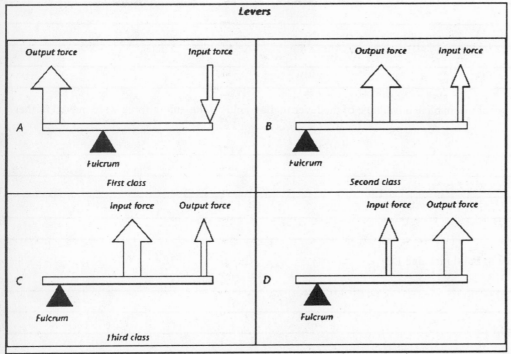

61. In what class of lever is the direction of the input force opposite to the direction of the output force?

_____

_____

_____

_____

_____

62. What class of lever is a pair of scissors? Explain your answer.

_____

_____

_____

_____

63. Which class of lever does not multiply the input force? What is its advantage?

_____

_____

_____

_____

_____

64. To which class of lever does each of the following belong: (a) fishing pole; (b) wheelbarrow; (c) bottle opener; (d) pliers?

_____

_____

_____

_____

65. What would happen to the ideal mechanical advantage of the lever in diagram B if the output force were moved farther from the fulcrum?

_____

_____

_____

_____

66. Why would it be impossible to build machine D?

_____

_____

_____

_____

Use the diagram to answer each question.

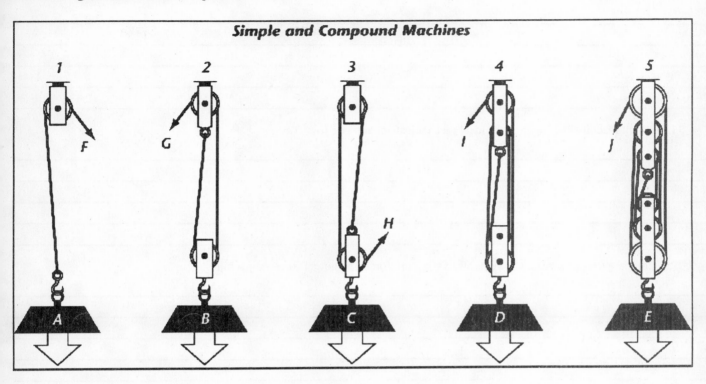

Simple and Compound Machines

67. Is machine 1 classified as a simple or compound machine?

_____

_____

_____

_____

_____

68. What is machine 1 used for?

_____

_____

_____

_____

_____

69. In machine 2, which letter represents the input force?

_____

_____

_____

_____

_____

70. Which machines multiply the input force?

_____

_____

_____

_____

71. Which machine has the greatest ideal mechanical advantage?

_____

_____

_____

_____

72. Compare the distances and directions of the input force and output force in machine 4.

_____

_____

_____

_____

_____

E. Essay

Write an answer to each of the following questions.

73. A bricklayer lifts a stack of bricks onto his shoulder, carries it across a room, and then lifts the bricks onto a ledge above his head. Explain if work is being done in each of these three situations.

_____

_____

_____

_____

_____

74. Explain how the ideal mechanical advantage and efficiency of a machine determine the machine's actual mechanical advantage.

_____
_____
_____
_____
_____
_____
_____

75. A constant push of 250 N is necessary to slide a crate weighing 400 N along a 2.0-m long ramp. If the ramp raises the crate 1.0 m, what is the efficiency of the ramp?

_____
_____
_____
_____
_____
_____
_____

76. Why is it more difficult to steer a bike when your hands are close together on the handlebars?

_____
_____
_____
_____
_____
_____

77. The output force of a lever with an ideal mechanical advantage of 3 is used as the input force of a pulley system with an ideal mechanical advantage of 2. Use the definition of ideal mechanical advantage to determine the ideal mechanical advantage of the compound machine.

_____

_____

_____

_____

_____

_____

_____

78. When you bite with your front teeth, your jaw acts as a third class lever. As you chew with your back teeth, your jaw acts as a second class lever. Explain how your jaw can act as two different classes of levers and how the ideal mechanical advantage of each helps you bite and chew food.

_____

_____

_____

_____

_____

_____

_____

79. Explain why wedges and screws are actually types of inclined planes.

_____

_____

_____

_____

_____

80. You push a food tray 1.5 m along a cafeteria table with a constant force of 18 N. How much work do you do?

_____

_____

_____

_____

Test 62 Book M, Chapter 4: Work and Machines
Answer Key (Short)

__b__	1.
__c__	2.
__a__	3.
__c__	4.
__a__	5.
__c__	6.
__d__	7.
__d__	8.
__d__	9.
__b__	10.
__a__	11.
__c__	12.
__c__	13.
__a__	14.
__b__	15.
__c__	16.
__c__	17.
__c__	18.
__c__	19.
__b__	20.
__d__	21.
__b__	22.
__c__	23.
__b__	24.
__b__	25.
__a__	26.
__b__	27.
__a__	28.
__a__	29.
__c__	30.

31.	false, 0 joules
32.	TRUE
33.	TRUE
34.	false, input work
35.	false, simple
36.	false, force
37.	false, divided by
38.	false, compound
39.	false, hip
40.	TRUE
41.	Earth

42.   horizontal (or forward)

43.   joule

44.   1

45.   input

46.   distance

47.   actual

48.   friction

49.   100

50.   70%

51.   lever

52.   screw

53.   wheel and axle

54.   inclined plane

55.   output

56.   decrease

57.   compound

58.   lever (or second-class lever)

59.   lever

60.   wedge

61.   first-class

62.   First class, because the fulcrum is between the input force and the output force.

63.   Third class. A third class lever multiplies the distance of the input force.

64.   (a) third, (b) second, (c) second, (d) first

65.   The ideal mechanical advantage would decrease.

66.   The machine multiplies both force and distance. The output work of this machine would be greater than the input work, which is impossible because a machine cannot do more output work than input work.

67.   simple machine

68.   lifting objects

69.   G

70.   machines 2, 3, 4, and 5, because at least 2 sections of the rope support the mass

71.   machine 5, because 6 sections of the rope support the mass

72.   The input force moves downward 4 times as far as the output force moves upward.

73.   Work is being done when the bricklayer lifts the stack of bricks to his shoulder and then raises the stack to the ledge. In both situations the bricklayer's force on the stack and the motion of the stack are in the same direction. When the bricklayer carries the stack, no work is being done because his force on the stack (vertical) and motion of the stack (horizontal) are perpendicular to each other.

74.   The actual mechanical advantage of a real machine is always less than the ideal mechanical advantage. The efficiency determines how close the actual mechanical advantage is to the ideal mechanical advantage. As friction is reduced and the efficiency approaches 100%, the actual mechanical advantage approaches the ideal mechanical advantage. If efficiency were 100%, the two would be equal.

75.   The output work is the work you would have to do without the ramp. The input work is the work you do with the ramp. *Efficiency = Output work / Input work* • 100% = 400 J / 500 J • 100% = 80%

76. The handlebars of a bike are an example of a wheel and axle. The center shaft of the handlebars is the axle. The handlebars make up the wheel. Using the handgrips at the ends of the handlebars gives the largest ideal mechanical advantage because the radius of the wheel is largest compared to the radius of the axle. When you move your hands together on the handlebars, the radius of the wheel decreases and the ideal mechanical advantage decreases. A lower ideal mechanical advantage makes steering (turning) the handlebars more difficult.

77. The ideal mechanical advantage of a compound machine is the product of the ideal mechanical advantages of the simple machines that make it up. So the ideal mechanical advantage of the compound machine is 2 times 3, or 6.

78. The fulcrum of the jaw is slightly below and in front of your ears. The input force is at the side of the cheek. When you bite, the output force is located in the front of the mouth. The output distance is greater than input distance. The jaw is a third class lever, so its ideal mechanical advantage is less than one. As a third class lever, the jaw multiplies distance, allowing you to bite quickly with your incisors. When chewing, the output force is near the back of the jaw; the input distance is greater than the output distance. Now the jaw is a second class lever, so its ideal mechanical advantage is greater than one. As a second class lever, the jaw multiplies force, allowing you to chew and grind food more easily.

79. A wedge is shaped like a double inclined plane. A screw is an inclined plane wrapped around a cylinder to form a spiral. Like an inclined plane, the wedge and the screw multiply the input force by having it move a greater distance along a sloping edge. In the case of the wedge and screw, the direction of the output force is perpendicular to the direction of the input force.

80. When pushing the tray, the force on the tray and the motion of the tray are in the same direction. Work = 18 N • 1.5 = 27 J

A. Multiple Choice
   Choose the letter of the correct answer.

_____ 1. The ability to do work is called

    a. velocity.

    b. energy.

    c. conversion.

    d. friction.

_____ 2. Energy is measured in units called

    a. joules.

    b. pounds.

    c. meters.

    d. horsepower.

_____ 3. The energy associated with motion is called

    a. kinetic energy.

    b. elastic potential energy.

    c. gravitational potential energy.

    d. nuclear energy.

_____ 4. Kinetic energy increases as

    a. mass increases and velocity decreases.

    b. mass decreases and velocity increases.

    c. both mass and velocity increase.

    d. both mass and velocity decrease.

_____ 5. The total energy of the particles in an object is called

    a. mechanical energy.

    b. thermal energy.

    c. chemical energy.

    d. electrical energy.

_____ 6. An example of something that stores chemical energy is

    a. lightning.

    b. a microwave.

    c. a match.

    d. the sun.

_____ 7. Moving water can be used to produce electricity because

    a. any form of energy can be converted into any other form.

    b. energy cannot be converted into other forms of energy.

    c. potential energy can be converted into kinetic energy, but not vice versa.

    d. kinetic energy can be converted into potential energy, but not vice versa.

_____ **8.** What type of conversion is taking place when natural gas is used to heat water?

    a. chemical energy into thermal energy

    b. thermal energy into mechanical energy

    c. mechanical energy into electromagnetic energy

    d. electromagnetic energy into chemical energy

_____ **9.** When you rub your hands together on a cold day, you use friction to convert

    a. mechanical energy into thermal energy.

    b. thermal energy into nuclear energy.

    c. nuclear energy into electrical energy.

    d. electrical energy into electromagnetic energy.

_____ **10.** The scientist who suggested that energy can be created under certain conditions was

    a. Newton.

    b. Einstein.

    c. Wright.

    d. Pascal.

_____ **11.** An example of a fossil fuel is

    a. wood.

    b. petroleum.

    c. the sun.

    d. water.

_____ **12.** Fossil fuels contain energy that originally came from

    a. tidal forces.

    b. Earth's core.

    c. the sun.

    d. dinosaurs.

_____ **13.** The process of burning a fuel is called

    a. combustion.

    b. meltdown.

    c. acceleration.

    d. conduction.

_____ **14.** When fossil fuels are burned, their chemical potential energy is converted into

    a. nuclear energy.

    b. electrical energy.

    c. mechanical energy.

    d. thermal energy.

_____ **15.** A device that is twice as powerful as another can do the same amount of work in

    a. half the time.

    b. twice the time.

    c. one third the time.

    d. the same amount of time.

_____ 16. Power equals work divided by

    a. energy.

    b. time.

    c. force.

    d. velocity.

_____ 17. The power of a light bulb that converts electrical energy at a rate of 100 joules per second is

    a. 50 watts.

    b. 200 watts.

    c. 100 watts.

    d. 40 watts.

_____ 18. One horsepower is equal to

    a. 100 watts.

    b. 746 watts.

    c. 746 watts.

    d. 1,769 watts.

_____ 19. The type of energy stored by fossil fuels such as coal is

    a. kinetic energy.

    b. mechanical energy.

    c. chemical potential energy.

    d. electromagnetic energy.

_____ 20. Which of the following has kinetic energy?

    a. a rock poised for a fall

    b. an archer's bow that is drawn back

    c. a rolling bowling ball

    d. a car waiting at a red light

_____ 21. Unlike kinetic energy, potential energy is

    a. energy of motion.

    b. stored.

    c. conserved.

    d. not measurable.

_____ 22. Potential energy that depends on height is called

    a. kinetic energy.

    b. gravitational potential energy.

    c. elastic potential energy.

    d. mechanical energy.

_____ 23. When generators are spun by turbines, they

    a. produce nuclear energy.

    b. store potential energy.

    c. produce electricity.

    d. burn fossil fuels.

_____ **24.** What type of energy does a spinning turbine have?

    a. electrical energy

    b. nuclear energy

    c. thermal energy

    d. mechanical energy

_____ **25.** The rate at which work is done is

    a. energy.

    b. power.

    c. velocity.

    d. force.

_____ **26.** Energy stored in the core of an atom is called

    a. electromagnetic energy

    b. nuclear energy

    c. mechanical energy

    d. chemical energy

_____ **27.** Visible light is an example of

    a. chemical energy.

    b. electrical energy.

    c. electromagnetic energy.

    d. nuclear energy.

_____ **28.** Power is measured in units called

    a. joules.

    b. pounds.

    c. watts.

    d. newtons.

_____ **29.** Niagara Falls is a good example of

    a. kinetic energy being converted into potential energy.

    b. potential energy being converted into kinetic energy.

    c. energy being lost.

    d. energy being created.

_____ **30.** The law of conservation of energy states that when one form of energy is converted into another,

    a. energy is destroyed in the process.

    b. no energy is destroyed in the process.

    c. energy is created in the process.

    d. some amount of energy cannot be accounted for.

B. True or False

If the statement is true, write true. If it is false, change the underlined word or words to make the statement true.

31. When work is done on an object, the object gains <u>energy</u>.

_____

_____

32. The <u>kinetic</u> energy of a book on a shelf is equal to the work done to lift the book to the shelf.

_____

_____

33. A compressed spring has <u>elastic potential</u> energy.

_____

_____

34. An ice cube melts when its <u>mechanical</u> energy increases.

_____

_____

35. A light bulb converts <u>electrical</u> energy into electromagnetic energy.

_____

_____

36. In a machine, work output is less than work input because some energy is converted into <u>thermal</u> energy.

_____

_____

37. <u>Animals</u>, algae, and certain bacteria convert energy from sunlight into chemical energy through the process of photosynthesis.

_____

_____

38. During combustion, a fuel's <u>electromagnetic</u> energy is converted into thermal energy.

_____

_____

39. <u>Energy</u> is the rate at which work is done.

_____

_____

40. A 100-watt light bulb converts electrical energy into electromagnetic energy at a <u>slower</u> rate than a 40 watt light bulb.

_____

_____

C. Completion
Fill in the word or phrase that best completes each statement.

41. A force pushes an object over a distance of 2 m. If 6 J of energy is transferred to the object, the size of the force is _____ N.

_____

_____

42. A truck and car are moving at the same speed. The truck has greater kinetic energy because its ___ is greater.

_____

_____

43. If the speed of an object is doubled, its kinetic energy is multiplied by ___.

_____

_____

44. The energy in the fuel of a rocket engine is _____ energy.

_____

_____

45. A baseball flying through the air has _____ energy because of its motion.

_____

_____

46. _____ energy, such as ultraviolet radiation, travels in the form of waves.

_____

_____

47. To maintain your body temperature, your body converts chemical potential energy into _____ energy.

_____

_____

48. As water runs over a waterfall, its potential energy is converted into _____ energy.

_____

_____

49. An electric motor converts electrical energy to _____ energy.

_____

_____

50. The law of _____ states that energy cannot be created or destroyed.

_____

_____

51. In nuclear reactions, huge amounts of energy are produced by destroying tiny amounts of _____.

_____

_____

52. Fossil fuels contain _____ potential energy stored millions of years ago.

_____

_____

53. Over long periods of time, buried animal and plant remains are converted into coal by high temperatures and _____ .

_____

_____

54. In power plants, generators convert mechanical energy into _____ energy.

_____

_____

55. In power plants, coal is burned to produce _____, which is then used to turn a turbine.

_____

_____

56. Power is equal to _____ divided by time.

_____

_____

57. A device that is twice as powerful as another can do _____ the amount of work in the same amount of time.

_____

_____

58. Power is the rate at which _____ is transferred from one object to another or converted from one form to another.

_____

_____

59. A 200-watt light bulb converts electrical energy at a rate of _____ J each second.

_____

_____

60. Work is the transfer of _____ from one object to another.

_____

_____

D. Interpreting Diagrams

Use the diagram to answer each question.

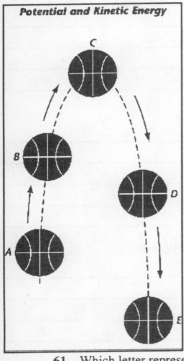

Potential and Kinetic Energy

61. Which letter represents the position at which the basketball has the greatest potential energy? Explain.

_____

_____

_____

_____

_____

62. Which letter represents the position at which the basketball has the greatest kinetic energy? Explain.

_____

_____

_____

_____

_____

63. Which letter represents the position at which the basketball has the least potential energy? Explain.

_____

_____

_____

_____

_____

64. Assume that the potential energy of the basketball is 0 J at position E. At which point is the ball's potential energy half of its maximum value? Explain.

_____

_____

_____

_____

65. Compare the speed of the basketball at positions A and D. Explain your comparison.

_____

_____

_____

_____

66. Which letter represents the position at which the basketball has the least kinetic energy? Explain.

_____

_____

_____

_____

Use the diagram to answer each question.

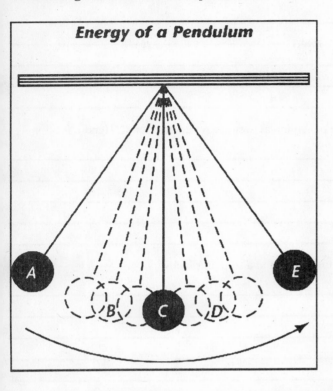

Energy of a Pendulum

67. Which letters represent the positions of maximum potential energy of the pendulum? Explain.

_____

_____

_____

_____

_____   _____

68. Describe how the kinetic and potential energies of the pendulum are changing at position B.

_____

_____

_____

_____

69. Describe how the kinetic and potential energies of the pendulum are changing at position D.

_____

_____

_____

_____

70. Is the potential energy of the pendulum changing at position E? Explain.

_____

_____

_____

_____

71. Compare the sum of the kinetic and potential energies of the pendulum at position A and position C. (Ignore friction.)

_____

_____

_____

_____

72. If the pendulum is allowed to continue to swing, it will eventually come to a stop. Explain why.

_____

_____

_____

_____

E. Essay
Write an answer to each of the following questions.

73. Describe the energy of a bowling ball as it rolls toward and hits a bowling pin.

_____

_____

_____

_____

_____

_____

74. Describe six different forms of energy.

_____

_____

_____

_____

_____

_____

_____

75. Describe two energy conversions that take place when you warm a cup of cocoa in a microwave oven.

_____

_____

_____

_____

_____

_____

_____

76. A 1-kg cart slams into a stationary 1-kg cart at 2 m/s. The carts stick together and move forward at a speed of 1 m/s. Determine whether kinetic energy was conserved in the collision. Use the law of conservation of energy to explain the collision.

_____

_____

_____

_____

_____

_____

77. Explain how both plants and animals stored the energy found in fossil fuels.

_____

_____

_____

_____

_____

78. A generator supplies 15,000 J of electrical energy each minute. Determine the maximum number of 100-W light bulbs that the generator can power.

_____

_____

_____

_____

_____

_____

79. A 1200-kg car reaches a speed of 11 m/s from rest in 10 seconds. Determine the car's power.

_____

_____

_____

_____

_____

_____

80. How high must you lift a 25-newton book for it to have the same increase in potential energy as a 20-newton book that was lifted 0.5 m?

_____

_____

_____

_____

_____

_____

Test 63 Book M, Chapter 5: Energy and Power
Answer Key (Short)

__b__	1.
__a__	2.
__a__	3.
__c__	4.
__b__	5.
__c__	6.
__a__	7.
__a__	8.
__a__	9.
__b__	10.
__b__	11.
__c__	12.
__a__	13.
__d__	14.
__a__	15.
__b__	16.
__c__	17.
__b__	18.
__c__	19.
__c__	20.
__b__	21.
__b__	22.
__c__	23.
__d__	24.
__b__	25.
__b__	26.
__c__	27.
__c__	28.
__b__	29.
__b__	30.

31.	TRUE
32.	false, gravitational potential
33.	TRUE
34.	false, thermal
35.	TRUE
36.	TRUE
37.	false, Plants
38.	false, chemical
39.	false, Power
40.	false, faster
41.	3

42.	mass
43.	four
44.	chemical potential
45.	mechanical
46.	Electromagnetic
47.	thermal
48.	kinetic
49.	mechanical
50.	conservation of energy
51.	matter
52.	chemical
53.	pressure
54.	electrical
55.	steam
56.	work
57.	twice
58.	energy
59.	200
60.	energy

61.   C. At this point, which is the highest point, all of the ball's energy is gravitational potential energy. The ball does not have kinetic energy because it is not moving at this point.

62.   E. As the ball falls from C to E, potential energy is converted to kinetic energy. The speed of the ball increases as it falls, which means that the ball attains its greatest speed at E.

63.   E. The potential energy of the ball depends on its height. Since E is the lowest point, the ball has the least amount of potential energy at this point.

64.   D. Potential energy decreases from its maximum value at C to its minimum value at E. The point halfway between C and E is the point at which the ball has half of its maximum potential energy.

65.   The speed of the ball is less at D than A. The sum of the kinetic and potential energies at A must equal the sum of the kinetic and potential energies at D. Because the basketball is at a lower position at A, it has less potential energy than at position D. So, at position A the basketball must have more kinetic energy than at position D. Because the mass of the basketball doesn't change, the difference in kinetic energies must be due to a faster speed at position A.

66.   C. Kinetic energy depends on the speed of the ball. As the ball rises from A to C, it slows down until the point at which it changes direction and begins to fall.

67.   A and E, because the pendulum is highest at these points

68.   The kinetic energy of the pendulum is increasing and the potential energy is decreasing. Potential energy is being converted to kinetic energy.

69.   The kinetic energy of the pendulum is decreasing and the potential energy is increasing. Kinetic energy is being converted to potential energy.

70.   No. The potential energy of the pendulum reaches its maximum value at position E, and is neither increasing nor decreasing at that point.

71.   From the law of conservation of energy, the sum of the kinetic and potential energies of the pendulum is constant, assuming no losses from friction. So the potential energy at A is equal to the kinetic energy at C.

72.   As the pendulum swings back and forth, the pendulum encounters friction in the air through which it moves. As a result of that friction, mechanical energy is converted to thermal energy. Eventually all the mechanical energy is converted to thermal energy and the pendulum comes to a stop.

73. Answers may vary. As the ball rolls, it has some energy. In other words, it has the ability to do work and move the pin some distance. When it hits the bowling pin, it does work on the pin. During this process, some energy is transferred from the ball to the pin. The pin then has the ability to do work. For example, the first pin might hit and move another bowling pin. After hitting the pin, the bowling ball has less energy than before, so it slows down.

74. Mechanical energy is energy associated with motion or position. Thermal energy is the total energy of the particles in an object. Chemical energy is energy stored in chemical bonds that hold compounds together. Electrical energy is energy associated with moving charges, or electric current. Electromagnetic energy is the energy of radiation, for example visible light or microwaves. Nuclear energy is stored in the core, or nucleus of an atom.

75. The microwave oven converts electrical energy to electromagnetic energy in the form of microwaves (and visible light as well.) When the cocoa absorbs energy from the microwaves, electromagnetic energy is converted to thermal energy, which causes the cocoa to become warm.

76. Before the collision: *Kinetic energy = Mass • Velocity^2 / 2 = (1 kg • (2 m/s)^2)/ 2 = 2 J* After the collision: *Kinetic energy = Mass • Velocity^2 / 2 = (2 kg • (1 m/s)^2) / 2 = 1 J* Kinetic energy was not conserved because the kinetic energy was reduced during the collision. However, energy is always conserved. The "lost energy" was converted into thermal energy.

77. During photosynthesis, plants, algae, and certain bacteria convert electromagnetic energy into chemical potential energy. Some of this chemical potential energy is stored in the plants. Animals that eat the plants obtain some of this energy and store it in their own cells. When ancient animals and plants died, the chemical potential energy was trapped within their remains, which were slowly changed into fossil fuels over time.

78. The power of the generator: Power = 15,000 J/60 s = 250 W. Because each light bulb requires 100 W, only 2 bulbs can be operated by the generator.

79. The work done by the engine is equal to the change in the car's kinetic energy. The change in kinetic energy of the car is its final kinetic energy minus its starting kinetic energy. Since its starting kinetic energy is zero (the car was at rest), the change in kinetic energy is equal to the final kinetic energy. *Kinetic energy = Mass • Velocity^2 / 2 =* (1,200 kg • (11 m/s)^2)/2 = 72,600 J So work is equal to 72,600 J. *Power = Work / Time =* 72,600J / 10s = 7,260 W

80. The increase in gravitational potential energy of the 20-newton book is 10 J. (20 N • 0.5 m = 10 J) The 25-newton book must be lifted to a height of 0.4 m to have an increase in gravitational potential energy of 10 J. (25 N • 0.4 m = 10 J)

A. Multiple Choice
   Choose the letter of the correct answer.

_____ 1.   No more energy can be removed from matter at

   a.   its freezing point.
   b.   0°C.
   c.   absolute zero.
   d.   273 K.

_____ 2.   The total energy of all the particles in a substance is called

   a.   temperature.
   b.   thermal energy.
   c.   degrees.
   d.   mass.

_____ 3.   The more particles a substance has at a given temperature,

   a.   the higher its temperature.
   b.   the more thermal energy it has.
   c.   the more degrees it has.
   d.   the more kelvins it has.

_____ 4.   The movement of thermal energy from a warmer object to a cooler object is called

   a.   heat.
   b.   temperature.
   c.   motion.
   d.   momentum.

_____ 5.   Heat, like work, is an energy transfer measured in

   a.   watts.
   b.   degrees.
   c.   joules.
   d.   kelvins.

_____ 6.   Heat is transferred from one particle of matter to another without the movement of matter itself in a process called

   a.   conduction.
   b.   convection.
   c.   radiation.
   d.   insulation.

_____ 7.   The transfer of energy by electromagnetic waves is called

   a.   conduction.
   b.   convection.
   c.   radiation.
   d.   insulation.

_____ **8.** Heat transfer occurs

    a. in many directions.

    b. both from warm objects to colder ones and from cold objects to warmer ones.

    c. only from warm objects to colder ones.

    d. only from cold objects to warmer ones.

_____ **9.** A material that does NOT conduct heat well is called a(n)

    a. insulator.

    b. conductor.

    c. metal.

    d. radiator.

_____ **10.** The amount of energy required to raise the temperature of 1 kilogram of a substance by 1 kelvin is called its

    a. specific heat.

    b. heat transfer.

    c. change of state.

    d. melting point.

_____ **11.** Which of these substances has the highest specific heat?

    a. aluminum

    b. glass

    c. sand

    d. water

_____ **12.** How many different forms, or states, does matter on Earth exist in?

    a. one

    b. two

    c. three

    d. fifty

_____ **13.** The addition or loss of thermal energy changes the arrangement of the particles during

    a. a change of state.

    b. conduction.

    c. convection.

    d. radiation.

_____ **14.** The temperature at which a solid changes into a liquid is called

    a. the boiling point.

    b. the freezing point.

    c. the melting point.

    d. absolute zero.

_____ **15.** Vaporization that takes place only at the surface of a liquid is called

    a. melting.

    b. boiling.

    c. evaporation.

    d. condensation.

_____ **16.** The expanding of matter when it is heated is known as

    a.   condensation.

    b.   evaporation.

    c.   thermal expansion.

    d.   vaporization.

_____ **17.** One common application of thermal expansion is

    a.   a toaster oven.

    b.   a microwave oven.

    c.   a refrigerator.

    d.   a thermometer.

_____ **18.** A steam engine is an example of a(n)

    a.   external combustion engine.

    b.   internal combustion engine.

    c.   four-stroke engine.

    d.   eight-cylinder engine.

_____ **19.** In an internal combustion engine, each up or down movement by a piston is called a

    a.   crank.

    b.   turn.

    c.   stroke.

    d.   combustion.

_____ **20.** A device that uses an outside energy source to transfer thermal energy from a cool area to a warm area is called

    a.   a thermometer.

    b.   a vaporizer.

    c.   a combustion engine.

    d.   a refrigerator.

_____ **21.** A refrigerator requires

    a.   combustion.

    b.   a refrigerant.

    c.   warm air.

    d.   radiation.

_____ **22.** Water freezes at 32 degrees on which temperature scale?

    a.   Fahrenheit

    b.   Celsius

    c.   Kelvin

    d.   absolute zero

_____ **23.** Absolute zero is shown as 0 on which scale?

    a.   Fahrenheit

    b.   Celsius

    c.   Kelvin

    d.   Centigrade

_____ 24. Which of the following is true of the Celsius scale?

     a. 212 degrees is the boiling point of water.

     b. 0 degrees is absolute zero.

     c. 0 degrees is the freezing point of water.

     d. 32 degrees is the freezing point of water.

_____ 25. The conversion of thermal energy into mechanical energy requires a

     a. thermometer.

     b. heat engine.

     c. vaporizer.

     d. thermostat.

_____ 26. Any temperature on the Kelvin scale can be changed to Celsius degrees by

     a. subtracting 100 from it.

     b. adding 212 to it.

     c. adding 273 to it.

     d. subtracting 32 from it.

_____ 27. Heated air moves from baseboard heaters to the rest of a room in a process called

     a. conduction.

     b. convection.

     c. radiation.

     d. insulation.

_____ 28. Which of these is a good conductor?

     a. wood

     b. paper

     c. silver

     d. air

_____ 29. Which statement is true of gases?

     a. The particles that make up gases are packed together in a relatively fixed position.

     b. Gases have a definite volume.

     c. Gases have a definite shape.

     d. Gases expand to fill all the space available.

_____ 30. A measure of the average kinetic energy of the individual particles in an object is called

     a. thermal energy.

     b. conduction.

     c. convection.

     d. temperature.

B. True or False

If the statement is true, write true. If it is false, change the underlined word or words to make the statement true.

31. A student lists three temperature measurements: 100°F, 100°C, and 100 K. Of the three measurements, <u>100 K</u> is the highest temperature.

_____

_____

32. The more particles a substance has at a given temperature, the more <u>thermal</u> energy it has.

_____

_____

33. Heat is <u>kinetic</u> energy moving from a warmer object to a cooler object.

_____

_____

34. During <u>conduction</u> heat is transferred by the movement of currents within a fluid.

_____

_____

35. Trapped air is a good <u>conductor</u> because it reduces heat transfer.

_____

_____

36. Particles of matter in the <u>solid</u> state are held together but can move around each other.

_____

_____

37. As most substances are cooled, they <u>expand</u>.

_____

_____

38. A material <u>gains</u> thermal energy as it freezes.

_____

_____

39. During the <u>power</u> stroke of a four-stroke engine, the fuel mixture is squeezed into a smaller volume.

_____

_____

40. A change in the thermal energy of an object is related to the object's specific heat, <u>temperature change</u>, and mass.

_____

_____

C. Completion
Fill in the word or phrase that best completes each statement.

41. If two glasses of water are at the same temperature, the average _____ energy of the particles of water in each glass is the same.

_____

_____

42. A one-degree change in temperature on the Celsius temperature scale is equal to a one-degree temperature change on the _____ temperature scale.

_____

_____

43. An increase in the total energy of the particles in a substance results in an increase in the _____ energy of the substance.

_____

_____

44. Even though the water in a filled bathtub may be at the same temperature as water in a teacup, the water in the bathtub has more _____ because it contains a greater number of water molecules.

_____

_____

45. The SI unit of heat is the _____.

_____

_____

46. If _____ is transferred from object A to object B, the thermal energy of object A decreases.

_____

_____

47. The handle of a spoon in a bowl of soup becomes warm due to heat transfer by the process of _____.

_____

_____

48. Stars transfer thermal energy by the process of _____.

_____

_____

49. The joule per kilogram-kelvin is the SI unit for _____.

_____

_____

50. Iron has a higher specific heat than silver. If 1 kg of iron and 1 kg of silver absorb equal amounts of heat, the temperature of the _____ will increase by a greater amount.

_____

_____

51. Fiberglass is a common _____, which is a material that reduces the transfer of heat.

_____

_____

52. Bare feet feel colder on a tile floor than on a rug because the tile floor is a better _____ of heat.

_____

_____

53. The most disorganized state of matter is the _____ state.

_____

_____

54. During a change of state, the addition or loss of _____ energy changes the arrangement of the particles in the substance.

_____

_____

55. A thermometer uses the fact that liquids, such as alcohol and mercury, _____ when heated.

_____

_____

56. The bimetallic strip in a thermostat bends as it is heated because the two metals in the strip _____ at different rates.

_____

_____

57. Boiling is vaporization that takes place at or _____ the surface of a liquid.

_____

_____

58. As a substance changes state, there is no change in the _____ of the substance.

_____

_____

59. Most gasoline engines are _____-stroke engines.

_____

_____

60. A refrigerator uses _____ energy to transfer thermal energy from a cool area to a warm area.

_____

_____

D. Interpreting Diagrams
Use the diagram to answer each question.

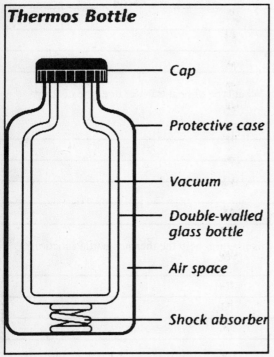

Thermos Bottle

- Cap
- Protective case
- Vacuum
- Double-walled glass bottle
- Air space
- Shock absorber

61. For what purpose is this device used?

_____

_____

_____

_____

62. What physical process is reduced by the device shown?

_____

_____

_____

63. What purpose do you think the air space serves?

_____

_____

_____

_____

64. Why do you think the device shown contains a vacuum, or space from which the air has been removed?

_____

_____

_____

_____

65. The glass walls of the device are covered with a shiny metallic coating. What type of heat transfer does the coating reduce? Explain.

_____

_____

_____

_____

66. The cap on the thermos bottle is made of plastic. How does the use of this material help the thermos bottle function?

_____

_____

_____

_____

Use the diagram to answer each question.

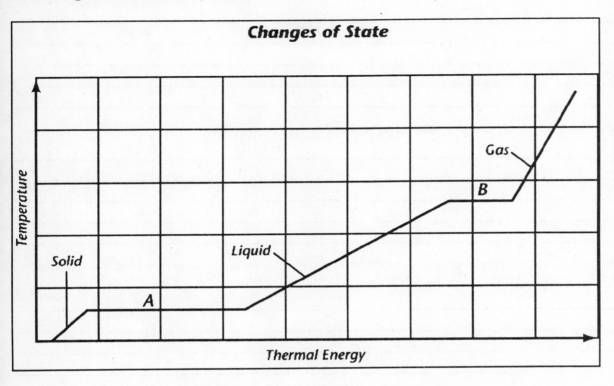

Changes of State

67. What states of matter of a pure substance are represented in the graph?

_____

_____

_____

_____

_____

68. What happens to each of the variables-temperature and thermal energy - during the changes indicated by line segments A and B?

_____

_____

_____

_____

69. Suppose the material is being heated. What change of state is represented by line segment A?

_____

_____

_____

_____

_____

70. Suppose the material is being cooled. What change of state is represented by line segment A?

_____

_____

_____

_____

71. What is the temperature of the change of state represented by line segment A called?

_____

_____

_____

_____

72. What is happening to the average kinetic energy of the particles during the change of state represented by line segment B? Explain.

_____

_____

_____

_____

E. Essay

Write an answer to each of the following questions.

73. Which is a larger change in temperature - a change of 1 Celsius degree or 1 Fahrenheit degree? Explain.

_____

_____

_____

_____

_____

74. Explain the role of density in the formation of convection currents.

_____

_____

_____

_____

_____

_____

_____

75. What is the difference between thermal energy and heat?

_____

_____

_____

_____

_____

_____

_____

76. In hot and dry climates, fountains of gently dripping water are often used to cool courtyards. Explain how.

_____

_____

_____

_____

_____

_____

77. Why is mercury used instead of alcohol in thermometers that are used to measure very high temperatures?

_____

_____

_____

_____

_____

_____

78. Why does steam at 100°C cause more severe burns than the same mass of water at 100°C?

_____

_____

_____

_____

_____

_____

_____

79. Why are two changes of state of the refrigerant necessary to operate a refrigerator?

_____

_____

_____

_____

_____

_____

_____

80. Why are most gasoline engines in automobiles called four-stroke heat engines?

_____

_____

_____

_____

_____

_____

_____

Test 64 Book M, Chapter 6: Thermal Energy and Heat

Answer Key (Short)

    __c__   **1.**

    __b__   **2.**

    __b__   **3.**

    __a__   **4.**

    __c__   **5.**

    __a__   **6.**

    __c__   **7.**

    __c__   **8.**

    __a__   **9.**

    __a__   **10.**

    __d__   **11.**

    __c__   **12.**

    __a__   **13.**

    __c__   **14.**

    __c__   **15.**

    __c__   **16.**

    __d__   **17.**

    __a__   **18.**

    __c__   **19.**

    __d__   **20.**

    __b__   **21.**

    __a__   **22.**

    __c__   **23.**

    __c__   **24.**

    __b__   **25.**

    __c__   **26.**

    __b__   **27.**

    __c__   **28.**

    __d__   **29.**

    __d__   **30.**

31.   false, 100°C

32.   TRUE

33.   false, thermal

34.   false, convection

35.   false, insulator

36.   false, liquid

37.   false, contract

38.   false, releases or loses

39.   false, compression

40.   TRUE

41.   kinetic

42.		Kelvin
43.		thermal
44.		thermal energy
45.		joule
46.		heat
47.		conduction
48.		radiation
49.		specific heat
50.		silver
51.		insulator
52.		conductor
53.		gas(eous)
54.		thermal
55.		expand
56.		expand
57.		below
58.		temperature
59.		four
60.		mechanical

61. It is a thermos bottle used to keep liquids hot or cold.

62. heat transfer

63. The air space is a good insulator, which reduces heat transfer.

64. The vacuum between the double walls of the glass bottle reduces heat transfer by convection. Because the vacuum contains little or no air, a convection current cannot form.

65. The metallic coating limits heat transfer by radiation, because the shiny surface reflects electromagnetic waves.

66. Plastic is a good insulator. Its use prevents heat transfer by conduction.

67. solid, liquid, and gas

68. Although thermal energy increases in each case, temperature remains constant. These lines indicate a change of state. There is no temperature change in a substance during a change of state.

69. melting

70. freezing

71. the freezing point or melting point

72. The average kinetic energy of the particles is not changing because the temperature of the substance is not changing.

73. A change of temperature of 1 Celsius degree is greater than a temperature change of 1 Fahrenheit degree because a Celsius degree is larger than a Fahrenheit degree. The Celsius degree is larger because there are 100 Celsius degrees between the freezing and boiling points of water, but there are 180 Fahrenheit degrees between the same points.

74. Convection currents are formed when a fluid is heated. As it absorbs heat, it expands, which causes its density to decrease. If a fluid is heated from below, the warmer, less dense fluid rises in the colder, denser fluid around it. Cooler, denser fluid sinks into its place. This fluid is warmed, becomes less dense, and rises. The warmer, less dense fluid transfers heat to the fluid around it as it rises. As it transfers heat, it cools, becomes denser, and sinks. The continuous rising of warmed fluid and the sinking of cooled fluid form convection currents.

75. Thermal energy is the total energy of all of the particles of a substance. Heat is the movement of thermal energy from a substance at a higher temperature to another at a lower temperature. Thermal energy is a form of energy, while heat is a form of energy transfer.

76.   As the water drips, it evaporates. As the water evaporates, it gains thermal energy from the surrounding air. As the air loses thermal energy, it cools.

77.   The boiling point of mercury is much higher than the boiling point of alcohol, so the mercury will remain a liquid at much higher temperatures than the alcohol. Alcohol might boil and give an inaccurate temperature reading or perhaps break the thermometer.

78.   Because the temperature and mass of the steam and water are the same, the average kinetic energy of the water vapor and liquid water molecules are the same. However, the water vapor molecules have absorbed heat because they are no longer held in an arrangement as a liquid. So, the steam has more thermal energy (total energy) than the liquid water.

79.   The liquid refrigerant must evaporate (change from a liquid to a gas) so that it can absorb heat from the interior of the refrigerator and cool the food. As a gas it must condense into a liquid so that it can release the absorbed heat to the outside and be recycled through the refrigerator to absorb more heat.

80.   The engine in a car is called a heat engine because it converts thermal energy to mechanical energy. It produces thermal energy by combustion, which is the burning of a fuel, inside a cylinder. The engine is called a four-stroke engine because four movements of the piston up or down in the cylinder (each called a stroke) are needed to (a) pull fuel into the cylinder (intake stroke-piston down), (b) compress the fuel (compression stroke-piston up), (c) have the combustion gases do work on the piston (power stroke-piston down), and (d) push the gases out of the cylinder (exhaust stroke-piston up).

Test 65 Book N, Chapter 1: Magnetism and Electromagnetism

A. Multiple Choice
Choose the letter of the correct answer.

_____ 1. What happens if you break a magnet in half?

    a. One half will have a north pole only and one half will have a south pole only.

    b. Neither half will have a pole.

    c. Each half will be a new magnet, with both a north and south pole.

    d. Neither half will be able to attract or repel.

_____ 2. Magnetic poles that are alike

    a. attract each other.

    b. repel each other.

    c. do not react to each other.

    d. always point toward the north.

_____ 3. The region around a magnet where the magnetic force is exerted is known as its

    a. magnetic pole.

    b. lodestone.

    c. magnetic field.

    d. magnetic domain.

_____ 4. A cluster of billions of atoms that all have magnetic fields lined up in the same way is known as a

    a. magnetic field line.

    b. magnetic pole.

    c. magnetic domain.

    d. permanent magnet.

_____ 5. An example of a common ferromagnetic material is

    a. plastic.

    b. hydrogen.

    c. nickel.

    d. copper.

_____ 6. Magnetic field lines around a bar magnet

    a. are perpendicular to the magnet.

    b. extend outward from the north pole only.

    c. are closest together at the poles.

    d. are perfectly straight.

_____ 7. Where is the magnetic north pole?

    a. at the geographic north pole

    b. at the geographic south pole

    c. along the coast of Antarctica

    d. in northern Canada

_____ 8. Streams of electrically charged particles flowing at high speeds from the sun make up the

    a. magnetosphere.

    b. solar wind.

    c. magnetic domain.

    d. magnetic field.

_____ 9. If you are in the northern hemisphere and see the Northern Lights, you are seeing

    a. an aurora.

    b. a magnetic field.

    c. the magnetosphere.

    d. magnesia.

_____ 10. Earth's magnetic field completely reverses about every

    a. day.

    b. lunar cycle.

    c. century.

    d. million years.

_____ 11. A magnetic field is produced by moving electrons, which carry an electric

    a. proton.

    b. charge.

    c. circuit.

    d. resistance.

_____ 12. An electric current produces a(an)

    a. magnetic domain.

    b. magnetic field.

    c. electrical resistance.

    d. permanent magnet.

_____ 13. A complete path through which electric charges can flow is a(an)

    a. electric circuit.

    b. electrical resistance.

    c. magnetic field line.

    d. magnetic pole.

_____ 14. What do toasters, radios, televisions, and electric guitars all have in common?

    a. They are all insulators.

    b. They all contain magnets.

    c. They all contain electric circuits.

    d. They are all superconductors.

_____ 15. Materials that allow the charges of an electric current to move freely through them are called

    a. insulators.

    b. conductors.

    c. resistors.

    d. magnets.

_____ **16.** An example of an insulator is

    a.   rubber.

    b.   copper.

    c.   silver.

    d.   iron.

_____ **17.** A solenoid with a ferromagnetic core is called a(n)

    a.   electromagnet.

    b.   magnetic pole.

    c.   lodestone.

    d.   temporary magnet.

_____ **18.** You can increase the strength of an electromagnet's field by

    a.   decreasing the current in the wire.

    b.   decreasing the number of loops in the wire.

    c.   using a stronger ferromagnetic material for the core.

    d.   increasing the thickness of the insulation on the wire.

_____ **19.** Every magnet, regardless of its shape, has two

    a.   magnetic poles.

    b.   magnetic charges.

    c.   magnetic fields.

    d.   magnetic domains.

_____ **20.** The magnetic properties of a material depend on its

    a.   shape.

    b.   atomic structure.

    c.   position.

    d.   magnetic poles.

_____ **21.** A magnet made from hard steel is most likely a(n)

    a.   permanent magnet.

    b.   temporary magnet.

    c.   electromagnet.

    d.   lodestone.

_____ **22.** How can you destroy a magnet's magnetism?

    a.   by putting it in water

    b.   by cooling it

    c.   by heating it

    d.   by breaking it into pieces

_____ **23.** A device that uses electrical energy as it interferes with the flow of current is a(n)

    a.   insulator.

    b.   conductor.

    c.   resistor.

    d.   superconductor.

_____ 24. An example of a conductor is

    a. wood.

    b. glass.

    c. plastic.

    d. aluminum.

_____ 25. The angle between geographic north and the north to which a compass needle points is known as

    a. the magnetic field line.

    b. the magnetic domain.

    c. magnetic declination.

    d. the magnetosphere.

_____ 26. Superconductors are not commonly used because they

    a. have a high electrical resistance.

    b. require very low temperatures.

    c. lose energy as current flows through them.

    d. are inefficient.

_____ 27. A current-carrying coil of wire with many loops is called a(n)

    a. insulator.

    b. solenoid.

    c. resistor.

    d. aurora.

_____ 28. Since Earth produces a strong magnetic field,

    a. Earth can make magnets.

    b. Earth can attract other planets.

    c. meteorites tend to move in Earth's direction.

    d. the ground will repel a magnet placed upside-down.

_____ 29. An electromagnet would most likely be used as a

    a. pocket compass.

    b. device on the end of a crane to lift junked cars.

    c. ski lift.

    d. refrigerator decoration.

_____ 30. The ampere is a unit of

    a. magnetism.

    b. electric current.

    c. electric charge.

    d. temperature.

B. True or False

If the statement is true, write true. If it is false, change the underlined word or words to make the statement true.

31. A magnetic pole is the part of a magnet where the magnetic effect is <u>weakest</u>.

_____

_____

32. In a magnetized material, most of the <u>domains</u> are lined up in the same direction.

_____

_____

33. Magnetic field lines curve out from one pole and return to the <u>same</u> pole.

_____

_____

34. The <u>magnetic domains</u> are two regions of space that surround Earth and contain electrons and protons traveling at high speeds.

_____

_____

35. Charged particles from the solar wind come closest to Earth at the <u>equator</u>, where Earth's magnetic field lines dip down to Earth's surface.

_____

_____

36. An electric current <u>cannot</u> be used to deflect a compass needle.

_____

_____

37. Copper is a good <u>conductor</u> of electric current.

_____

_____

38. The electrons in an insulator are <u>loosely</u> bound to their atoms.

_____

_____

39. A straight, unbroken line in a circuit diagram represents a <u>switch</u>.

_____

_____

40. Increasing the number of loops in an electromagnet will cause the strength of its magnetic field to <u>decrease</u>.

_____

_____

C. Completion

Fill in the word or phrase that best completes each statement.

41. When placed near each other, unlike magnetic poles _____ each other.

_____

_____

42. A maglev train is pushed off the ground because magnets in the bottom of the train and magnets in the guideway beneath the train have ___ magnetic poles.

_____

_____

43. A magnetic _____ is a cluster of billions of atoms that all have magnetic fields lined up in the same way.

_____

_____

44. An atom can act as a tiny magnet due to the spinning and orbiting motion of negatively charged particles called _____.

_____

_____

45. A _____ material, such as iron, shows strong magnetic effects.

_____

_____

46. A _____ is the region of magnetic force around a magnet.

_____

_____

47. Earth's magnetism is thought to be due to the circulation of molten iron and nickel within Earth's _____.

_____

_____

48. The angle between true north and the north to which a compass needle points is known as _____.

_____

_____

49. Alternating bands of magnetic materials on the sea floor show that Earth's magnetic field occasionally _____ .

_____

_____

50. Molten rock that formed the ocean floor contained _____, which lined up in the direction of Earth's magnetic field.

_____

_____

51. Protons and electrons have a property called electric _____.

_____

_____

52. The magnetic field lines near a straight, current-carrying wire are in the shape of a _____.

_____

_____

53. A(n) _____ is a material in which charges are not able to move freely.

_____

_____

54. Superconductors allow electric current to flow without resistance, but only at very low _____.

_____

_____

55. The flow of charge through a material is called electric _____.

_____

_____

56. In a flashlight, the battery acts as a source of electrical _____.

_____

_____

57. A switch can be used to open and close an electric _____.

_____

_____

58. A _____ uses electrical energy as it interferes with the flow of charge.

_____

_____

59. A current-carrying coil of wire with many loops is called a(n) _____.

_____

_____

60. A solenoid with a ferromagnetic core is called a(n) _____.

_____

_____

D. Interpreting Diagrams
Use the diagram to answer each question.

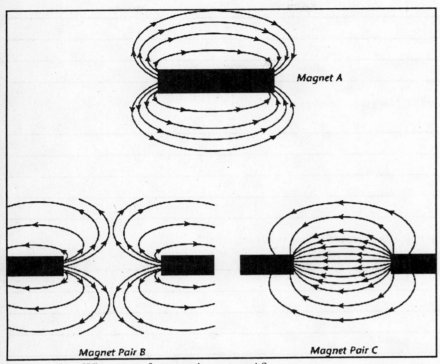

Magnet A

Magnet Pair B   Magnet Pair C

61. What type of magnet is magnet A?

_____
_____
_____
_____
_____

62. What is each end of magnet A called?

_____
_____
_____
_____
_____

63. What is each curved line around magnet A called?

_____
_____
_____
_____
_____

64. Based on the direction of the lines around magnet A, where are the north and south magnetic poles? Explain.

_____

_____

_____

_____

_____

65. Which pair of magnets is arranged so that like poles are placed near each other?

_____

_____

_____

_____

_____

66. Which pair of magnets is arranged so that opposite poles are placed near each other?

_____

_____

_____

_____

_____

Use the diagram to answer each question.

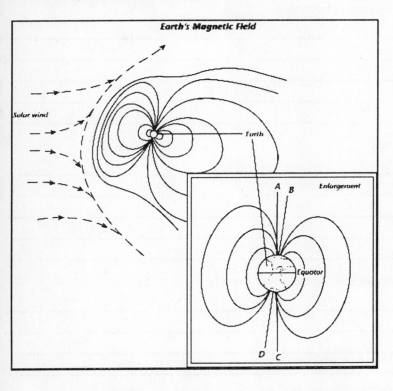

67. In what direction does a compass needle point? Explain how Earth's magnetic field lines are related to magnetic declination.

_____

_____

_____

_____

_____

68. In the enlargement in the diagram, what does point A represent?

_____

_____

_____

_____

69. In the enlargement in the diagram, what does point B represent?

_____

_____

_____

_____

70. Earth's magnetic field is similar to that of a huge bar magnet. If such a bar were buried within Earth, between what points in the enlargement in the diagram would this magnet be located?

_____

_____

_____

_____

71. What makes up the solar wind shown in the diagram?

_____

_____

_____

_____

_____

72. Why are the field lines of the magnetosphere closer together on the side of Earth facing toward the sun?

_____

_____

_____

_____

E. Essay

Write an answer to each of the following questions.

73. Suppose that a bar magnet is suspended a few millimeters above another bar magnet. If the north pole of the bottom magnet is on the left, where is the north pole of the top magnet? Explain.

_____

_____

_____

_____

_____

_____

_____

74. Why might a permanent magnet become unmagnetized if it is dropped?

_____
_____
_____
_____
_____
_____

75. The north pole of a magnet will point toward the magnetic pole of Earth that is located near Earth's geographic north. What does this tell you about Earth's northern magnetic pole?

_____
_____
_____
_____
_____
_____
_____
_____

76. What is an aurora and how is an aurora formed?

_____
_____
_____
_____
_____
_____

77. How does a conductor differ from an insulator? Give an example of each.

_____
_____
_____
_____
_____
_____
_____

78. How can the strength of an electromagnet be increased?

_____

_____

_____

_____

_____

_____

79. How can iron filings be used to map the magnetic field of a bar magnet?

_____

_____

_____

_____

80. What are the basic features of an electric circuit?

_____

_____

_____

_____

_____

_____

Name _____   Date _____

Test 65 Book N, Chapter 1: Magnetism and Electromagnetism

Answer Key (Short)

c	1.	
b	2.	
c	3.	
c	4.	
c	5.	
b	6.	
d	7.	
b	8.	
a	9.	
d	10.	
b	11.	
b	12.	
a	13.	
c	14.	
b	15.	
a	16.	
a	17.	
c	18.	
a	19.	
b	20.	
a	21.	
c	22.	
c	23.	
d	24.	
c	25.	
b	26.	
b	27.	
a	28.	
b	29.	
b	30.	

31.	false, strongest
32.	TRUE
33.	false, opposite
34.	false, Van Allen belts
35.	false, magnetic poles
36.	false, can
37.	TRUE
38.	false, tightly
39.	false, conducting wire
40.	false, increase
41.	attract

42.	like (or similar)
43.	domain
44.	electrons
45.	ferromagnetic
46.	magnetic field
47.	core
48.	magnetic declination
49.	reverses direction
50.	iron
51.	charge
52.	circle
53.	insulator
54.	temperatures
55.	current
56.	energy
57.	circuit
58.	resistor
59.	solenoid
60.	electromagnet
61.	a bar magnet
62.	a magnetic pole
63.	a magnetic field line
64.	North is on the left and south is on the right. Magnetic field lines are drawn from the north magnetic pole to the south magnetic pole.
65.	magnet pair B
66.	magnet pair C
67.	A compass needle points to magnetic north. The needle lines up with Earth's magnetic field lines. At any point on Earth, the angle between Earth's magnetic field lines and the direction of geographic north is the magnetic declination.
68.	the north geographic pole
69.	the north magnetic pole
70.	between points B and D
71.	The solar wind is a stream of electrically charged particles flowing at high speeds from the sun.
72.	The solar wind pushes against the magnetosphere, compressing it on the side facing the sun.
73.	The north pole of the top magnet is on the left also. Because the top magnet is hovering over the bottom magnet, the magnets must be repelling each other. Magnets repel each other when like magnetic poles are brought together.
74.	A permanent magnet is strongly magnetic because all or most of its domains are aligned. If the magnet is dropped, the domains can be knocked into random alignments. If the domains are unaligned, the permanent magnet will lose its magnetic properties.
75.	Since opposite poles attract each other, the north pole of the bar magnet will be attracted to a south magnetic pole. So the magnetic pole located near geographic north must really be a south magnetic pole.
76.	An aurora is a glowing region near Earth's magnetic poles. An aurora is formed by electrically charged particles from the sun that become trapped by Earth's magnetic field. Some of the particles collide with atoms in the atmosphere. The collisions cause the atoms to give off light. The region of visible light is called an aurora.

77. Electric current moves freely through conductors, but not through insulators. The reason is that some of the electrons in a conductor are only loosely bound to their atoms. These electrons are able to move throughout the conductor, forming an electric current. In an insulator, the electrons are bound tightly to their atoms and do not flow easily. Examples of conductors include copper, silver, and iron. Examples of insulators include rubber, glass, and wood.

78. There are several ways to increase the strength of an electromagnet. One way is to increase the current. Another is to increase the number of loops of wire. A third way is to wind the loops of wire closer together. And a fourth way is to use a stronger ferromagnetic material for the core.

79. Because iron is a ferromagnetic substance, it is attracted to a magnet. When iron filings are sprinkled on top of a sheet of paper or plastic placed on top of a bar magnet, the magnetic forces act on the iron filings so they line up with the field of the magnet. This causes the filings to trace a pattern of magnetic field lines.

80. A circuit has a source of electrical energy, such as a battery. A circuit also has a device that is run by electrical energy, such as a light bulb. Conducting wires and a switch are used to connect the elements of a circuit, and to turn the circuit on and off.

Test 66 Book N, Chapter 2: Electric Charges and Current

A. Multiple Choice
Choose the letter of the correct answer.

_____ 1.   Electric field lines show that the force an electron exerts on a proton is

       a.   zero.

       b.   toward the proton.

       c.   toward the electron.

       d.   always upward.

_____ 2.   As in the case of unlike magnetic poles, unlike electric charges

       a.   attract each other.

       b.   repel each other.

       c.   exist in pairs.

       d.   do not interact.

_____ 3.   The buildup of charges on an object is called

       a.   static discharge.

       b.   static electricity.

       c.   positive charge.

       d.   negative charge.

_____ 4.   Clothes in a dryer acquire static cling by

       a.   friction.

       b.   conduction.

       c.   induction.

       d.   static discharge.

_____ 5.   The loss of static electricity as electric charges move off an object is called

       a.   friction.

       b.   conduction.

       c.   induction.

       d.   static discharge.

_____ 6.   Suppose you acquire a positive charge from walking across a carpet. You then touch a doorknob and receive a shock. This leaves you

       a.   positively charged.

       b.   negatively charged.

       c.   supercharged.

       d.   electrically neutral.

_____ 7.   The type of energy that depends on position is called

       a.   potential energy.

       b.   electrical energy.

       c.   magnetic energy.

       d.   solar energy.

_____ 8. The potential energy per unit of electric charge is called

    a. a discharge.

    b. a voltmeter.

    c. current.

    d. electrical potential.

_____ 9. What causes current to flow?

    a. voltage

    b. energy

    c. electricity

    d. magnetism

_____ 10. An example of a voltage source is a(n)

    a. electrical wire.

    b. battery.

    c. car engine.

    d. magnet.

_____ 11. The amount of water that flows through a pipe does NOT depend on

    a. the length of the pipe.

    b. whether the pipe is thin or wide.

    c. what type of metal the pipe is made of.

    d. whether the pipe is clogged or clean.

_____ 12. An electric current will always follow

    a. the path of least resistance.

    b. a path toward the north pole.

    c. a path toward the south pole.

    d. the path that leads through insulators.

_____ 13. According to Ohm's law, what is the resistance of a light if the voltage is 9.0 volts and the current is 0.30 amps?

    a. 0.033 ohms.

    b. 2.7 ohms.

    c. 30 ohms.

    d. 8.7 ohms.

_____ 14. According to Ohm's law, resistance is equal to voltage divided by

    a. time.

    b. conduction.

    c. current.

    d. potential.

_____ 15. In a series circuit with three bulbs,

    a. there are many paths for the current to take.

    b. the remaining two bulbs are not affected if one bulb burns out.

    c. all of the bulbs become dimmer as more bulbs are added.

    d. a switch is never used.

_____ **16.** In a series circuit with three bulbs, the current in the third bulb

    a.   is twice the current in the first bulb.

    b.   is half the current in the first bulb.

    c.   is half the current in the second bulb.

    d.   is the same as the current in the first bulb.

_____ **17.** In a parallel circuit with three bulbs,

    a.   the bulbs must all be located on the same branch.

    b.   there is only one path for the current to take.

    c.   each bulb can have its own path from one terminal of the battery to the other.

    d.   the overall resistance increases if a new branch is added.

_____ **18.** To measure the voltage across a device, a voltmeter should be wired

    a.   in series with the device.

    b.   in parallel with the device.

    c.   in a separate circuit from the device.

    d.   in the central branch of the circuit within the device.

_____ **19.** A connection that allows current to take an unintended path is called a

    a.   short circuit.

    b.   series circuit.

    c.   parallel circuit.

    d.   grounded circuit.

_____ **20.** If you accidentally become part of a circuit, your greatest chance of avoiding serious injury might come from

    a.   being barefoot.

    b.   standing in water.

    c.   wearing rubber-soled shoes.

    d.   using the drop-and-roll technique.

_____ **21.** What is a disadvantage of using fuses?

    a.   When a fuse burns out, it cannot be used again.

    b.   A fuse uses an electromagnet, so it shuts off when the current gets too high.

    c.   Compared with circuit breakers, fuses are a newer, easier way to protect circuits.

    d.   You cannot blow a fuse by plugging in too many appliances at once.

_____ **22.** The function of a lightning rod is to

    a.   produce lightning.

    b.   make an object lighter.

    c.   protect a building from damage due to lightning.

    d.   prevent short circuits in a building's wiring.

_____ **23.** If you are outside during a storm, the best way to protect yourself from lightning is to

    a.   stay low and dry.

    b.   use your umbrella.

    c.   stand under a tall tree.

    d.   drop and roll.

_____ 24. What effect would a current of greater than 0.2 amp have on your body?

    a.   It would be almost unnoticeable.

    b.   It might cause an irregular heartbeat and disrupt the flow of blood.

    c.   It could cause burns and stop your heart.

    d.   It would feel like a shock you get from touching a doorknob.

_____ 25. The charge on a proton is

    a.   negative, and the charge on an electron is positive.

    b.   positive, and the charge on an electron is negative.

    c.   the same as the charge on an electron.

    d.   can change according to the situation.

_____ 26. A situation in which you might want to increase static electricity is when you are

    a.   combing your hair.

    b.   taking clothes out of a dryer.

    c.   wrapping leftover food in plastic wrap.

    d.   throwing away a small piece of packing foam.

_____ 27. An instrument that uses the interaction between like charges to detect the presence of an electric charge is a(n)

    a.   magnet.

    b.   electroscope.

    c.   generator.

    d.   conductor.

_____ 28. How many terminals does a voltage source have?

    a.   one

    b.   two

    c.   three

    d.   four

_____ 29. When lightning strikes a lightning rod, the last place the charge flows is

    a.   into the rod itself.

    b.   into the building the rod is on.

    c.   back into the air.

    d.   into Earth.

_____ 30. When charges are able to flow directly from the circuit into the ground connection, the circuit is electrically

    a.   exposed.

    b.   grounded.

    c.   shorted.

    d.   shocking.

B. True or False

If the statement is true, write true. If it is false, change the underlined word or words to make the statement true.

31. Electric charges that are different <u>repel</u> each other.

_____

_____

32. Conduction is the transfer of electrons from a charged object to another object by <u>rubbing</u>.

_____

_____

33. The unit of measure of potential difference is the <u>ohm</u>.

_____

_____

34. The <u>potential difference</u> between the terminals of a voltage source causes current to flow in a circuit.

_____

_____

35. As the temperature of most conductors increases, the resistance <u>decreases</u>.

_____

_____

36. For a constant voltage, increasing the resistance will cause the current to <u>decrease</u>.

_____

_____

37. In a <u>parallel</u> circuit, there is only one path for current to take.

_____

_____

38. If one light bulb is removed from a parallel circuit with three bulbs, the brightness of the other bulbs will <u>decrease</u>.

_____

_____

39. A <u>circuit breaker</u> must be replaced after a short circuit occurs.

_____

_____

40. Living cells have a <u>high</u> resistance to electric current.

_____

_____

C. Completion

Fill in the word or phrase that best completes each statement.

41. Like electric charges _____ each other.

_____

_____

42. The strength of the electric field of a charged particle becomes greater as the distance from the particle ____.

_____

_____

43. The law of _____ of charge states that charges are not created or destroyed.

_____

_____

44. Plastic wrap clings to the edges of a container because the wrap charges the edges of the container by _____.

_____

_____

45. A(n) _____ is an instrument in which two leaves move apart in response to electric charge.

_____

_____

46. Potential difference is also called _____.

_____

_____

47. Batteries and generators are examples of _____, which create a potential difference in a circuit.

_____

_____

48. An increase in voltage causes a greater flow of electric ___ in a circuit.

_____

_____

49. The greater the _____, the less current there is for a given voltage.

_____

_____

50. If two wires of the same material have the same thickness but different lengths, the _____ wire will have a greater resistance.

_____

_____

51. For a current of 3 amps and a voltage of 9 volts, the resistance is _____.

_____

_____

52. To measure the current through a device in an electric circuit, a(n) _____ should be connected in series with the device.

_____

_____

53. Adding bulbs to a _____ circuit causes all of the bulbs to shine less brightly.

_____

_____

54. In a _____ circuit, different parts of the circuit are on separate branches.

_____

_____

55. The resistance of a parallel circuit _____ as you add more branches.

_____

_____

56. A _____ is a safety device that uses an electromagnet to shut off a circuit when the current becomes too great.

_____

_____

57. A circuit is electrically _____ if it is designed to carry electric current from a short circuit directly to Earth.

_____

_____

58. Benjamin Franklin invented the _____, which carries charge through a wire to Earth during a storm.

_____

_____

59. A lightning rod works because its _____ attracts the electrons in a lightning bolt.

_____

_____

60. The severity of an electric shock depends on the amount of _____.

_____

_____

D. Interpreting Diagrams
   Use the diagram to answer each question.

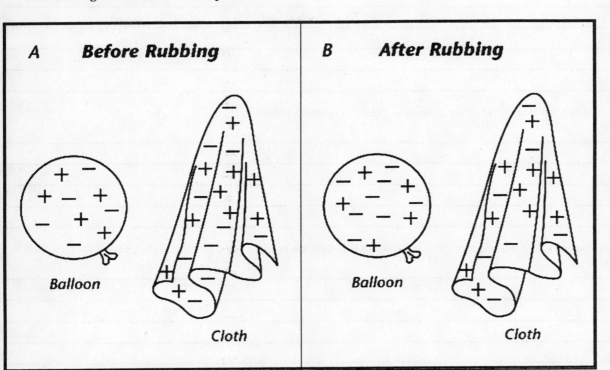

61. What is the overall electric charge, if any, on the balloon and on the cloth in Diagram A?

_____

_____

_____

_____

_____

62. What type of overall charge, if any, does the balloon in Diagram B have? Explain how you determined your answer.

_____

_____

_____

_____

_____

63. What type of overall charge, if any, does the cloth in Diagram B have?

_____

_____

_____

_____

_____

64. What has rubbing done to the charges on the objects shown in diagrams A and B?

_____

_____

_____

_____

65. What would happen if you placed the balloon in Diagram B near a wall?

_____

_____

_____

_____

66. What will happen to the balloon and cloth in Diagram B if they are brought close together without touching? Explain.

_____

_____

_____

_____

Use the diagram to answer each question.

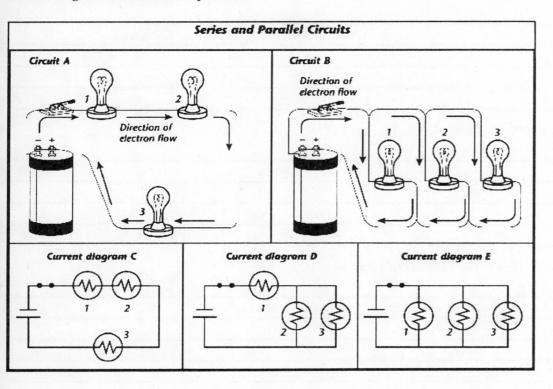

Series and Parallel Circuits

Circuit A

1
2
Direction of
electron flow

− +

3

Circuit B

Direction of
electron flow

1
2
3

− +

Current diagram C

1
2
3

Current diagram D

1
2
3

Current diagram E

1
2
3

67. Which circuit - A or B - represents a series circuit? Explain your answer.

_____

_____

_____

_____

_____

68. Which circuit - A or B - is a parallel circuit? Explain your answer.

_____

_____

_____

_____

69. Which circuit diagram represents circuit B?

_____

_____

_____

_____

_____

70. What will happen to bulb 1 in circuit A if the switch is opened?

_____

_____

_____

_____

71. Will removing bulb 1 in circuit B cause bulb 3 to go out? Explain.

_____

_____

_____

_____

72. What will happen to bulb 2 in circuit diagram D if bulb 1 burns out?

_____

_____

_____

_____

E. Essay
Write an answer to each of the following questions.

73. How are conduction and induction alike and how are they different?

_____

_____

_____

_____

_____

_____

© Prentice-Hall, Inc.

74. Explain why you may produce a static discharge if you touch a metal doorknob after walking on a wool carpet.

_____

_____

_____

_____

_____

_____

75. How is current related to resistance?

_____

_____

_____

_____

_____

_____

_____

76. Three identical flashlight bulbs in a parallel circuit are connected to a flashlight battery. If the current through each bulb is 0.3 amp, what current is the battery supplying to the circuit? Explain.

_____

_____

_____

_____

_____

77. How does a fuse protect against a short circuit?

_____

_____

_____

_____

_____

78. Why is it dangerous to stand under a tree during an electrical storm?

_____

_____

_____

_____

_____

_____

_____

79. Three identical flashlight bulbs in a series circuit are connected to a flashlight battery. If the current through each bulb is 0.3 amp, what is the current in the circuit? Explain.

_____

_____

_____

_____

_____

_____

_____

80. What is the resistance of a lamp operating at 115 volts and using 0.25 amp of current? What relationship did you use to find the answer?

_____

_____

_____

_____

_____

_____

_____

Name _____ Date _____

Test 66 Book N, Chapter 2: Electric Charges and Current

Answer Key (Short)

__c__	1.	
__b__	2.	
__b__	3.	
__a__	4.	
__d__	5.	
__d__	6.	
__a__	7.	
__d__	8.	
__a__	9.	
__b__	10.	
__c__	11.	
__a__	12.	
__c__	13.	
__c__	14.	
__c__	15.	
__d__	16.	
__c__	17.	
__b__	18.	
__a__	19.	
__c__	20.	
__a__	21.	
__c__	22.	
__a__	23.	
__b__	24.	
__b__	25.	
__c__	26.	
__b__	27.	
__b__	28.	
__d__	29.	
__b__	30.	

31.	false, attract
32.	false, direct contact
33.	false, volt
34.	TRUE
35.	false, increases
36.	TRUE
37.	false, series
38.	false, remain the same
39.	false, fuse
40.	false, low
41.	repel

42.	decreases
43.	conservation
44.	induction
45.	electroscope
46.	voltage
47.	voltage sources
48.	current
49.	resistance
50.	longer
51.	3 ohms
52.	ammeter
53.	series
54.	parallel
55.	decreases
56.	circuit breaker
57.	grounded
58.	lightning rod
59.	pointed end
60.	current
61.	Both the balloon and cloth are neutral.
62.	The charge is negative. Counting reveals that the number of negative charges exceeds the number of positive charges.
63.	The charge is positive.
64.	Rubbing has transferred negative charge from the cloth to the balloon.
65.	The balloon would stick to the wall for a short time. The negative balloon will induce a slight positive charge in the wall. The positive wall and negative balloon will then be attracted to each other.
66.	The two will attract each other. In Diagram B, the balloon has a negative charge and the cloth has a positive charge. Opposite charges attract.
67.	Circuit A is a series circuit because there is only one path through which current can flow.
68.	Circuit B is a parallel circuit. There is more than one path through which current can flow.
69.	circuit diagram E
70.	Bulb 1 will go out.
71.	No, because the three bulbs in circuit B are in parallel, removing bulb 1 will still allow current to flow through bulbs 2 and 3.
72.	Bulb 2 will go out as well. Even though bulbs 2 and 3 are wired in parallel, bulb 1 is wired in series with the other two bulbs. So if one bulb in a series circuit goes out, they all go out.
73.	Both conduction and induction involve a movement of electrons. Conduction is the transfer of electrons from a charged object to another object by direct contact. Induction does not involve direct contact. Instead, induction is the movement of electrons from one part of an object to another as a result of the electric field of the second object.
74.	Friction between your shoe and the wool causes a transfer of electrons from the carpet to you. Your body now has a static charge. When you touch the metal knob, electrons suddenly move from your body through your fingertips to the metal doorknob as a static discharge.
75.	The amount of current flowing in a circuit depends on the resistance offered by the material in the circuit. The greater the resistance, the less current there is for a given voltage.

76.   The battery is supplying 0.9 amp. In a parallel circuit, the current from the battery separates so that part of the current flows through each of the branches. The current supplied by the battery must equal the sum of the currents in the branches of the circuit because no charge is lost. The sum of the three currents in the branches of this circuit is 0.9 amp.

77.   A fuse contains a small strip of metal through which current flows. If a large amount of current flows through the circuit, the current through the metal strip will cause it to become hot enough to melt. When the strip melts, it breaks and no more current can flow through the fuse or the circuit.

78.   The tall, wet tree can act as a conductor, allowing electrons to flow through it from a lightning bolt. The discharge through the tree would travel downward toward the ground and could pass through you as well.

79.   The current is 0.3 amp. In a series circuit, the amount of current that moves through each bulb is the same as the amount of current that moves through the circuit as a whole because there is only one path for the current. The current supplied by the battery equals the current through each bulb, which in this circuit is 0.3 amp.

80.   Ohm's law was used.

$$\text{Resistance} = \frac{\text{Voltage}}{\text{Current}} = \frac{115 \text{V}}{0.25 \text{ A}} = 460 \, \Omega$$

Test 67 Book N, Chapter 3: Electricity and Magnetism at Work

A. Multiple Choice
Choose the letter of the correct answer.

_____ 1. Which type of energy is associated with electric currents?

    a.   mechanical energy

    b.   electrical energy

    c.   magnetic energy

    d.   geothermal energy

_____ 2. When a current-carrying wire is placed in a magnetic field,

    a.   electrical energy is converted to mechanical energy.

    b.   mechanical energy is converted to electrical energy.

    c.   the wire becomes a permanent magnet.

    d.   the current stops flowing.

_____ 3. What is one difference between a galvanometer and an electric motor?

    a.   An electric motor causes something to move.

    b.   A galvanometer uses an electric current.

    c.   In an electric motor, a loop of current-carrying wire spins continuously.

    d.   An electric motor uses electricity.

_____ 4. In a motor, the direction of current is reversed by

    a.   brushes.

    b.   an armature.

    c.   a commutator.

    d.   a pointer.

_____ 5. The process of generating an electric current from the motion of a conductor in a magnetic field is

    a.   conduction.

    b.   induction.

    c.   motion.

    d.   magnetism.

_____ 6. The type of current produced by a battery is

    a.   direct current.

    b.   alternating current.

    c.   magnetic current.

    d.   induced current.

_____ 7. An electric generator is the opposite of a(n)

    a.   electric motor.

    b.   AC generator.

    c.   DC generator.

    d.   electric current.

_____ **8.** What kind of energy turns the huge turbines in electric generating plants?

    a. electrical energy

    b. mechanical energy

    c. magnetic energy

    d. induction energy

_____ **9.** What kind of energy involves steam from Earth's interior?

    a. geothermal

    b. solar

    c. tidal

    d. nuclear

_____ **10.** Which of the following types of energy is nonrenewable?

    a. wind energy

    b. solar energy

    c. tidal energy

    d. energy from fossil fuels

_____ **11.** If a household's voltage is 120 volts, what is the power rating of a light bulb with 0.5 amps of current flowing through it?

    a. 120 watts

    b. 600 watts

    c. 60 watts

    d. 6 watts

_____ **12.** One kilowatt equals

    a. 10 watts.

    b. 100 watts.

    c. 1,000 watts.

    d. 10,000 watts.

_____ **13.** A device that increases or decreases voltage is called a(n)

    a. alternator.

    b. transformer.

    c. generator.

    d. turbine.

_____ **14.** What is produced when a current flows in the primary coil of a transformer?

    a. magnetic field

    b. nuclear field

    c. electric field

    d. solar field

_____ **15.** What did Nikola Tesla's system of alternating current replace?

    a.   galvanometers

    b.   generating plants

    c.   direct current

    d.   transformers

_____ **16.** Electric current from the generating plant is

    a.   direct current transmitted at high voltages, but usually used at low voltages.

    b.   alternating current transmitted at high voltages, but usually used at low voltages.

    c.   alternating current transmitted at low voltages, but usually used at high voltages.

    d.   direct current transmitted at low voltages, but usually used at high voltages.

_____ **17.** To provide electrical energy, a generator converts mechanical energy and batteries convert

    a.   solar energy.

    b.   magnetic energy.

    c.   nuclear energy.

    d.   chemical energy.

_____ **18.** What parts of the cell are used to connect an electrochemical cell to a circuit?

    a.   electrodes

    b.   electrolytes

    c.   wet cells

    d.   terminals

_____ **19.** Several electrochemical cells can be combined to make a

    a.   wet cell.

    b.   dry cell.

    c.   battery.

    d.   electrolyte.

_____ **20.** The voltage of a battery is equal to the

    a.   voltage of the smallest cell.

    b.   voltage of the largest cell.

    c.   average voltage of all the cells.

    d.   sum of the voltages of all the cells.

_____ **21.** Energy = Power x

    a.   Time.

    b.   Current.

    c.   Voltage.

    d.   Kilowatts.

_____ **22.** A device used to measure small currents is a(n)

    a.   electric motor.

    b.   commutator.

    c.   armature.

    d.   galvanometer.

_____ 23. An alternating current

    a. turns on and off repeatedly.

    b. reverses direction repeatedly.

    c. flows in one direction only.

    d. flows in one direction in some devices and changes direction in others.

_____ 24. One example of a turbine is

    a. a magnet.

    b. a windmill.

    c. the ocean's tides.

    d. a dam.

_____ 25. Which type of energy makes use of the sun's rays?

    a. geothermal energy

    b. nuclear energy

    c. solar energy

    d. tidal energy

_____ 26. When you turn on a toaster, stove, or microwave oven, you are converting electrical energy into

    a. heat.

    b. mechanical energy.

    c. nuclear energy.

    d. magnetic energy.

_____ 27. A device that converts stored chemical energy into electrical energy is a(n)

    a. electrolyte.

    b. electrode.

    c. electrochemical cell.

    d. terminal.

_____ 28. The rate at which energy is converted from one form to another is known as

    a. voltage.

    b. current.

    c. power.

    d. electricity.

_____ 29. You can calculate power by multiplying

    a. voltage by current.

    b. voltage by heat.

    c. time by current.

    d. time by voltage.

_____ 30. The symbol for current is

    a. C.

    b. I.

    c. P.

    d. V.

B. True or False

If the statement is true, write true. If it is false, change the underlined word or words to make the statement true.

31. When a current-carrying wire is moved by a magnetic field, electrical energy is converted into <u>mechanical</u> energy.

_____

_____

32. In a motor, the arrangement of an iron core and a number of wire loops is called an <u>armature</u>.

_____

_____

33. When a coil of wire is moved across the lines of a magnetic field, a <u>current</u> is induced in the wire.

_____

_____

34. A <u>motor</u> uses motion to produce an electric current.

_____

_____

35. <u>Nuclear power</u> plants near the bases of dams and waterfalls produce electricity by using falling water to turn turbines.

_____

_____

36. Power equals voltage times <u>resistance</u>.

_____

_____

37. A <u>transformer</u> is a device that increases or decreases voltage.

_____

_____

38. The voltage of the electricity produced by a generating plant is <u>lower than</u> the voltage of the electricity carried by transmission lines.

_____

_____

39. An electrochemical cell consists of two different metals called <u>electrolytes</u>.

_____

_____

40. A <u>generator</u> is a device made up of two or more electrochemical cells connected in series.

_____

_____

C. Completion
Fill in the word or phrase that best completes each statement.

41. The direction in which a current-carrying wire placed in a magnetic field moves depends on the _____ of the current.

_____

_____

42. A galvanometer is a device that measures small amounts of _____.

_____

_____

43. The amount of rotation of the loops of wire and pointer in a galvanometer depends on the strength of the _____ field produced by the loops of wire.

_____

_____

44. A current consisting of charges moving back and forth in a circuit is called a(n) _____ current.

_____

_____

45. When a _____ is moved up or down repeatedly through a coil of wire, an alternating current is induced in the wire.

_____

_____

46. In a(n) ____ generator, slip rings and brushes allow current to travel from the moving armature to the rest of the circuit.

_____

_____

47. In an alternating-current generator, each time the armature rotates, the current changes _____.

_____

_____

48. A large generator may be connected to a(n) _____, which is a circular device made up of many blades.

_____

_____

49. In most electrical generating plants, a turbine is attached to the _____ of a generator.

_____

_____

50. The ____ rating of an electrical device is a measure of the rate at which the device uses or produces electrical energy.

_____

_____

51. The kilowatt-hour is a unit of electrical _____.

_____

_____

52. A step-up transformer is a device that increases _____.

_____

_____

53. In a transformer, an induced current is produced in the ____ coil.

_____

_____

54. Tesla was a scientist who championed the use of _____ current.

_____

_____

55. A _____ transformer is used to change the voltage of electricity in transmission lines before it enters houses in a neighborhood.

_____

_____

56. An electrolyte is a substance that _____ electric current.

_____

_____

57. An electrochemical cell produces current because of chemical reactions that occur between the electrolyte and the _____.

_____

_____

58. A ____ cell is an electrochemical cell in which the electrolyte is a paste.

_____

_____

59. A _____ battery uses electric current to convert the products of its chemical reaction back into reactants.

_____

_____

60. The energy that an object has due to its movement or position is called ____ energy.

_____

_____

D. Interpreting Diagrams

Use the diagram to answer each question.

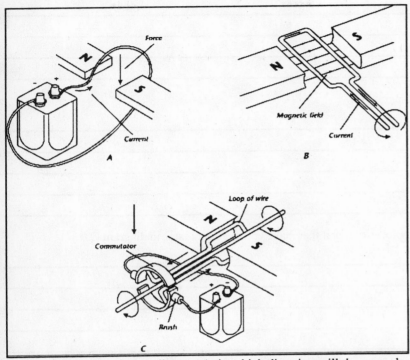

61. According to diagram A, in which direction will the upper loop of the wire move?

_____

_____

_____

_____

_____

62. In which direction would the wire move in diagram A if both the direction of the current and the direction of the magnetic field were reversed?

_____

_____

_____

_____

_____

63. In diagram B, is the loop of wire rotating clockwise or counterclockwise?

_____

_____

_____

_____

_____

64. Describe two ways of causing the loop to rotate in the opposite direction in diagram B.

_____

_____

_____

_____

_____

65. What common electrical device is shown in diagram C?

_____

_____

_____

_____

66. Explain why there is a break between the two pieces of metal that make up the commutator in diagram C.

_____

_____

_____

_____

Use the diagram to answer each question.

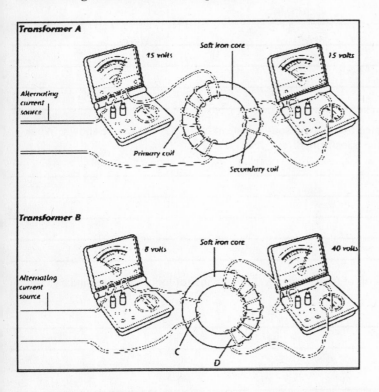

Transformer A

15 volts   Soft iron core   15 volts

Alternating current source

Primary coil

Secondary coil

Transformer B

8 volts   Soft iron core   40 volts

Alternating current source

C

D

67. By what process is current generated in the secondary coils of the two transformers shown in the diagram?

_____

_____

_____

_____

_____

68. What type of transformer is transformer A?

_____

_____

_____

_____

69. What type of transformer is transformer B?

_____

_____

_____

_____

_____

70. Identify the parts labeled C and D.

_____

_____

_____

_____

71. Suppose the primary coil of transformer A is connected to a 15-volt source instead of the 45-volt source shown. What will be the voltage reading in the secondary coil of the transformer?

_____

_____

_____

_____

72. What would happen to the voltage in the secondary coil of transformer A if the number of loops in the secondary coil were reduced?

_____

_____

_____

_____

E. Essay

Write an answer to each of the following questions.

73. What would happen to the force on a current-carrying wire placed between the poles of a magnet if the current in the wire were continually reversing direction? Explain why.

_____

_____

_____

_____

_____

_____

74. What is the purpose of the spring in a galvanometer?

_____
_____
_____
_____
_____
_____

75. How are turbines used in generating electricity?

_____
_____
_____
_____
_____
_____
_____

76. A clock radio has a power rating of 12 watts and uses a standard voltage of 120 volts. What is the current going to the radio? How did you determine your answer?

_____
_____
_____
_____
_____
_____
_____

77. What is electromagnetic induction and how is it used in a transformer?

_____
_____
_____
_____
_____
_____

78. How are step-up and step-down transformers used in the transmission of electric current from power stations to homes?

_____
_____
_____
_____
_____
_____
_____

79. How do chemical reactions in electrochemical cells produce electricity?

_____
_____
_____
_____
_____
_____
_____

80. A 12-volt automobile battery consists of six identical wet cells connected together. What is the voltage of each cell? Explain your answer.

_____
_____
_____
_____
_____
_____
_____

Test 67 Book N, Chapter 3: Electricity and Magnetism at Work
Answer Key (Short)

__b__	**1.**
__a__	**2.**
__c__	**3.**
__c__	**4.**
__b__	**5.**
__a__	**6.**
__a__	**7.**
__b__	**8.**
__a__	**9.**
__d__	**10.**
__c__	**11.**
__c__	**12.**
__b__	**13.**
__a__	**14.**
__c__	**15.**
__b__	**16.**
__d__	**17.**
__d__	**18.**
__c__	**19.**
__d__	**20.**
__a__	**21.**
__d__	**22.**
__b__	**23.**
__b__	**24.**
__c__	**25.**
__a__	**26.**
__c__	**27.**
__c__	**28.**
__a__	**29.**
__b__	**30.**

31.	TRUE
32.	TRUE
33.	TRUE
34.	false, generator
35.	false, Hydroelectric
36.	false, current
37.	TRUE
38.	TRUE
39.	false, electrodes
40.	false, battery
41.	direction

42.	current
43.	magnetic
44.	alternating
45.	magnet
46.	AC, or alternating current
47.	direction
48.	turbine
49.	armature
50.	power
51.	energy
52.	voltage
53.	secondary
54.	alternating
55.	step-down
56.	conducts
57.	electrodes
58.	dry
59.	rechargeable
60.	mechanical
61.	It will move downward.
62.	It would move downward.
63.	It is rotating counterclockwise.
64.	Reverse the direction of the current or reverse the direction of the magnetic field.
65.	an electric motor
66.	Each half of the commutator is attached to one end of the loop of wire. When the loop rotates, the commutator rotates as well. Each half of the commutator is connected to the current source by contacts called brushes. The break allows the current to continue to flow in one direction in the loop of wire even though the loop is spinning.
67.	the process of electromagnetic induction
68.	step-down transformer
69.	step-up transformer
70.	C: primary coil; D: secondary coil
71.	5 volts
72.	The voltage would be lower. For example, if there were two loops in the secondary coil, the voltage would drop to 10 V.
73.	The force would change direction repeatedly. The force on a current-carrying wire in a magnetic field depends on the direction of the current. When the current is in one direction, the force would act downward. When the current is in the opposite direction, the force on the wire would act upward.
74.	The spring exerts a force on the pointer. This force opposes the force caused by current in the wire loops in the magnetic field of the permanent magnet. When the current is turned off, the unbalanced force of the spring returns the pointer to its original position.
75.	The armature of a generator must be turned by some source of mechanical energy, which in many situations is a turbine. The energy of the spinning turbine may come from the mechanical energy of wind or flowing water, or from the thermal energy of steam.

76.

Power = Voltage x Current P = V x I Power is equal to voltage times current. The equation can be rearranged to solve for current. Current is equal to power divided by voltage.

$$I = \frac{P}{V} = \frac{12 \text{ watts}}{20 \text{ volts}} = 0.1 \text{ amp}$$

77. Electromagnetic induction is the process by which an electric current is produced in a closed, conducting loop that is exposed to a changing magnetic field. In a transformer, an alternating current in one coil (primary coil) produces a changing magnetic field. This induces an electric current in another coil (secondary coil).

78. Step-up transformers are used to increase the voltage of electricity before it is sent out over transmission lines from generating plants. Step-down transformers are used to reduce the voltage of electricity from high-voltage transmission lines before it enters homes and businesses. Some devices, such as televisions, contain step-up transformers that increase the voltage once again.

79. Chemical reactions occur between the electrolyte and the electrodes in an electrochemical cell. These reactions cause one electrode to become negatively charged and the other to become positively charged. There is a potential difference (voltage) between the electrodes because they have opposite charges. If the electrodes are connected by a conducting wire, current will flow in the wire as a result of the potential difference.

80. Each cell has 2 volts. A battery is an arrangement of cells in which the voltage of the battery is equal to the sum of the voltages of the individual cells. In this case, each of the six cells has the same voltage because they are identical. The voltage of each cell must be one sixth the voltage of the battery. One-sixth of 12 volts is 2 volts.

A. Multiple Choice
   Choose the letter of the correct answer.

_____ 1. An electric current that is varied in some way to represent information is a(n)

    a. electronic signal.

    b. digital signal.

    c. integrated circuit.

    d. electromagnetic wave.

_____ 2. A digital signal differs from an analog signal because it

    a. consists of a current that changes smoothly.

    b. consists of a current that changes in steps.

    c. carries information.

    d. is used in electronic devices.

_____ 3. A thermometer that shows temperature as the height of a column of liquid is an analog device because its measurements

    a. are an indication of the weather.

    b. change continuously.

    c. are in degrees.

    d. do not rely on electricity.

_____ 4. A material that conducts electricity under certain conditions only is a(n)

    a. conductor.

    b. insulator.

    c. semiconductor.

    d. vacuum tube.

_____ 5. In the binary system,

    a. 0 is represented by a pulse.

    b. 1 is represented by the absence of a pulse.

    c. each 1 or 0 is called a bit.

    d. 10 numbers are used.

_____ 6. What does a transistor do?

    a. allow a current to flow in one direction only

    b. amplify an electronic signal

    c. convert an analog signal into a digital signal

    d. combine thousands of diodes and resistors

_____ 7. The number of electromagnetic waves passing a given point each second is the

    a. frequency.

    b. amplitude.

    c. crest.

    d. trough.

_____ **8.** A solid-state device that allows current to flow in one direction only is called a

    a. diode.

    b. bit.

    c. transistor.

    d. vacuum tube.

_____ **9.** Changing the height of the carrier wave to match that of the signal is called

    a. frequency modulation.

    b. amplitude modulation.

    c. crest modulation.

    d. trough modulation.

_____ **10.** What electronic component was widely used in electronic devices before solid-state components were developed?

    a. bit

    b. amplifier

    c. transistor

    d. vacuum tube

_____ **11.** Which part of your radio receives the electromagnetic waves sent out from a radio station?

    a. power switch

    b. speakers

    c. antenna

    d. tuning dial

_____ **12.** Cathode-ray tubes are found in

    a. televisions.

    b. radios.

    c. telephones.

    d. cellular telephones.

_____ **13.** Without wires, electronic signals are carried over long distances by

    a. transistors.

    b. carbon granules.

    c. electromagnetic waves.

    d. integrated circuits.

_____ **14.** All computer information is represented in the

    a. numeric language.

    b. binary system.

    c. decimal system.

    d. English language.

_____ **15.** A modern device that often has its signals carried through wires or glass optical fibers is a

    a. satellite

    b. radio

    c. telephone

    d. cellular telephone

_____ **16.** Bytes are arrangements of

    a.   2 bits.

    b.   8 bits.

    c.   100 bits.

    d.   one million bits.

_____ **17.** Computer programs, called software, are

    a.   permanent components of the computer.

    b.   part of a central processing unit.

    c.   memory storage devices.

    d.   detailed sets of instructions directing the computer to perform in a certain way.

_____ **18.** The brain of a computer is the

    a.   random access memory.

    b.   central processing unit.

    c.   input device.

    d.   output device.

_____ **19.** Scientists can make a semiconductor by adding atoms of other elements to

    a.   aluminum.

    b.   steel.

    c.   silicon.

    d.   zinc.

_____ **20.** A group of computers connected by cables or telephone lines is called a(n)

    a.   computer network.

    b.   encryption.

    c.   RAM.

    d.   central processing unit.

_____ **21.** A set of computers connected in one classroom is an example of

    a.   a wide area network.

    b.   a local area network.

    c.   the Internet.

    d.   the World Wide Web.

_____ **22.** The Internet is a

    a.   local area network.

    b.   method of encryption.

    c.   wide area network.

    d.   collection of freeware.

_____ **23.** Prior to the World Wide Web, computer users could get information only in the form of

    a.   pictures.

    b.   sounds.

    c.   words and numbers.

    d.   movies.

_____ 24. The process of coding data so that only the intended user can read them is known as

    a.   encryption.

    b.   solid-state storage.

    c.   binary.

    d.   read only memory.

_____ 25. A program that interferes with the normal operation of a computer is called a(n)

    a.   web.

    b.   computer virus.

    c.   network.

    d.   encryption.

_____ 26. Which of these is an example of external memory?

    a.   a computer game

    b.   a floppy disk

    c.   RAM

    d.   ROM

_____ 27. What is the first step a programmer takes in creating software?

    a.   developing a flowchart

    b.   writing the instructions for the computer

    c.   outlining exactly what the program will do

    d.   testing the program

_____ 28. Computer networks are useful because they

    a.   are free to use.

    b.   are protected from computer viruses.

    c.   allow people in different locations to communicate.

    d.   do not require telephone lines or wires.

_____ 29. Chat rooms are

    a.   convenient and safe for all users.

    b.   a feature of local area networks only.

    c.   possibly risky because users are not screened.

    d.   no longer popular.

_____ 30. Electronics treats electric currents as a means of carrying

    a.   voltage.

    b.   amps.

    c.   electricity.

    d.   information.

B. True or False

If the statement is true, write true. If it is false, change the underlined word or words to make the statement true.

31. In the study of <u>electrical</u> devices, current is treated as a means of carrying information.

_____

_____

32. Sundials are examples of <u>digital</u> devices.

_____

_____

33. <u>Semiconductors</u> are materials that conduct electric current better than insulators but not as well as conductors.

_____

_____

34. An electromagnetic wave is a wave that consists of changing electric and magnetic <u>charges</u>.

_____

_____

35. The transmitter of a radio station combines an electronic signal with a <u>sound</u> wave.

_____

_____

36. The term <u>byte</u> is short for binary digit.

_____

_____

37. Information in Read Only Memory (ROM) <u>cannot</u> be changed by a computer's central processing unit.

_____

_____

38. Computers connected across large distances form a <u>local</u> area network.

_____

_____

39. The World Wide Web is a system that allows you to display and view files, called <u>pages</u>, on the Internet.

_____

_____

40. <u>Decryption</u> is the process of coding data so that it can be read only by the intended user.

_____

_____

C. Completion

Fill in the word or phrase that best completes each statement.

41. An electronic _____ is an electric current that is altered in some way to represent information.

_____

_____

42. The lighted display timers on microwave ovens are examples of _____ devices.

_____

_____

43. A CD, or compact disc, stores sound information as _____ signals.

_____

_____

44. A(n) _____ circuit is a circuit that has been manufactured on a tiny slice of semiconductor called a chip.

_____

_____

45. A _____, which allows current to flow in one direction only, consists of two types of semiconductors joined together.

_____

_____

46. The height of a wave from the center line to a crest or trough is the wave's _____.

_____

_____

47. Changing the frequency of the carrier wave to match the signal is called frequency _____.

_____

_____

48. The receiver located in a telephone earpiece contains a speaker that changes electric current into _____.

_____

_____

49. A communications _____ revolves around Earth, receiving signals from one part of the planet and transmitting them to the other.

_____

_____

50. The _____ system uses combinations of two digits, 0 and 1, to represent information.

_____

_____

51. The digits 0 and 1 can represent whether a(n) _____ is closed or open on a computer chip.

_____

_____

52. Random Access Memory (RAM) is the _____ storage area for data while the computer is operating.

_____

_____

53. A(n) ____ disc is a memory device on which information is written and read by lasers.

_____

_____

54. A computer ___ allows people in different locations to share information and software.

_____

_____

55. In ____ area networks, very powerful computers may serve as a support connection for hundreds of less powerful computers across long distances.

_____

_____

56. The Internet, along with other, smaller networks, is sometimes called the _____ superhighway.

_____

_____

57. When you download a file from a network, you should use _____.

_____

_____

58. A computer _____ is a program that interferes with the normal operation of a computer, destroying information and even disabling the computer.

_____

_____

59. An idea or artistic creation is considered _____ property, and is often protected by law.

_____

_____

60. The use of electricity to control, communicate, and process information is called _____.

_____

_____

D. Interpreting Diagrams

Use the diagram to answer each question.

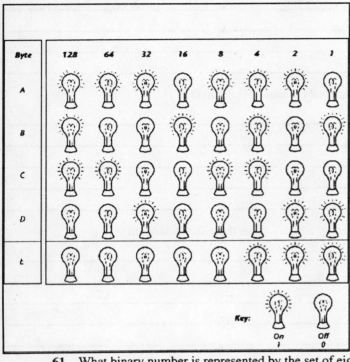

61. What binary number is represented by the set of eight bulbs in byte A?

_____

_____

_____

_____

_____

62. In the base-10 numbering system, what numeral is represented by byte B?

_____

_____

_____

_____

_____

63. Which byte in the diagram represents the binary number 00100011?

_____

_____

_____

_____

_____

64. What byte in the diagram represents the base-10 numeral 204?

_____

_____

_____

_____

_____

65. What is true of any binary representation of a numeral that is odd in base-10 notation?

_____

_____

_____

_____

_____

66. What is the largest base-10 numeral that can be represented by a byte such as those in the diagram?

_____

_____

_____

_____

_____

Use the diagram to answer each question.

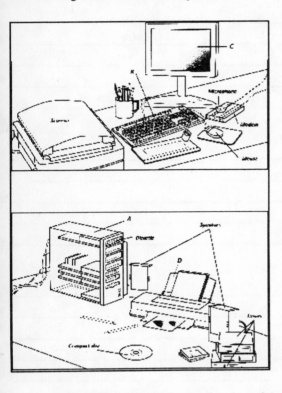

67. What is the name and function of the computer component labeled A?

_____

_____

_____

_____

_____

68. What is the name and function of the computer component labeled B?

_____

_____

_____

_____

69. What is the name and function of the computer component labeled C?

_____

_____

_____

_____

_____

70. What is the name and function of the computer component labeled D?

_____

_____

_____

_____

71. Which objects in the diagram are used for external memory?

_____

_____

_____

_____

72. What is the function of the modem?

_____

_____

_____

_____

E. Essay

Write an answer to each of the following questions.

73. How is sound produced when you play a compact disc?

_____

_____

_____

_____

_____

_____

74. What are the two functions of a transistor?

_____

_____

_____

_____

_____

_____

75. What is an electromagnetic wave? Give an example.

_____

_____

_____

_____

_____

_____

76. How does a radio enable you to select and hear the transmission of only one station?

_____

_____

_____

_____

_____

_____

77. How can magnetic tapes record and store computer information?

_____

_____

_____

_____

_____

_____

78. In a computer system, what is the function of each of the following kinds of devices: input device, output device, and memory device?

_____
_____
_____
_____
_____
_____
_____

79. What is the Internet and how can it be accessed?

_____
_____
_____
_____
_____
_____
_____

80. How is freeware different from shareware?

_____
_____
_____
_____
_____
_____
_____

Test 68 Book N, Chapter 4: Electronics

Answer Key (Short)

__a__	**1.**
__b__	**2.**
__b__	**3.**
__c__	**4.**
__c__	**5.**
__b__	**6.**
__a__	**7.**
__a__	**8.**
__b__	**9.**
__d__	**10.**
__c__	**11.**
__a__	**12.**
__c__	**13.**
__b__	**14.**
__c__	**15.**
__b__	**16.**
__d__	**17.**
__b__	**18.**
__c__	**19.**
__a__	**20.**
__b__	**21.**
__c__	**22.**
__c__	**23.**
__a__	**24.**
__b__	**25.**
__b__	**26.**
__c__	**27.**
__c__	**28.**
__c__	**29.**
__d__	**30.**

31.	false, electronic
32.	false, analog
33.	TRUE
34.	false, fields
35.	false, electromagnetic
36.	false, bit
37.	TRUE
38.	false, wide
39.	TRUE
40.	false, encryption
41.	signal

42.   digital

43.   digital

44.   integrated

45.   diode

46.   amplitude

47.   modulation

48.   sound

49.   satellite

50.   binary

51.   switch

52.   temporary

53.   optical

54.   network

55.   wide

56.   information

57.   virus-checking software

58.   virus

59.   intellectual

60.   electronics

61.   11101110

62.   149 (128 + 16 + 4 + 1)

63.   D

64.   C; 204 = 128 + 64 + 8 + 4

65.   The last (rightmost) digit in the binary byte is 1.

66.   255 (128 + 64 + 32 + 16 + 8 + 4 + 2 + 1)

67.   It is a central processing unit (CPU). It processes and stores information, and coordinates the functions of other parts of the computer.

68.   It is a keyboard. A keyboard is an input device used to type data and instructions directly into a computer.

69.   It is a monitor. It is used to display information.

70.   It is a printer. A printer is an output device that prints information on paper.

71.   diskettes and compact discs

72.   It connects a computer to a telephone line. A modem acts as both an input and output device as information is both sent out and retrieved through it.

73.   When a CD is played, a beam of light scans the pits and flats, where digital information is stored. As the light hits them, it produces flashes. The light flashes are converted to a digital signal. The digital signal is fed into an amplifier and then a speaker, where it is changed into sound.

74.   A transistor can act as an amplifier by increasing the strength of a signal. It can also act as a switch by either letting current through or cutting it off.

75.   An electromagnetic wave is a wave that consists of changing electric and magnetic fields at right angles to each other. Since a changing electric field produces a changing magnetic field and a changing magnetic field produces a changing electric field, the two fields continue to produce each other over and over again. Examples of electromagnetic waves include microwaves, X-rays, and visible light.

76. A tuner in the radio selects the frequency of the carrier wave of the station you want from carrier waves of other frequencies. The radio then amplifies the signal and separates it from the carrier wave. The signal is then sent to the radio speaker, where it is converted into sound.

77. Computer information is stored in binary form using two digits, 0 and 1. Magnetic tapes can record information by changes in the arrangement of the magnetic domains in them. The magnetic domains can be oriented in one direction to represent 1's and in the opposite direction to represent 0's.

78. An input device feeds data to the central processing unit. An output device presents data from the central processing unit. A memory device stores information.

79. The Internet is a network of host computers that extends around the world. It can be accessed through computers of subscribers, who must have an electronic address at which they can be reached.

80. Both are programs that are available through the Internet. Freeware is software that an author has decided to let people use at no charge. Shareware is software that an author allows people to try out for use at a very low fee.

Name _____ Date _____

A. Multiple Choice
Choose the letter of the correct answer.

_____ 1. A disturbance that transfers energy from place to place is called a

    a. wave.

    b. medium.

    c. vibration.

    d. compression.

_____ 2. Waves are created when a source of energy causes a medium to

    a. move.

    b. compress.

    c. expand.

    d. vibrate.

_____ 3. The highest parts of a wave are called

    a. troughs.

    b. crests.

    c. nodes.

    d. wavelengths.

_____ 4. Waves that move the particles of the medium parallel to the direction that the waves are traveling are called

    a. longitudinal waves.

    b. transverse waves.

    c. surface waves.

    d. combination waves.

_____ 5. The maximum distance that the particles of a medium move from the rest position is the

    a. amplitude of the wave.

    b. wavelength of the wave.

    c. frequency of the wave.

    d. speed of the wave.

_____ 6. The distance between two corresponding parts of a wave is the wave's

    a. amplitude.

    b. wavelength.

    c. frequency.

    d. speed.

_____ 7. The speed of a wave is its wavelength multiplied by its

    a. amplitude.

    b. vibration.

    c. frequency.

    d. reflection.

_____ **8.** Which of the following affects the speed of sound waves traveling through the air?

    a. how loud the sound is

    b. the air temperature

    c. how often the sound is repeated

    d. the amplitude of the waves

_____ **9.** The bending of waves due to a change in speed is called

    a. reflection.

    b. refraction.

    c. diffraction.

    d. interference.

_____ **10.** The bending of waves around the edge of a barrier is known as

    a. reflection.

    b. refraction.

    c. diffraction.

    d. interference.

_____ **11.** The interaction between two waves that meet is called

    a. reflection.

    b. refraction.

    c. diffraction.

    d. interference.

_____ **12.** Waves combine to make a wave with larger amplitude in a process called

    a. destructive interference.

    b. constructive interference.

    c. reflection.

    d. refraction.

_____ **13.** When an incoming wave combines with a reflected wave in such a way that the combined wave appears to be standing still, the result is a

    a. longitudinal wave.

    b. standing wave.

    c. transverse wave.

    d. surface wave.

_____ **14.** What occurs when vibrations traveling through an object match the object's natural frequency?

    a. reflection

    b. refraction

    c. diffraction

    d. resonance

_____ **15.** Waves produced by earthquakes are called

     a. standing waves.

     b. transverse waves.

     c. seismic waves.

     d. longitudinal waves.

_____ **16.** In which direction(s) do seismic waves travel from their point of origin?

     a. north to south only

     b. toward the equator only

     c. in all directions

     d. inward, toward Earth's core

_____ **17.** Longitudinal seismic waves are known as

     a. primary waves.

     b. secondary waves.

     c. surface waves.

     d. transverse waves.

_____ **18.** Secondary waves CANNOT travel through

     a. rock.

     b. liquids.

     c. Earth's mantle.

     d. Earth's crust.

_____ **19.** Which waves arrive at a seismograph first?

     a. P waves

     b. P waves

     c. transverse waves

     d. surface waves

_____ **20.** What is another use of a seismograph aside from detecting earthquakes?

     a. measuring tsunamis

     b. locating pockets of valuable substances underground

     c. predicting accurately when and where volcanoes will erupt

     d. locating gold dust in rivers

_____ **21.** What are the highest and lowest points on a standing wave called?

     a. nodes

     b. antinodes

     c. compressions

     d. rarefactions

_____ **22.** The material through which a wave travels is called a

     a. vibration.

     b. medium.

     c. crest.

     d. trough.

_____ **23.** Waves are classified according to

    a.   their size.

    b.   their shape.

    c.   how they move.

    d.   their source.

_____ **24.** Waves in a pond or lake are

    a.   longitudinal waves.

    b.   transverse waves.

    c.   surface waves.

    d.   standing waves.

_____ **25.** Frequency is measured in units called

    a.   amps.

    b.   hertz.

    c.   nodes.

    d.   antinodes.

_____ **26.** Scientists on the side of Earth opposite to the epicenter of an earthquake mainly detect

    a.   P waves.

    b.   S waves.

    c.   transverse waves.

    d.   surface waves.

_____ **27.** Which type of wave caused by an earthquakes does the most above-ground damage?

    a.   surface waves

    b.   P waves

    c.   S waves

    d.   longitudinal waves

_____ **28.** An earthquake that occurs under water can cause huge surface waves on the ocean called

    a.   P waves.

    b.   S waves.

    c.   transverse waves.

    d.   tsunamis.

_____ **29.** When a wave hits a surface through which it CANNOT pass and bounces back, it undergoes

    a.   reflection.

    b.   refraction.

    c.   constructive interference.

    d.   destructive interference.

_____ **30.** Waves combine to produce a smaller or zero-amplitude wave in a process called

    a.   destructive interference.

    b.   constructive interference.

    c.   reflection.

    d.   refraction.

B. True or False

If the statement is true, write true. If it is false, change the underlined word or words to make the statement true.

31. Waves that require a medium through which to pass are called <u>electromagnetic</u> waves.

_____

_____

32. In <u>transverse</u> waves, the medium moves at right angles to the direction in which the wave is traveling.

_____

_____

33. The unit associated with <u>amplitude</u> is the hertz.

_____

_____

34. Sound waves travel at <u>different</u> speeds in different mediums.

_____

_____

35. <u>Refraction</u> is a bending that occurs when a wave moves from one medium to another.

_____

_____

36. <u>Constructive</u> interference occurs when the amplitudes of two waves combine to produce a wave with a smaller amplitude.

_____

_____

37. Nodes are points on a standing wave where the energy of the wave is <u>maximum</u>.

_____

_____

38. The waves produced by earthquakes are known as <u>seismic</u> waves.

_____

_____

39. Tsunamis are huge ocean <u>secondary</u> waves caused by underwater earthquakes.

_____

_____

40. A seismograph records the <u>air</u> movement caused by seismic waves.

_____

_____

C. Completion
Fill in the word or phrase that best completes each statement.

41. A mechanical wave is created when a medium _____, or moves back and forth or up and down.

_____

_____

42. In a longitudinal wave moving along a spring, areas where the coils are farthest apart are called _____.

_____

_____

43. In _____ waves, each particle of the medium moves in a circle.

_____

_____

44. The _____ of a mechanical wave is a direct measure of its energy.

_____

_____

45. If a longitudinal wave has very crowded compressions and very uncrowded rarefactions, it has a large _____.

_____

_____

46. You hear thunder several seconds after you see lightning because light travels at a _____ speed than sound.

_____

_____

47. As the frequency of a wave traveling at constant speed increases, its _____ decreases.

_____

_____

48. _____ occurs when a wave goes around the edge of a barrier.

_____

_____

49. The law of reflection states that the angle of _____ equals the angle of reflection.

_____

_____

50. In _____ interference, the energy of the combined wave is greater than the energy of each of the two waves.

_____

_____

51. When the crests of one wave align with the _____ of an identical wave, the amplitude of the resulting wave is zero.

_____

_____

52. The crests and troughs of a standing wave are called ____.

_____

_____

53. ____ occurs when an object that is vibrating at its natural frequency absorbs energy from objects that vibrate at the same frequency.

_____

_____

54. _____ zones are areas in which there are no seismic waves.

_____

_____

55. When the _____ in rock builds up enough, the rock breaks or changes shape, releasing energy in the form of waves.

_____

_____

56. Transverse seismic waves are known as ____ waves.

_____

_____

57. ____ waves are longitudinal seismic waves.

_____

_____

58. A(n) _____ is an instrument used to detect and measure earthquakes.

_____

_____

59. Scientists can identify the location of an earthquake by comparing readings from at least ____ seismographs at different locations.

_____

_____

60. The material through which a wave travels is called a(n) _____.

_____

_____

D. Interpreting Diagrams
Use the diagram to answer each question.

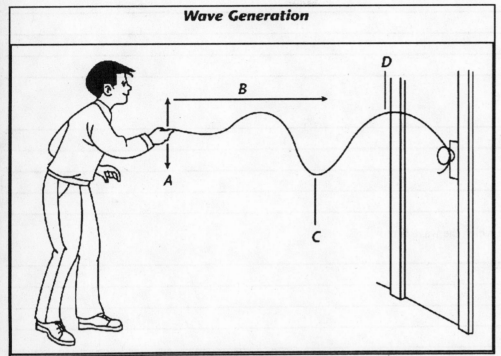

Wave Generation

61. What does the person transfer to the rope by pulling it up and down at point A?

_____

_____

_____

_____

62. What does the direction of arrow B indicate?

_____

_____

_____

_____

_____

63. In what direction does the medium move relative to the direction of the wave? Explain.

_____

_____

_____

_____

_____

64. What kind of wave is being generated?

_____

_____

_____

_____

65. What does point C represent?

_____

_____

_____

_____

66. What is the medium through which the wave is moving?

_____

_____

_____

_____

Use the diagram to answer each question.

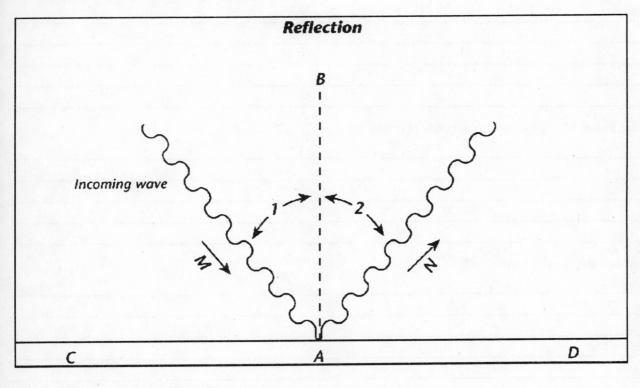

Reflection

67. What does arrow M indicate?

_____

_____

_____

_____

_____

68. What does arrow N indicate?

_____

_____

_____

_____

_____

69. What does the dotted line AB represent?

_____

_____

_____

_____

_____

70. Which numbered angle represents the angle of incidence?

_____

_____

_____

_____

71. Which numbered angle represents the angle of reflection?

_____

_____

_____

_____

72. What does the line CAD represent?

_____

_____

_____

_____

E. Essay

Write an answer to each of the following questions.

73. How does the motion of the particles of the medium differ among transverse, longitudinal, and surface waves?

_____

_____

_____

_____

_____

_____

74. How can you measure the wavelength of a transverse wave? Of a longitudinal wave?

_____

_____

_____

_____

_____

_____

75. Describe how to calculate each of wavelength, speed, and frequency if you know the other two factors. What is the wavelength of a 25-hertz wave traveling at 35 cm/s?

_____

_____

_____

_____

_____

_____

_____

_____

76. Suppose that a reflected light wave has an angle of reflection of 30°. What must be the angle of incidence and what must be the angle between the reflecting surface and the incoming wave? Explain.

_____

_____

_____

_____

_____

_____

77. What is interference? Describe the effect of each of the two types of wave interference on amplitude.

_____

_____

_____

_____

_____

_____

78. How is it possible for a sound to shatter a glass?

_____

_____

_____

_____

_____

_____

79. Why is it that S waves cannot be detected on the side of Earth opposite an earthquake?

_____

_____

_____

_____

_____

_____

80. How do scientists use a seismograph to determine how far away an earthquake has occurred?

_____

_____

_____

_____

_____

_____

Test 69 Book O, Chapter 1: Characteristics of Waves

Answer Key (Short)

__a__	1.
__d__	2.
__b__	3.
__a__	4.
__a__	5.
__b__	6.
__c__	7.
__b__	8.
__b__	9.
__c__	10.
__d__	11.
__b__	12.
__b__	13.
__d__	14.
__c__	15.
__c__	16.
__a__	17.
__b__	18.
__a__	19.
__b__	20.
__b__	21.
__b__	22.
__c__	23.
__c__	24.
__b__	25.
__a__	26.
__a__	27.
__d__	28.
__a__	29.
__a__	30.

31.	false, mechanical
32.	TRUE
33.	false, frequency
34.	TRUE
35.	TRUE
36.	false, Destructive
37.	false, zero
38.	TRUE
39.	false, surface
40.	false, ground
41.	vibrates

42.   rarefactions

43.   surface

44.   amplitude

45.   amplitude

46.   greater (or higher)

47.   wavelength

48.   Diffraction

49.   incidence

50.   constructive

51.   troughs

52.   antinodes

53.   Resonance

54.   Shadow

55.   stress

56.   secondary

57.   Primary

58.   seismograph

59.   three

60.   medium

61.   energy

62.   the direction in which the wave is moving

63.   Perpendicular; the rope moves up and down vertically and the wave moves horizontally.

64.   a transverse wave

65.   a trough

66.   the rope

67.   the direction of the incoming wave

68.   the direction of the reflected wave

69.   an imaginary line drawn perpendicular to the reflecting surface

70.   angle 1

71.   angle 2

72.   the surface of the material from which the wave is reflected

73.   The particles of the medium move perpendicular to the direction in which a transverse wave is traveling. The particles of the medium move parallel to the direction in which a longitudinal wave is traveling. The particles of the medium move in circular paths as a surface wave passes.

74.   In general, you measure the distance between two corresponding parts of the wave. For example, in transverse waves, you might measure the distance from one crest to the next or from one trough to the next. In longitudinal waves, you might measure the distance between one compression and the next or between one rarefaction and the next.

75.   Wavelength is equal to speed divided by frequency. Speed is equal to frequency times wavelength. Frequency is equal to speed divided by wavelength.   Wavelength = Speed/Frequency = (35 cm/s) / 25 hertz = (35 cm/s) / (25/s) = 1.4 cm

76. For the angle of reflection to be 30°, the angle of incidence must be 30°, too, because these two angles are always equal. So the angle between an imaginary line perpendicular to the surface of the barrier and the incoming wave must be 30°. For this to happen, the angle between the surface of the barrier and the incoming wave must be 90° - 30° = 60°.

77. Wave interference occurs when two waves meet and have an effect on each other. Constructive interference increases wave amplitude. Destructive interference decreases wave amplitude.

78. The frequency of the sound could match the natural frequency of the glass. Resonance would occur and the increased energy of the vibrations could cause the glass to shatter.

79. S waves cannot travel through liquids. So they cannot travel through the liquid core of Earth to the side opposite the earthquake.

80. P waves arrive at a seismograph earlier than S waves because P waves travel faster. By measuring the time between the arrival of the P waves and the S waves, scientists can tell how far away the earthquake was.

Test 70 Book O, Chapter 2: Sound

A. Multiple Choice
   Choose the letter of the correct answer.

_____ 1. Sound is a disturbance that travels through a medium as a

   a. longitudinal wave.

   b. surface wave.

   c. standing wave.

   d. transverse wave.

_____ 2. Sound does NOT travel through

   a. air.

   b. liquids.

   c. solids.

   d. outer space.

_____ 3. The speed of sound depends on

   a. the loudness of the sound.

   b. the pitch of the sound.

   c. the source of the sound.

   d. the properties of the medium it travels through.

_____ 4. The ability of a material to bounce back after being disturbed is called

   a. density.

   b. elasticity.

   c. intensity.

   d. frequency.

_____ 5. The first person to break the sound barrier was

   a. Orville Wright.

   b. Andy Green.

   c. Chuck Yeager.

   d. John Glenn.

_____ 6. Why did Chuck Yeager's team chose a high altitude to try to break the sound barrier?

   a. The temperature is lower, so the speed of sound is higher.

   b. The temperature is lower, so the speed of sound is lower.

   c. The temperature is higher, so the speed of sound is higher.

   d. The temperature is higher, so the speed of sound is lower.

_____ 7. The amount of energy a sound wave carries per second through a unit area is its

   a. loudness.

   b. intensity.

   c. frequency.

   d. pitch.

_____ 8. Loudness, or sound level, is measured in units called

    a. decibels.

    b. hertz.

    c. meters per second.

    d. watts per square meter.

_____ 9. Which term refers to how high or low a sound seems to a person?

    a. loudness

    b. intensity

    c. frequency

    d. pitch

_____ 10. The pitch of a sound that you hear depends on the sound wave's

    a. loudness.

    b. frequency.

    c. intensity.

    d. speed.

_____ 11. The changing pitch of a police car's siren as it moves by you is an example of

    a. the Doppler effect.

    b. resonance.

    c. the speed of sound.

    d. intensity.

_____ 12. As a sound source moves toward a listener, the pitch

    a. appears to decrease.

    b. appears to increase.

    c. stays the same.

    d. goes up and down repeatedly.

_____ 13. A fundamental tone is a sound wave of only one

    a. frequency.

    b. pitch.

    c. timbre.

    d. intensity.

_____ 14. What is a set of tones combined in a way that is pleasing to the ear?

    a. noise

    b. sound

    c. music

    d. timbre

_____ 15. What occurs when two or more sound waves interact?

    a. interference

    b. Doppler effect

    c. resonance

    d. ultrasound

_____ **16.** How well sounds can be heard in a particular room or hall is described by

    a. pitch.

    b. resonance.

    c. acoustics.

    d. timbre.

_____ **17.** Which part of your ear do sound waves enter through?

    a. ear canal

    b. eardrum

    c. earlobe

    d. cochlea

_____ **18.** Which part of your ear sends the message to your brain that you've heard a sound?

    a. the outermost part of your ear

    b. the vibrating eardrum

    c. the hammer, anvil, and stirrup located in your middle ear

    d. the cochlea hairs that are attached to nerve cells

_____ **19.** Which of the following can cause hearing loss?

    a. listening to soft music

    b. going outside in cold weather

    c. viral or bacterial infections

    d. working in a quiet office

_____ **20.** The most common type of hearing loss is due to

    a. injury.

    b. infection.

    c. loud noise or music.

    d. aging.

_____ **21.** A system of detecting reflected sound waves is

    a. dissonance.

    b. infrasound.

    c. sonar.

    d. acoustics.

_____ **22.** What do bats use to locate food and to navigate?

    a. dissonance

    b. echolocation

    c. infrasound

    d. acoustics

_____ **23.** Sound waves with frequencies above 20,000 Hz are called

    a. ultrasound.

    b. infrasound.

    c. sonar.

    d. echolocation.

_____ **24.** Doctors are able to make sonograms through the use of

    a.   ultrasound.

    b.   infrasound.

    c.   sonar.

    d.   acoustics.

_____ **25.** You can hear sounds from around corners because of

    a.   refraction.

    b.   reflection.

    c.   diffraction.

    d.   elasticity.

_____ **26.** Sound travels more slowly

    a.   in dense materials.

    b.   in mediums that have a high degree of elasticity.

    c.   in very cold temperatures.

    d.   at low altitudes.

_____ **27.** At what level does sound become painful to most people?

    a.   10 dE

    b.   40 dB

    c.   85 dB

    d.   120 dB

_____ **28.** Sound waves with frequencies above the normal human range of hearing are called

    a.   ultrasound.

    b.   infrasound.

    c.   resonance.

    d.   decibels.

_____ **29.** What is a mixture of sound waves that do not sound pleasing together called?

    a.   music

    b.   noise

    c.   timbre

    d.   pitch

_____ **30.** Which household item might use ultrasound?

    a.   toaster oven

    b.   coffee machine

    c.   hair dryer

    d.   electric toothbrush

B. True or False

If the statement is true, write true. If it is false, change the underlined word or words to make the statement true.

31. Sound waves are <u>longitudinal.</u>

_____

_____

32. The speed of sound in air <u>decreases</u> with increasing temperature.

_____

_____

33. The loudness of a sound that can just barely be heard is <u>100</u> dB.

_____

_____

34. The frequency of the sound waves produced by a string increases as the tension of the string <u>decreases.</u>

_____

_____

35. Timbre describes the <u>loudness</u> of a sound you hear.

_____

_____

36. Interference occurs when two or more sound waves <u>interact.</u>

_____

_____

37. The hammer, anvil, and stirrup are bones that make up the <u>inner</u> ear.

_____

_____

38. It is not safe to put objects into your ear, even to clean it, because you may puncture the <u>eardrum.</u>

_____

_____

39. The ability of fish to hear <u>low-frequency</u> sound waves may allow them to escape animals that use echolocation to find prey.

_____

_____

40. <u>Ultrasonic</u> cleaners use the vibrations of sound waves to shake dirt away from objects.

_____

_____

C. Completion
Fill in the word or phrase that best completes each statement.

41. The _____ of a sound wave is the distance between a compression or rarefaction and the next compression or rarefaction.

_____

_____

42. Because of _____, sound waves entering through a doorway spread to all parts of a room.

_____

_____

43. The _____ of a medium is the amount of mass there is in a given amount of space, or volume.

_____

_____

44. The state of matter that is generally the poorest transmitter of sound is the _____ state.

_____

_____

45. An object that travels faster than sound is said to travel at _____ speed.

_____

_____

46. The unit associated with _____ is the watt per square meter (W/m^2).

_____

_____

47. If two sound waves differ in intensity, the wave that is more intense sounds _____.

_____

_____

48. Sound waves with frequencies _____ than the normal human range of hearing are called infrasound.

_____

_____

49. A short string under a certain tension generally produces a sound with a higher _____ than a long string under the same tension.

_____

_____

50. A sonic _____ is a huge amount of energy released in the form of a shock wave.

_____

_____

51. Sound that generally has no pleasing timbre and no identifiable pitch is referred to as _____.

_____

_____

52. The repeating changes in loudness of two sound waves that are interfering are called _____.

_____

_____

53. The acoustics of a good concert hall should have no echoes and little _____ interference.

_____

_____

54. The ear canal ends at a tightly stretched membrane called the _____.

_____

_____

55. The _____ is a liquid-filled cavity in the inner ear.

_____

_____

56. Earplugs prevent the ___ of the cochlea from becoming damaged by long exposure to loud sounds.

_____

_____

57. An echo is a _____ sound wave.

_____

_____

58. The use of sound waves by bats to navigate and find food is called _____.

_____

_____

59. A(n) _____ is a picture of the inside of the human body produced by ultrasound.

_____

_____

60. A sonogram analyzes both the intensity and _____ of reflected ultrasonic waves.

_____

_____

D. Interpreting Diagrams
Use the diagram to answer each question.

Speed of Sound	
Medium	**Speed (m/s)**
Gases	
Air (0°C)	331
Air (20°C)	340
Liquids	
Fresh water	1,490
Salt water	1,531
Solids (25°C)	
Lead	1,210
Plastic	1,800
Silver	2,680
Copper	3,100
Gold	3,240
Brick	3,650
Hard wood	4,000
Glass	4,540
Iron	5,000
Steel	5,200

61. In which medium listed in the table does sound travel slowest?

_____
_____
_____
_____
_____

62. In which medium listed in the table does sound travel fastest?

_____
_____
_____
_____
_____

63. Compare the speed of sound in iron with the speed of sound in lead. How are these speeds related to each metal's density?

_____
_____
_____
_____
_____

64. Explain why there is a difference between the speed of sound in air at 0°C and the speed of sound in air at 20°C.

_____

_____

_____

_____

_____

65. What is the speed of sound in glass at 25°C?

_____

_____

_____

_____

_____

66. Explain why there is a difference between the speed of sound in fresh water and the speed of sound in salt water.

_____

_____

_____

_____

_____

Use the diagram to answer each question.

Sonar

Ocean floor

67. What is happening in the diagram?

_____

_____

_____

_____

68. Where is the sonar device located?

_____

_____

_____

_____

69. What type of sound waves does the sonar device produce?

_____

_____

_____

_____

70. What do the arrows that run from A to B represent?

_____

_____

_____

_____

71. What do the arrows that run from B to C represent?

_____

_____

_____

_____

72. Suppose that the sound waves of a sonar device on the ship are sent down and reflected back up by the sunken ship. If it takes 3 seconds for the waves to travel from their source to the sunken ship and back, what is the depth of sunken ship? (Assume that the speed of the sound waves is 1,520 m/s.)

_____

_____

_____

_____

E. Essay

   Write an answer to each of the following questions.

73. How does a drum make a sound when it is struck?

_____

_____

_____

_____

_____

316

74. Why can you hear a sound around a corner of a building?

_____

_____

_____

_____

_____

_____

_____

75. Explain how the speed of sound in a medium is related to the temperature of the medium.

_____

_____

_____

_____

_____

_____

_____

76. Give an example of the Doppler effect, and explain how it occurs.

_____

_____

_____

_____

_____

_____

_____

77. How is the timbre of an instrument related to the overtones it produces?

_____

_____

_____

_____

_____

_____

_____

78. Describe the functions of the three main sections of the ear.

_____

_____

_____

_____

_____

_____

_____

79. Give an example of noise. Explain what makes a sound a noise.

_____

_____

_____

_____

_____

_____

_____

80. How does a camera use ultrasound to focus automatically?

_____

_____

_____

_____

_____

_____

Name _____ Date _____

Test 70 Book O, Chapter 2: Sound
Answer Key (Short)

__a__	1.
__d__	2.
__d__	3.
__b__	4.
__c__	5.
__b__	6.
__b__	7.
__a__	8.
__d__	9.
__b__	10.
__a__	11.
__b__	12.
__a__	13.
__c__	14.
__a__	15.
__c__	16.
__a__	17.
__d__	18.
__c__	19.
__d__	20.
__c__	21.
__b__	22.
__a__	23.
__a__	24.
__c__	25.
__a__	26.
__d__	27.
__a__	28.
__b__	29.
__d__	30.

31. TRUE
32. false, increases
33. false, 0
34. false, increases
35. quality
36. TRUE
37. false, middle
38. TRUE
39. false, high-frequency
40. TRUE
41. wavelength

42.		diffraction
43.		density
44.		gas (or gaseous)
45.		supersonic
46.		intensity
47.		louder
48.		lower
49.		pitch
50.		boom
51.		noise
52.		beats
53.		destructive
54.		eardrum
55.		cochlea
56.		hairs
57.		reflected
58.		echolocation
59.		sonogram
60.		frequency
61.		air at 0°C
62.		steel

63.   Sound travels more than four times as fast in iron as it does in lead. Both metals are in the same state, but the density of lead is greater than that of iron. The particles in a dense solid do not move as quickly as particles in a less-dense solid, so the speed of sound is lower.

64.   At the lower temperature, the particles of the air tend to move more slowly and respond less readily to the energy of the sound wave, making the speed of sound in air lower at 0°C than at 20°C.

65.   4,540 m/s

66.   Both are in the same state, but salt water is denser than fresh water. The particles in a dense liquid do not move as quickly as particles in a less-dense liquid, so the speed of sound is lower.

67.   Sonar is being used to locate sunken objects and determine depth.

68.   on the ship above

69.   ultrasonic

70.   ultrasonic sound waves sent out from the ship

71.   reflected ultrasonic sound waves

72.   The time for the sound waves to reach the sunken ship is half the time for the round trip, or $1/2 \cdot 3\ s = 1.5\ s$.
        $Distance = Speed \cdot Time = 1{,}520\ m/s \cdot 1.5\ s = 2{,}280\ m$

73.   When a drum is struck, it begins to vibrate. As it vibrates, it pushes up and down on the air around it. The up-and-down motion produces compressions and rarefactions in the air, which form a longitudinal wave. If the frequency of the wave is within the range of human hearing, the wave will be heard as a sound.

74.   When sound waves pass near a barrier, such as a building, they diffract, or spread out and bend around it. The waves are thus able to reach you even though you are around the corner.

75.   The speed of sound increases as the temperature of the medium increases. This occurs because the particles that make up the medium move faster at higher temperatures.

76. Answers will vary. One example is the sound of a racecar engine as it moves past a stationary listener. As the car approaches, the pitch of the engine sounds higher than when the car is standing still. This is because the sound waves bunch up in front of the car, which means that the frequency increases. As the car passes, the pitch seems to drop. This is because the waves spread out behind the car. The frequency decreases, and the pitch sounds lower as the car moves away than when it is standing still.

77. When an instrument plays a note, the fundamental tone of the note has a certain frequency. The instrument also produces overtones, which are sounds that have frequencies that are multiples of the fundamental frequency. The blending of the fundamental tone and overtones make up the characteristic sound of the instrument, which is instrument's timbre.

78. The outer ear collects sound waves and funnels them into the ear canal and to the eardrum, which vibrates. The middle ear transmits the waves inward by means of three small bones. The inner ear contains a liquid-filled cochlea lined with hairs that sway as a result of the vibrations. Nerves carry the information to the brain.

79. Examples will vary, but should include any sound generally perceived as unpleasant (jackhammer, subway train, lawnmower). Noise lacks pleasing quality and usually has no identifiable pitch.

80. As you push the button to take a picture of an object, the camera sends out ultrasound waves. The waves reflect off the object and return to the camera. The camera measures the time it takes for the waves to return and calculates the distance. It then adjusts the lens accordingly.

A. Multiple Choice
Choose the letter of the correct answer.

_____ 1. Which waves have some electrical properties and some magnetic properties?

    a. longitudinal waves

    b. transverse waves

    c. mechanical waves

    d. electromagnetic waves

_____ 2. Electromagnetic waves can transfer energy without a(n)

    a. medium.

    b. electric field.

    c. magnetic field.

    d. change in either a magnetic or an electric field.

_____ 3. Light that has passed through a polarizing filter is called

    a. transverse light.

    b. polarized light.

    c. white light.

    d. photoelectric light.

_____ 4. In 1905, Albert Einstein suggested that light energy travels in tiny packets or particles called

    a. neutrons.

    b. electrons.

    c. photons.

    d. gamma rays.

_____ 5. All electromagnetic waves have the same

    a. wavelength.

    b. frequency.

    c. speed.

    d. amplitude.

_____ 6. Visible light has a higher frequency than

    a. X-rays.

    b. ultraviolet rays.

    c. infrared rays.

    d. gamma rays.

_____ 7. The range of electromagnetic waves placed in a certain order is called the

    a. electromagnetic spectrum.

    b. electromagnetic wavelength.

    c. electromagnetic frequency.

    d. electromagnetic field.

_____ 8. The electromagnetic waves with the highest frequencies are called

    a. radio waves.

    b. gamma rays.

    c. X-rays.

    d. visible light.

_____ 9. When a police officer uses radar for speed control, the officer is using what kind of electromagnetic waves?

    a. radio waves

    b. gamma rays

    c. ultraviolet rays

    d. X-rays

_____ 10. White light can be separated into the various colors of the visible spectrum to form a(n)

    a. rainbow.

    b. thermogram.

    c. MRI.

    d. X-ray picture.

_____ 11. Which type of light bulb glows when a filament inside it gets hot?

    a. incandescent

    b. fluorescent

    c. sodium vapor

    d. neon

_____ 12. Which light bulbs are coated on the inside with a powder?

    a. incandescent

    b. fluorescent

    c. neon

    d. sodium vapor

_____ 13. If something vibrates one million times per second, it has a frequency of

    a. 1 hertz.

    b. 10 hertz.

    c. 1 megahertz.

    d. 1 kilohertz.

_____ 14. FM signals travel as changes in

    a. the speed of the wave.

    b. the amplitude of the wave.

    c. the frequency of the wave.

    d. the loudness of the wave.

_____ 15. What kind of waves do cellular telephones use to transmit and receive signals?

    a. gamma rays

    b. microwaves

    c. ultraviolet rays

    d. infrared rays

_____ **16.** Small electronic communication devices that people carry in their pockets or attach to their clothes are called

    a.   cordless telephones.

    b.   pagers.

    c.   televisions.

    d.   satellites.

_____ **17.** Broadcasting stations can send their signals around the world using

    a.   cellular telephones.

    b.   television satellites.

    c.   pagers.

    d.   the Global Positioning System.

_____ **18.** Global Positioning System signals can tell you

    a.   what television station you are tuned to.

    b.   your exact location on Earth.

    c.   how many satellites are in orbit.

    d.   who is sending a message to your pager.

_____ **19.** What is transferred by electromagnetic waves?

    a.   sound

    b.   electricity

    c.   electromagnetic radiation

    d.   resonance

_____ **20.** About how much faster than sound are electromagnetic waves?

    a.   ten times faster

    b.   one million times faster

    c.   one hundred times faster

    d.   one thousand times faster

_____ **21.** Which type of light bulb is commonly used in advertising signs and decoration?

    a.   incandescent

    b.   fluorescent

    c.   neon

    d.   sodium vapor

_____ **22.** Which type of light bulb is used in overhead projectors?

    a.   tungsten-halogen

    b.   neon

    c.   sodium vapor

    d.   fluorescent

_____ **23.** Which electromagnetic waves have the longest wavelengths and lowest frequencies?

    a.   infrared waves

    b.   radio waves

    c.   ultraviolet rays

    d.   gamma rays

_____ **24.** On AM broadcasts, what remains constant?

   a. the amplitude
   b. the music
   c. the frequency
   d. the speech

_____ **25.** Microwaves can be used to

   a. treat cancer.
   b. make rainbows.
   c. heat food.
   d. create an X-ray image.

_____ **26.** The process that uses radio waves and magnetism to produce images of tissues in the human body is called

   a. ultrasound.
   b. radar.
   c. magnetic resonance imaging.
   d. radiation treatment.

_____ **27.** The images made by an infrared camera are called

   a. X-rays.
   b. thermograms.
   c. magnetic resonance images.
   d. ultraviolet images.

_____ **28.** Which of the following is true of ultraviolet rays?

   a. They are visible.
   b. They carry information to televisions and radios.
   c. They help your body produce vitamin D.
   d. They provide the energy that makes your morning toast.

_____ **29.** The Global Positioning System (GPS) was originally designed for use by the

   a. citizens of the United States.
   b. transportation industry, worldwide.
   c. United States military.
   d. radio and television stations in the United States.

_____ **30.** An instrument used to view different colors of light produced by each type of light bulb is called a(n)

   a. thermogram.
   b. spectroscope.
   c. radar gun.
   d. MRI machine.

B. True or False

If the statement is true, write true. If it is false, change the underlined word or words to make the statement true.

31. Electromagnetic waves are classified as <u>longitudinal</u> waves.

_____

_____

32. <u>Polarized</u> light consists of waves that vibrate in one direction only.

_____

_____

33. Electromagnetic waves with the longest wavelengths have the <u>highest</u> frequencies.

_____

_____

34. The tuner on a radio allows you to select a station based on the <u>amplitude</u> of the radio waves transmitted from the radio station.

_____

_____

35. Electromagnetic waves that have wavelengths slightly shorter than those of visible light are called <u>ultraviolet rays</u>.

_____

_____

36. Thermograms are produced by <u>X-rays</u>.

_____

_____

37. In a sodium vapor light, neon and argon gas are heated until they cause sodium to change from a <u>liquid</u> into a gas.

_____

_____

38. Each radio and television station is assigned a basic broadcast frequency known as the <u>carrier</u> frequency.

_____

_____

39. Cellular telephones transmit and receive signals using high-frequency <u>gamma rays</u>.

_____

_____

40. <u>Satellite</u> telephone systems make long-distance telephone calls more easily available and less costly.

_____

_____

C. Completion
Fill in the word or phrase that best completes each statement.

41. Energy that does not require a medium and is transferred by electromagnetic waves is called electromagnetic _____.

_____

_____

42. In electromagnetic waves, the magnetic fields are _____ to the electric fields.

_____

_____

43. In the phenomenon known as the _____ effect, electric current will flow when light shines on certain substances.

_____

_____

44. For two polarizing filters to block light passing through them, one filter should be rotated ___ degrees from the other.

_____

_____

45. The _____ rays in sunlight can cause sunburn.

_____

_____

46. The radio waves with the shortest wavelengths and the highest frequencies are called _____.

_____

_____

47. Red light has the longest _____ of any color of visible light.

_____

_____

48. The part of the electromagnetic spectrum you can see is called _____ light.

_____

_____

49. The electromagnetic waves that have the lowest frequencies are called _____ waves.

_____

_____

50. _____ are used to make images of bones inside the human body.

_____

_____

51. A thermogram identifies the warm and cool parts of an object by analyzing _____ rays.

_____

_____

52. Most of the energy produced by an incandescent bulb is given off as _____ rays.

_____

_____

53. As an electric _____ passes through the gas in a neon light, gas particles absorb energy.

_____

_____

54. AM signals travel as changes in the _____ of a radio wave.

_____

_____

55. Radio transmissions are produced when charged particles move back and forth in instruments such as transmission _____.

_____

_____

56. Each cell in a cellular system has its own transmitter and _____.

_____

_____

57. The information of a pager message is coded at the _____ station and then sent as electromagnetic waves to the correct pager.

_____

_____

58. _____ satellites are satellites orbiting Earth that receive radio, television, and telephone signals and then transmit them around the world.

_____

_____

59. Signals from at least _____ satellites in the Global Positioning System are needed to determine the position of an object.

_____

_____

60. An electromagnetic wave consists of changing electric and magnetic _____.

_____

_____

D. Interpreting Diagrams
Use the diagram to answer each question.

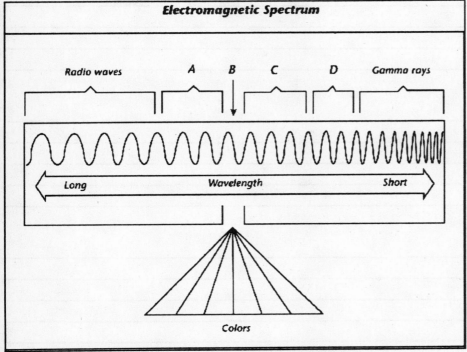

Electromagnetic Spectrum

Radio waves   A   B   C   D   Gamma rays

Long   Wavelength   Short

Colors

61. Name the type of wave that has the highest frequency.

_____

_____

_____

_____

_____

62. Name the type of wave labeled C.

_____

_____

_____

_____

63. Name the type of wave that has the greatest energy.

_____

_____

_____

_____

64. Which letter shows the type of wave that can be seen by the human eye?

_____

_____

_____

_____

_____

65. Name the type of wave labeled A.

_____

_____

_____

_____

66. Which letter indicates X-rays?

_____

_____

_____

_____

Use the diagram to answer each question.

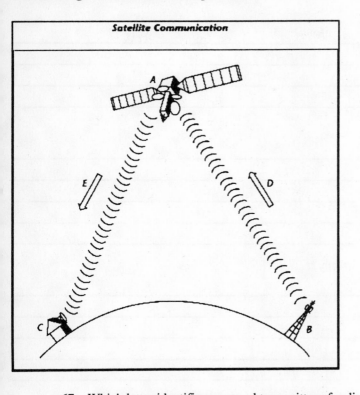

Satellite Communication

67. Which letter identifies a ground transmitter of radio waves?

_____
_____
_____
_____
_____

68. Which letter represents a ground receiver of radio waves?

_____
_____
_____
_____
_____

69. What is the object labeled A?

_____
_____
_____
_____
_____

70. What does object A do when it acts a receiver?

_____

_____

_____

_____

71. What does object A do when it acts as a transmitter?

_____

_____

_____

_____

72. What prevents the radio waves from B from reaching C directly?

_____

_____

_____

_____

E. Essay

Write an answer to each of the following questions.

73. Look at the following group of terms and decide which term does not belong: *star, candle flame, moon,* and *glowing light bulb filament.* Give a reason for your choice.

_____

_____

_____

_____

_____

_____

74. Explain how light can be thought of as both a particle and a wave.

_____

_____

_____

_____

_____

_____

_____

_____

75. Compare and contrast the properties of visible light, ultraviolet rays, and X-rays.

_____

_____

_____

_____

_____

_____

_____

_____

76. What properties of gamma rays make them useful in medicine? Explain.

_____

_____

_____

_____

_____

_____

_____

77. How is light produced in a fluorescent bulb? In an incandescent bulb?

_____

_____

_____

_____

_____

_____

78. Which type of radio broadcast has a greater distance range, AM or FM? Explain.

_____

_____

_____

_____

_____

_____

_____

79. Contrast the transmission of signals by a cellular telephone with the transmission of signals by a cordless telephone.

_____

_____

_____

_____

_____

_____

_____

80. How do television networks use communications satellites?

_____

_____

_____

_____

_____

_____

_____

Test 71 Book O, Chapter 3: The Electromagnetic Spectrum
Answer Key (Short)

__d__	**1.**
__a__	**2.**
__b__	**3.**
__c__	**4.**
__c__	**5.**
__c__	**6.**
__a__	**7.**
__b__	**8.**
__a__	**9.**
__a__	**10.**
__a__	**11.**
__b__	**12.**
__c__	**13.**
__c__	**14.**
__b__	**15.**
__b__	**16.**
__b__	**17.**
__b__	**18.**
__c__	**19.**
__b__	**20.**
__c__	**21.**
__a__	**22.**
__b__	**23.**
__c__	**24.**
__c__	**25.**
__c__	**26.**
__b__	**27.**
__c__	**28.**
__c__	**29.**
__b__	**30.**

31.   false, transverse

32.   TRUE

33.   false, lowest

34.   false, frequency

35.   TRUE

36.   false, infrared rays

37.   false, solid

38.   TRUE

39.   false, radio waves (or microwaves)

40.   TRUE

41.   radiation

42.	perpendicular
43.	photoelectric
44.	90
45.	ultraviolet
46.	microwaves
47.	wavelength
48.	visible
49.	radio
50.	X-rays
51.	infrared
52.	infrared
53.	current
54.	amplitude
55.	antennas
56.	receiver
57.	receiving
58.	Communications
59.	three
60.	fields
61.	gamma rays
62.	ultraviolet
63.	gamma rays
64.	B
65.	infrared
66.	D
67.	B
68.	C
69.	communications satellite
70.	It receives radio, television, and telephone signals from Earth.
71.	The satellite relays signals it receives from Earth back to other receivers on Earth and may strengthen them.
72.	the curvature of Earth
73.	Moon; the moon is an illuminated object, which reflects light. A star, candle flame, and glowing light bulb filament are luminous objects, which produce light.
74.	Light can be described as made up of a stream of particles called photons, but also as electromagnetic wave. Light acts like a stream of particles in the photoelectric effect, but acts like a wave when it becomes polarized. Both the particle and wave models are necessary to explain all the properties of electromagnetic radiation.
75.	Visible light, ultraviolet rays, and X-rays are all parts of the electromagnetic spectrum, and travel at about 300,000,000 m/s in a vacuum. Visible light can be seen, but not ultraviolet rays or X-rays. Ultraviolet rays have shorter wavelengths, higher frequencies, and higher energy than visible light. X-rays have shorter wavelengths, higher frequencies, and higher energy than ultraviolet rays.
76.	Gamma rays have the highest energy of the electromagnetic spectrum. They are the most penetrating because of their energy. Gamma rays can be used to kill cancer cells in radiation therapy. Gamma rays can also be used to examine the body's internal structures. For example, a patient can be injected with a fluid that emits gamma rays. A gamma-ray detector can then form an image of the inside of the body.

77.   In a fluorescent bulb, an electric current passes through a gas in the bulb, causing the gas to emit ultraviolet rays. The ultraviolet rays hit a powder that coats the inside of the bulb, which causes the coating to emit visible light. In an incandescent light bulb, an electric current passes through and heats a thin wire filament made of tungsten. The filament then glows white, emitting all colors of visible light.

78.   AM; the ionosphere reflects transmitted AM waves back toward Earth, so that they "bend" around the curvature of Earth. For that reason, the broadcast of AM waves can reach great distances. FM waves more readily pass through the ionosphere because they have higher frequencies and more energy than AM waves. They are not reflected back toward Earth and thus cannot bend around Earth's curvature.

79.   Cellular telephones transmit signals using high-frequency radio waves, called microwaves, from one cell to another nearby cell. Cordless telephones are connected to the telephone system in the same way as ordinary telephones. Information is transferred from the handset to the base of the telephone by radio waves rather than by electric signals through a cord.

80.   Television networks use communications satellites to send their signals to local stations across the world. The television signals are changed into radio waves using frequency modulation. Some people can receive signals directly from the satellite by using dish-shaped antennas called satellite dishes.

Test 72 Book O, Chapter 4: Light

A. Multiple Choice
Choose the letter of the correct answer.

_____ 1. A material that reflects or absorbs any light that strikes it is

     a. opaque.

     b. transparent.

     c. translucent.

     d. concave.

_____ 2. Frosted glass and wax paper are

     a. transparent.

     b. translucent.

     c. clear.

     d. opaque.

_____ 3. What happens when parallel rays of light hit a smooth surface?

     a. diffuse reflection

     b. diffraction

     c. refraction

     d. regular reflection

_____ 4. When the surface of a mirror curves inward, like the inside of a bowl, it is called a

     a. plane mirror.

     b. convex mirror.

     c. concave mirror.

     d. diffuse mirror.

_____ 5. The bending of light rays as they enter a new medium is called

     a. diffuse reflection.

     b. regular reflection.

     c. refraction.

     d. diffraction.

_____ 6. What happens when light passes from air into water?

     a. The light speeds up.

     b. The light continues at the same speed.

     c. The light slows down.

     d. The light forms a mirage.

_____ 7. A curved piece of glass or other transparent material that is used to refract light is called a(n)

     a. mirror.

     b. lens.

     c. reflector.

     d. optical fiber.

_____ 8. Because the light rays never meet, a concave lens can produce

    a. no image.

    b. both real and virtual images.

    c. only a real image.

    d. only a virtual image.

_____ 9. What happens when white light strikes a black object?

    a. Blue light is reflected.

    b. Red light is reflected.

    c. No light is reflected.

    d. All of the light is reflected.

_____ 10. How would a tomato look under blue light?

    a. The tomato will seem to disappear.

    b. The tomato still appears red.

    c. The tomato appears black.

    d. The tomato appears white.

_____ 11. The primary colors of light are

    a. red, yellow, and blue.

    b. yellow, cyan, and magenta.

    c. red, green, and blue.

    d. red, orange, yellow, green, blue, and violet.

_____ 12. Opaque substances that are used to color other materials are called

    a. pigments.

    b. lenses.

    c. mirages.

    d. filters.

_____ 13. The colored ring of muscle that controls the size of the pupil is called the

    a. cornea.

    b. iris.

    c. lens.

    d. retina.

_____ 14. The signals generated by the rods and cones are carried to your brain by the

    a. cornea.

    b. pupil.

    c. optic nerve.

    d. lens.

_____ 15. A person is nearsighted if he or she

    a. can see far away things very well.

    b. has eyeballs that are a little too short.

    c. has eyeballs that are a little too long.

    d. sees nearby objects as blurry.

_____ **16.** Farsightedness can usually be corrected using

    a.   convex mirrors.

    b.   concave mirrors.

    c.   convex lenses.

    d.   concave lenses.

_____ **17.** What instruments use lenses or mirrors to collect and focus light from distant objects?

    a.   microscopes

    b.   optical fibers

    c.   telescopes

    d.   lasers

_____ **18.** Which device uses lenses to focus light rays and record an image of an object on photographic film?

    a.   microscope

    b.   reflecting telescope

    c.   refracting telescope

    d.   camera

_____ **19.** A laser produces light that

    a.   is incoherent.

    b.   has many different colors.

    c.   is coherent.

    d.   has many different wavelengths.

_____ **20.** What instrument is used in holography?

    a.   telescope

    b.   microscope

    c.   laser

    d.   camera

_____ **21.** Long, thin strands of glass or plastic that carry light for long distances without allowing the light to fade are called

    a.   lasers.

    b.   holograms.

    c.   optical fibers.

    d.   compact discs.

_____ **22.** A laser beam can travel through a curled up optical fiber due to

    a.   diffuse reflection.

    b.   holography.

    c.   total internal reflection.

    d.   regular reflection.

_____ **23.** Clear glass, water, and air are examples of what kind of material?

    a.   opaque

    b.   fluid

    c.   translucent

    d.   transparent

_____ **24.** What occurs when parallel rays of light hit a rough or bumpy surface?

    a. regular reflection

    b. diffuse reflection

    c. refraction

    d. diffraction

_____ **25.** An image of a distant object caused by refraction of light is called a

    a. prism.

    b. mirage.

    c. rainbow.

    d. hologram.

_____ **26.** A photographic slide is an example of a(n)

    a. color filter.

    b. opaque material.

    c. transparent material.

    d. reflecting material.

_____ **27.** Why are lasers useful in surgery?

    a. They increase the amount of blood loss from an incision.

    b. Laser incisions usually heal faster than scalpel cuts.

    c. They add light to the operating room.

    d. The beam of light is very weak.

_____ **28.** Any two primary colors of light combined in equal amounts produce

    a. a complematary color.

    b. a secondary color.

    c. a fluorescent color.

    d. the third primary color.

_____ **29.** The transparent front surface of the eye is called the

    a. cornea.

    b. iris.

    c. pupil.

    d. retina.

_____ **30.** Rods and cones are the light-sensitive cells on the

    a. cornea.

    b. iris.

    c. pupil.

    d. retina.

B. True or False

   If the statement is true, write true. If it is false, change the underlined word or words to make the statement true.

31. A transparent material <u>absorbs</u> light.

_____

_____

32. A <u>virtual</u> image is formed where light rays meet at a point.

_____

_____

33. A mirage is caused by <u>reflection</u> as light passes through layers of air at different temperatures.

_____

_____

34. A convex lens is <u>thicker</u> in the center than at its edges.

_____

_____

35. A white carpet will appear red when viewed through a red filter because the filter <u>absorbs</u> red light only.

_____

_____

36. A secondary color of light is produced by mixing <u>three</u> primary colors together.

_____

_____

37. To focus light, muscles in the eye change the length and thickness of the <u>retina</u>.

_____

_____

38. Nearby objects appear blurry to a person who is <u>farsighted</u>.

_____

_____

39. The <u>eyepiece</u> of a telescope or microscope magnifies an image.

_____

_____

40. Light waves that are in step, or have crests aligned with crests, are said to be <u>focused</u>.

_____

_____

C. Completion
Fill in the word or phrase that best completes each statement.

41. A _____ material is one that allows light to pass through it, but not very well.

_____

_____

42. Glare from a glass window pane is an example of light that has been _____ from a transparent material.

_____

_____

43. Diffuse _____ occurs when parallel rays of light hit a bumpy, or uneven, surface.

_____

_____

44. A material's index of refraction is a measure of how much a ray of light ___ when it enters that material at an angle.

_____

_____

45. Because of refraction, glass prisms separate white light into a visible _____ of colors.

_____

_____

46. As parallel rays of light pass through a(n) _____ lens, they are bent toward the center of the lens.

_____

_____

47. A(n) _____ image formed by a lens is always on the side of the lens opposite the object.

_____

_____

48. An opaque object has a particular color because it reflects some wavelengths of light and _____ the rest.

_____

_____

49. A red tomato will appear _____ when viewed under blue light.

_____

_____

50. When the three primary pigments are mixed, the resulting color is _____.

_____

_____

51. Any two colors that combine to form _____ light are called complementary colors.

_____

_____

52. The _____ is the transparent front surface of the eye.

_____

_____

53. When you focus on a _____ object, the lens in your eye becomes longer and thinner.

_____

_____

54. The vision of a nearsighted person can be improved if the person wears _____ lenses.

_____

_____

55. In a(n) _____ person, the lens of the eye focuses an image in front of the retina.

_____

_____

56. A(n) _____ uses a combination of lenses to magnify images of very small objects.

_____

_____

57. The type of image formed by the lens of a camera is a(n) ___ image.

_____

_____

58. A(n) _____ is a three-dimensional photograph created by using a laser.

_____

_____

59. To send signals through optical fibers, lasers convert electrical signals into pulses of _____.

_____

_____

60. A convex mirror reflects incoming parallel rays of light as though they came from _____ the mirror.

_____

_____

D. Interpreting Diagrams
Use the diagram to answer each question.

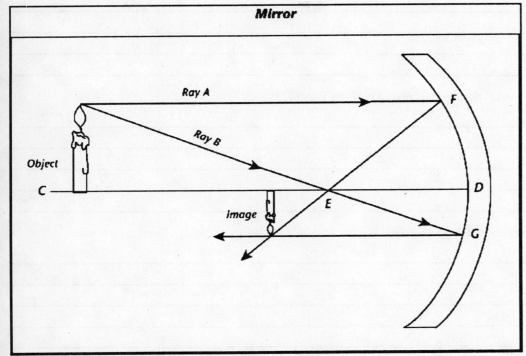

61. What type of mirror is shown?

_____

_____

_____

_____

62. Name and define point E.

_____

_____

_____

_____

63. What type of image does this mirror form?

_____

_____

_____

_____

64. Relate the size and orientation of the image formed by the mirror to the size and orientation of the original object.

_____

_____

_____

_____

65. What type of image will form if the candle is placed between E and D?

_____

_____

_____

_____

66. What will happen to the reflected light if the candle is placed at point E?

_____

_____

_____

_____

Use the diagram to answer each question.

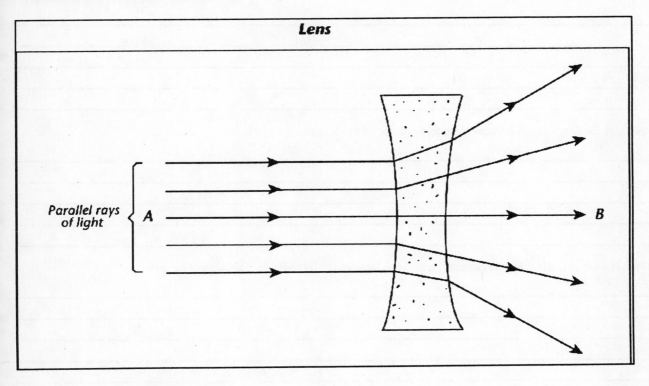

Lens

Parallel rays of light { A

B

67. What type of lens is shown?

_____

_____

_____

_____

_____

68. What effect does the lens have on parallel light rays passing through it?

_____

_____

_____

_____

69. On which side of the lens - left or right - would the focal point appear to be?

_____

_____

_____

_____

_____

70. What type of image does this lens form?

_____

_____

_____

_____

71. How does the shape of the lens compare to the shape of the lens in your eye?

_____

_____

_____

_____

72. Which condition could this lens correct - nearsightedness or farsightedness? Explain your answer.

_____

_____

_____

_____

E. Essay

   Write an answer to each of the following questions.

   73. Compare and contrast regular and diffuse reflection.

_____

_____

_____

_____

_____

74. You look at your reflection on the inner surface of a spoon held about 30 centimeters away. Then you turn the spoon around and look at the reflection on the back of the spoon. Compare and contrast the two images.

_____

_____

_____

_____

_____

_____

_____

75. Suppose a ray of light strikes a block of clear ice at an angle of 40°. A similar ray strikes a block of glass at the same angle. If the light ray is bent less in ice, which material has the greater index of refraction? Explain.

_____

_____

_____

_____

_____

_____

_____

76. What is the only type of image that can be formed by both a concave lens and a convex lens? For each lens, explain the relative position of the object that will produce that type of image.

_____

_____

_____

_____

_____

_____

_____

77. A piece of cloth appears red under red light, green under green light, and blue under blue light. What color is the cloth? Explain why it cannot be any other color.

_____

_____

_____

_____

_____

_____

78. Explain what happens to the shape of the eye lens when the muscles that control it contract. What happens when they relax?

_____

_____

_____

_____

_____

79. Explain what a hologram is and how it is produced. Why is the light from a laser split into two beams to record a hologram?

_____

_____

_____

_____

_____

80. Describe two uses of optical fibers.

_____

_____

_____

_____

Test 72 Book O, Chapter 4: Light
Answer Key (Short)

__a__	1.
__b__	2.
__d__	3.
__c__	4.
__c__	5.
__c__	6.
__b__	7.
__d__	8.
__c__	9.
__c__	10.
__c__	11.
__a__	12.
__b__	13.
__c__	14.
__c__	15.
__c__	16.
__c__	17.
__d__	18.
__c__	19.
__c__	20.
__c__	21.
__c__	22.
__d__	23.
__b__	24.
__b__	25.
__a__	26.
__b__	27.
__b__	28.
__a__	29.
__d__	30.

31.	false, transmits
32.	false, real
33.	false, refraction
34.	TRUE
35.	false, transmits
36.	false, two
37.	false, lens
38.	TRUE
39.	TRUE
40.	false, coherent
41.	translucent

42. reflected

43. reflection

44. bends

45. spectrum

46. convex

47. real

48. absorbs

49. black

50. black

51. white

52. cornea

53. distant

54. concave

55. nearsighted

56. microscope

57. real

58. hologram

59. light

60. behind

61. concave

62. E is the focal point, the point at which rays of light meet.

63. real

64. The image is reduced and upside down.

65. virtual

66. The rays of light will reflect from the mirror as parallel rays.

67. concave

68. It causes them to move apart.

69. the left side

70. virtual

71. The lens in the diagram is thinner in the middle than at the edges, or concave. The lens in your eye is a convex lens, which means that it is thicker in the middle than at the edges.

72. Nearsightedness; in the nearsighted eye, the lens of the eye focuses the light in front of the retina because the eyeball is too long from back to front. Using of a concave lens, such as the one shown in the diagram, would spread out incoming rays before they enter the lens of the eye. That would cause the image to form farther back in the eyeball, on the retina.

73. In both regular and diffuse reflection, each ray of light obeys the law of reflection. In regular reflection, all parallel rays of light are reflected from a smooth surface at the same angle. In diffuse reflection, each of the parallel rays is reflected at a different angle because the surface is bumpy or uneven.

74. The first image would be a real image that is reduced and inverted. The second image would be a virtual image that is reduced and right-side up.

75. Glass; the index of refraction is a measure of how much a light ray bends as it enters a material. The higher the index of refraction of a medium is, the more it bends the light. Glass has the greater index of refraction because it bent a light ray more than ice bent a similar light ray under the same conditions.

76. Virtual; the image formed by a concave lens is always virtual. A convex lens will form a virtual image when the object is between the focal point and the lens.

77. White; if the cloth were any other color, it would appear black when seen through at least one of the filters because it would absorb the colored light. Only a white cloth reflects all colors of light.

78. When the muscles contract, they pull on the lens and make it longer and thinner. When they relax, the lens becomes shorter and thicker.

79. A hologram is a three-dimensional photograph. The three-dimensional image of an object that is recorded on a hologram is made by the interference of light rays from two beams of light from the same laser. The light rays of one beam strike the film. The light rays of the other beam also strike the film after they are reflected from the object. The interference of the light rays from the two beams forms a three-dimensional image of the object.

80. Answers may vary. Optical fibers are used in communications to carry light signals over long distances. They are also used in medical-examination instruments.